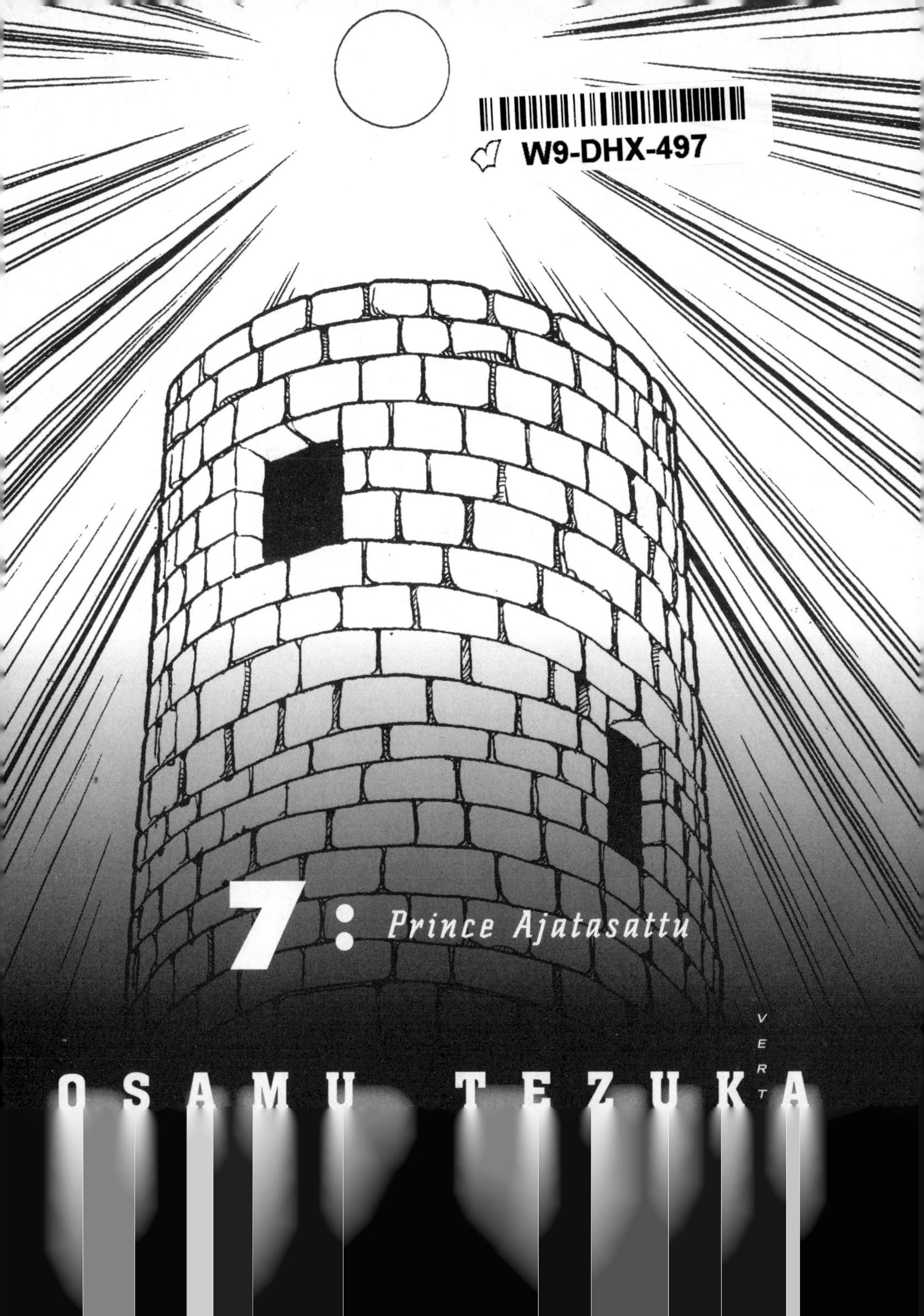

W9-DHX-497
7: Prince Ajatasattu
VERT
OSAMU TEZUKA

THE JOURNEY

NEPA

ROHTAK
MEERUT
MORADABAD
DELHI
BAREILLY
ALIGARH
SHAHJAHANPUR
MATHURA
CAPITAL OF KOSALA
JE
SAVATTHI
AGRA
UTTAR PRADESH
KOSALA
JAIPUR
SAKETA
LUCKNOW
FAIZABAD
CHAMBAL R.
KANPUR
GWALIOR
YAMUNA R.
THE GANGES
PRAY
ALLAHABAD
KOSAMBI

JETAVANA

KAPILAVASTU

KUSINAGARA

DEER PARK

LUMBINI ANCIENT PLACE NAMES
MAJOR ROUTES
● PLACES VISITED BY THE BUDDHA

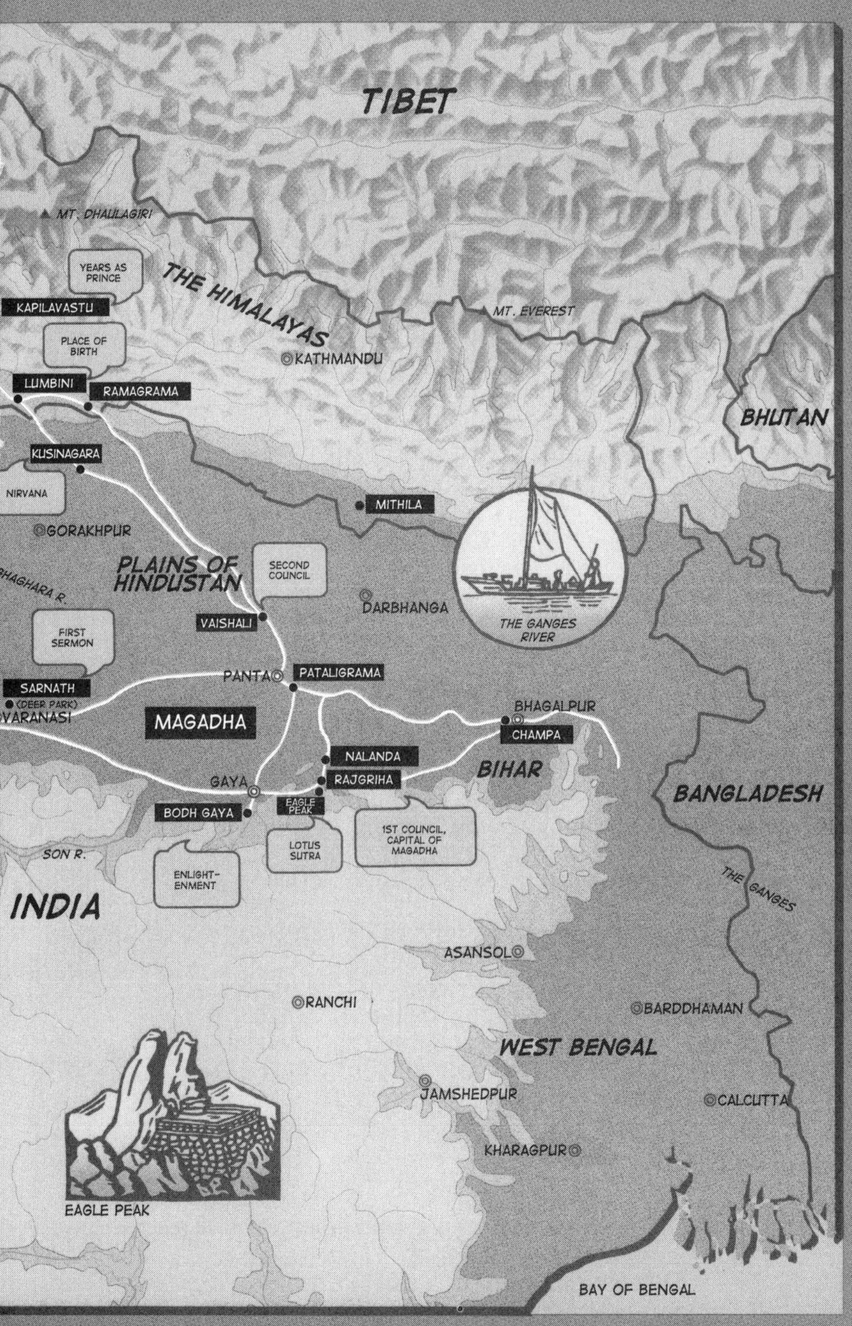

TIBET
MT. DHAULAGIRI
YEARS AS PRINCE
THE HIMALAYAS
KAPILAVASTU
MT. EVEREST
PLACE OF BIRTH
KATHMANDU
LUMBINI
RAMAGRAMA
BHUTAN
KUSINAGARA
NIRVANA
MITHILA
GORAKHPUR
PLAINS OF HINDUSTAN
SECOND COUNCIL
DARBHANGA
VAISHALI
THE GANGES RIVER
FIRST SERMON
PANTA
PATALIGRAMA
SARNATH
(DEER PARK)
VARANASI
BHAGALPUR
MAGADHA
CHAMPA
NALANDA
BIHAR
GAYA
RAJGRIHA
BANGLADESH
EAGLE PEAK
BODH GAYA
1ST COUNCIL, CAPITAL OF MAGADHA
LOTUS SUTRA
SON R.
ENLIGHT-ENMENT
THE GANGES
INDIA
ASANSOL
RANCHI
BARDDHAMAN
WEST BENGAL
JAMSHEDPUR
CALCUTTA
KHARAGPUR
EAGLE PEAK
BAY OF BENGAL

TRANSLATION- MAYA ROSEWOOD
PRODUCTION- HIROKO MIZUNO
AYAKO FUKUMITSU
YUKA NAGATE
SHINOBU SATO

PUBLISHED BY VERTICAL, INC., NEW YORK.

ORIGINALLY PUBLISHED IN JAPANESE AS *BUDDA DAI NANAKAN AJASE* BY USHIO SHUPPANSHA, TOKYO, 1988.

ISBN 978-1-932234-62-6

MANUFACTURED IN THE UNITED STATES OF AMERICA

FIRST PAPERBACK EDITION. THE ARTWORK OF THE ORIGINAL HAS BEEN PRODUCED AS A MIRROR-IMAGE IN ORDER TO CONFORM WITH THE ENGLISH LANGUAGE. THIS WORK OF FICTION CONTAINS CHARACTERS AND EPISODES THAT ARE NOT PART OF THE HISTORICAL RECORD.

THIRD PRINTING

VERTICAL, INC.
1185 AVE. OF THE AMERICAS 32ND FLOOR
NEW YORK, NY 10036
WWW.VERTICAL-INC.COM

CONTENTS

PART FIVE (CONTINUED)

PART SIX

PART FIVE (CONTINUED)

CHAPTER NINE

VENUVANA

KAKLOP
KAKLOP
KAKLOP
KAKLOP

A THOUSAND MONKS ARE APPROACHING THE CASTLE GATES!

THEY'RE LED BY BUDDHA!

WHAT? BUDDHA?

BUDDHA IS COMING! HE'S LESS THAN A HUNDRED YARDS FROM THE CASTLE!
PREPARE A RECEPTION !
WHOA, BUDDHA! I, BUDDHA I WANNA SEE BUDDHA! I MISS BUDDHA!
YATALA, SIDDOWN, YOU'RE ROCKIN' THE CASTLE!
DEVADATTA, IS THIS THE MIRACLE WORKER YOU ALWAYS TALK ABOUT?
YES, MILORD. HE LEFT THIS CASTLE BEFORE YOU WERE BORN. IT'S BEEN 15 YEARS!

BUDDHA...
LONG TIME NO SEE...

I PROMISED THAT ONE DAY I WOULD RETURN
AND REPORT TO YOU WHAT I'VE LEARNED.
HOW I'VE WAITED! OH, HOW LONG THOSE DAYS FELT TO ME!

LEAD BUDDHA AND HIS DISCIPLES INTO THE BANQUET HALL!
PREPARE A FEAST! WELCOME THEM AS YOU WOULD A BROTHER!
GET TO IT!

THIS WAY, BUDDHA...

PLEASE, EVERYONE! DON'T PUSH, NOW.
A FULL THOUSAND OF 'EM.
WONDER IF THEY'LL ALL FIT ?

HEY, BUDDHA! BUDDHA! BUDDHAAA!

YOU DARE—

WATCH IT, PAL! YOU'RE TALKIN' TO THE MAN'S DISCIPLE!

IT'S ALL RIGHT. TATTA, COME HITHER.

HA! JERK!

ACTUALLY, THERE'S SOMETHING I WANT TO TELL YOU.

ENOUGH FOR NOW. SAVE THAT UNTIL LATER.
TATTA

ALL RIGHT, COME IN!
SHUT UP! THIS IS IMPOR-TANT!

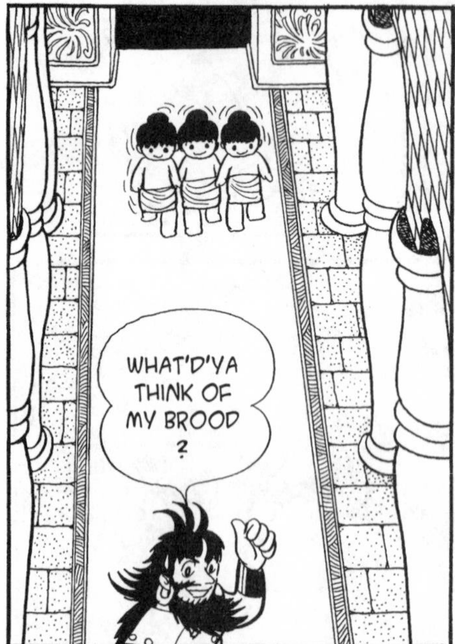
WHAT'D'YA THINK OF MY BROOD ?

TRIPLETS. MAKES A MAN PROUD.

HOW OLD ?
THEY'RE THREE ALREADY.

WHAT SPLENDID CHIL-DREN
CONGRAT-ULATIONS, TATTA, MIGAILA. WHAT ARE THEIR NAMES?

THEY HAVEN'T GOT ANY YET.

THREE YEARS OLD, AND NO NAMES ?
YOU SEE, I WAS HOPING YOU'D BE THEIR GODFATHER.
SO I LEFT THEM NAMELESS ON PURPOSE. DO US THE FAVOR!

A FAVOR! BUDDHA MUST BE EXHAUSTED. DON'T TASK HIM NOW!

BU BU BUDDHA? I, WANNA... WANTED TO SEE YOU! BUDDHA, I WORK FOR KING BIMBISARA NOW.
HEY, BUTT OUT, BIG GUY!
OWWW

SPLAT

BUDDHA, DO YOU REMEMBER ME? I'M DEVADATTA.
THERE'S SOMEONE I'D LIKE TO INTRODUCE TO YOU.

THE SUCCESSOR TO THE THRONE, PRINCE AJATA-SATTU!

...

I'M THE PRINCE, ALL RIGHT?
YOU OUGHT TO KNEEL TO ME, YOU KNOW?

NOT ONE OF YOUR SERVANTS
I AM BUDDHA

ARE YOU REALLY SO GREAT?
I SAW MY FATHER KNEEL BEFORE YOU, JUST NOW.

MILORD, BUDDHA IS A MIRACLE WORKER WHO CAN SPEAK TO US OF COSMIC TRUTHS.

I DON'T THINK THAT MAKES HIM GREAT.

EACH OF US DECIDES ON OUR OWN WHO IS OR ISN'T GREAT.

UHM, MI... MILORD...
WHY? BECAUSE HE'S LIKE A WALKING ENCYCLOPEDIA AND HE TEACHES ME ALL SORTS OF THINGS.
I THINK DEVADATTA HERE IS FAR GREATER THAN YOU.

MY FATHER CAN THINK WHAT HE DAMN WELL PLEASES, BUT I DON'T AGREE.

THAT'S THE PRINCE AJATASATTU. SURELY YOU REMEMBER, IT WAS PROPHESIED THAT
WHEN THE KING TURNED 41, HIS OWN SON WOULD KILL HIM!

WE ALL LAUGHED IT OFF AS NONSENSE, BUT IN TRUTH, EVERYONE
THE KING INCLUDED, FEARS THE PROPHECY WILL COME TRUE.

HE'S 36 YEARS OLD!
ONLY FIVE MORE YEARS UNTIL THE FATED YEAR!

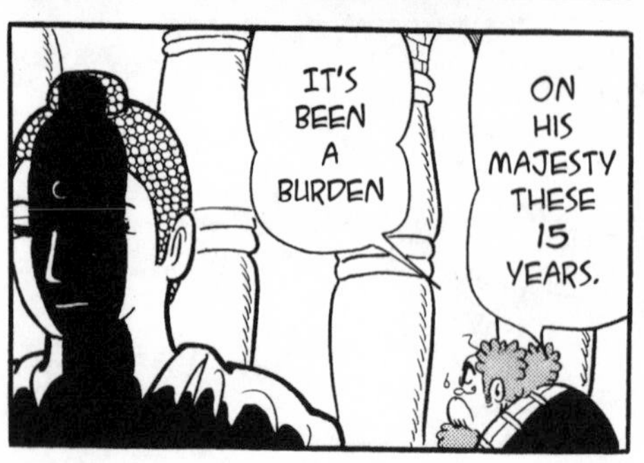
IT'S BEEN A BURDEN
ON HIS MAJESTY THESE 15 YEARS.

DO YOU REMEMBER THIS, BUDDHA?
AS IF I SAW IT YESTER-DAY

I OFFERED THIS JEWEL-FILLED CASKET TO YOU. BUT AS A SAMANNA, YOU HAD TO REFUSE ANY CHARITY OTHER THAN A FEW SCRAPS OF FOOD.
YOU WERE QUITE FIRM IN YOUR REFUSAL.

THAT WAS SO, KING.

DON'T CALL ME THAT!
SUCH FORMALITIES FROM YOU FEEL ICE COLD. JUST CALL ME SENIYA, LIKE YOU USED TO.

SO, I THREW THIS CASKET INTO THE POOL.
ONCE YOU RETURNED, I'D USE THIS TREASURE TO BUILD YOU A FINE TEMPLE! UNTIL THEN, I WOULDN'T TOUCH A SINGLE RUBY!

IT'S BEEN 15 YEARS.
YOU'VE COME BACK A HOLY MAN

ONCE MORE, I'D LIKE TO OFFER THIS TREASURE TO YOU, WITH SOME LAND ON WHICH TO BUILD THE TEMPLE.
AND WITH A THOUSAND DISCIPLES!

PLEASE ACCEPT MY GIFT, AS A SYMBOL OF OUR FRIENDSHIP.

A COUPLE OF MILES FROM THIS CASTLE LIES A GROVE THAT I OWN. THERE'S A FRESH SPRING, AND FLOWERS EVERYWHERE. I THINK YOU'LL LIKE IT.

SINCE I'LL HAVE NO USE FOR SUCH THINGS...

WHEN I DIE...
I WON'T NEED ANYTHING, WILL I?!

ONLY FIVE MORE YEARS.
I CAN ALREADY HEAR DEATH'S FOOTSTEPS APPROACHING.
I'LL BE BRANDED THE WORLD'S CRUELEST FATHER.
KILL THE PRINCE? IMPRISON HIM? BANISH HIM?
WHAT IS THERE TO DO? SHOULD I FLEE?
BUT WHAT CAN BE DONE ?

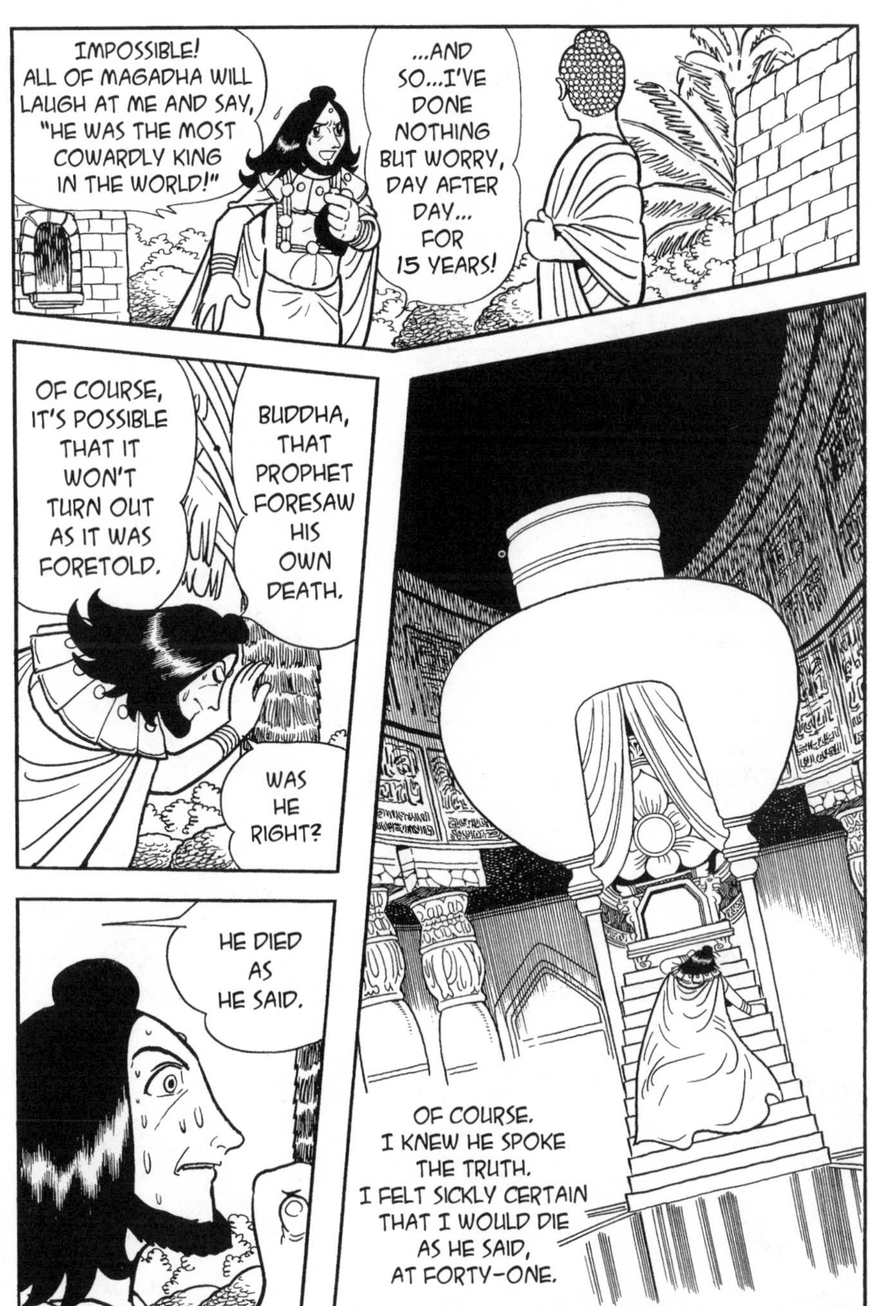
IMPOSSIBLE! ALL OF MAGADHA WILL LAUGH AT ME AND SAY, "HE WAS THE MOST COWARDLY KING IN THE WORLD!"
...AND SO...I'VE DONE NOTHING BUT WORRY, DAY AFTER DAY... FOR 15 YEARS!
OF COURSE, IT'S POSSIBLE THAT IT WON'T TURN OUT AS IT WAS FORETOLD.
BUDDHA, THAT PROPHET FORESAW HIS OWN DEATH.
WAS HE RIGHT?
HE DIED AS HE SAID.
OF COURSE. I KNEW HE SPOKE THE TRUTH. I FELT SICKLY CERTAIN THAT I WOULD DIE AS HE SAID, AT FORTY-ONE.

BUDDHA, PLEASE HELP ME!

HOW CAN I BE FREE FROM THIS PAIN?

TREES WITHER AND DIE. IF NOT, THEY ARE CUT DOWN.
WHAT DOES A TREE FEEL WHEN IT'S BEING AXED?
"IT HURTS"? "THEY'RE KILLING ME"? "POOR ME"?

TREE... IF YOU HAD A MOUTH, YOU'D SCREAM.
IF YOU HAD EYES, YOU'D WEEP.
IF YOU COULD MOVE, YOU'D TRY TO RUN AWAY...

BUT A TREE CAN DO NONE OF THOSE THINGS, SO IT CALMLY AWAITS THE DAY.

SENIYA, YOU TOO.
IF YOUR FATE IS INESCAPABLE, THEN BE BRAVE AND BE PREPARED.
LIVE RIGHTLY, ACT RIGHTLY UNTIL THAT DAY!

JUST AS ASSAJI DID...

WHO IS THAT?
ASSAJI ?

A MAN WHO KNEW FOR YEARS WHEN HE WOULD DIE, BUT WHO CALMLY GREETED THAT DAY.
THE MAN WHO PREDICTED YOUR FATE.

...

FATHER!
OH, AJATA-SATTU.

HAVE YOU BECOME BUDDHA'S DISCIPLE ?
YES... I AM NOW A LAY FOLLOWER.*

WHY ?!
WHY MUST A GREAT MAN LIKE MY FATHER TAKE ADVICE FROM SOME SAMANNA?
SHUT UP !

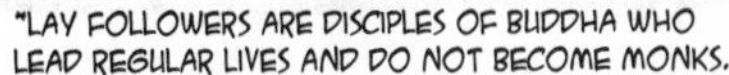
*LAY FOLLOWERS ARE DISCIPLES OF BUDDHA WHO LEAD REGULAR LIVES AND DO NOT BECOME MONKS.

AJATASATTU! BUDDHA IS THE ONLY HUMAN ALIVE WHO CAN EASE MY WORRIED MIND!
WHAT'S HE WORTH? A FLOCK OF PEOPLE TRAIL HIM EVERYWHERE, BUT HE LOOKS FEEBLE AND ALL HE DOES IS SIT!
YOU MEAN YOU'RE WORRIED THAT I MIGHT KILL YOU?
YES?
HAH! RIDICULOUS! HOW CAN YOU BELIEVE THAT CRAP?
WHEN I WAS LITTLE, I ADORED YOU! YOU WERE SO BRAVE, SO DIGNIFIED! YOU BURNED WITH AN AURA OF CONVICTION!
FATHER!
BUT NOW, YOU SEEM SO SCARED! YOU SEEM SO WEAK AND AIMLESS.
SHUT YOUR MOUTH
FATHER, HAVE SOME GUTS!

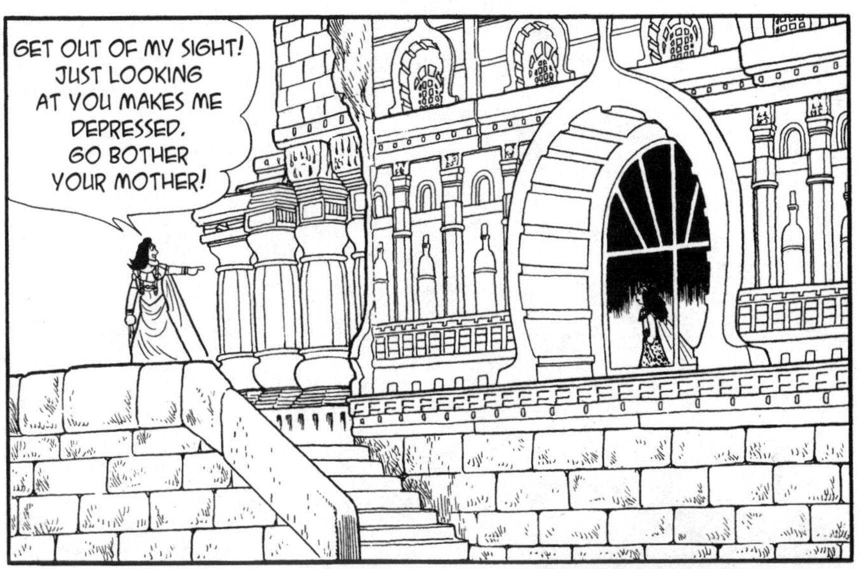
GET OUT OF MY SIGHT! JUST LOOKING AT YOU MAKES ME DEPRESSED. GO BOTHER YOUR MOTHER!

FATHER ...

WHY WOULD I EVER KILL YOU?
YOU'VE BEEN TRICKED BY THAT BUDDHA.

I'LL GO FIND DEVADATTA. HE'LL KNOW WHAT TO DO.

EVERYONE, THANKS FOR JOINING ME!

ALLOW ME TO INTRODUCE MYSELF. MY NAME IS DEVADATTA. I, TOO, AM A DISCIPLE OF BUDDHA. THINK OF ME AS YOUR COLLEAGUE.
COLLIE? DOES HE FETCH?

WE'RE ALL FOLLOWERS OF BUDDHA. TO FURTHER THE TEACHINGS OF BUDDHA...
WE SHALL FORM AN ORGANI-ZATION.

TO HELL WITH THAT. I JUST WANT TO LEARN FROM BUDDHA, THAT'S ALL.
ORGANI-ZATION?

OF COURSE WE'LL LEARN FROM BUDDHA. BUT LOOK, HE HAS OVER 1,000 DISCIPLES NOW!

I TAKE YOUR POINT. WE NEED TO FORM SOME SORT OF ORGANIZATION.

KASSAPA, YOU USED TO HEAD ONE, RIGHT? YOU KNOW HOW IMPORTANT THEY ARE.

THE POINT IS THAT WE CAN'T REMAIN A DISORGANIZED GROUP! MY FELLOW DISCIPLES, I'M SURE YOU UNDERSTAND!
IF YOU PREFER, AN "ASSOCIA-TION"!

AN ASSOCIATION HAS RULES TO GUIDE ITS ACTIONS. A TYPICAL GROUP JUST TALKS UP A STORM WITHOUT ACCOMPLISHING ANYTHING!
ANY OBJECTIONS?
FURTHERMORE, AS ASCETICS, WE NEED ESPECIALLY STRICT RULES!
WHAT KIND OF RULES?
LET'S START WITH RULES FOR A DAILY ROUTINE.
HOW DO YOU MEAN?
LIKE, BRUSHING OUR TEETH EVERY MORNING?
NOT PICKING OUR NOSES IN PUBLIC?
I'M TALKING ABOUT WAKING AT 5 A.M!

FIRST THING, WE'LL SCRUB THE FLOORS AND WASH OUR ROBES.
THEN MEDITATION!
ONCE THE SUN HAS RISEN, WE'LL TAKE OUR BOWLS AND SET OUT TO BEG FOR ALMS.
WE EAT JUST ONCE A DAY, AND IN THE MORNING! AFTER NOON, ANYTHING OTHER THAN WATER OR FRUIT IS STRICTLY PROHIBITED!
NO MORE THAN FOUR HOURS OF SLEEP!
MEALS SHOULD BE TAKEN OUTDOORS, IN A QUIET SPOT.
IF WE HAVE AN INVALID OR ELDERLY COLLEAGUE, WE FIRST OFFER HIM ANY FOOD WE'VE RECEIVED AND EAT WHAT'S LEFT.
WHAT WE CAN'T FINISH WE'LL SHARE WITH WILD BIRDS AND ANIMALS.
THE DAILY ROUTINE OF AN ORDAINED MONK...
MUST BE THIS STRICT, IF NOT MORE.

IMPOSSIBLE!
I DON'T WANNA END UP A SACK OF BONES!

I CAN'T FOLLOW THOSE RULES.

YOUNG MAN, THEY'RE NOTHING COMPARED TO THE RULES OF A JAIN SECT!

OKAY, THEN LET'S TAKE SUNDAYS OFF, AT LEAST
SO WE CAN GO TO THE MOVIES, MAYBE
OR PLAY MAH-JONG
DO SO, IF YOU WANT. BUT YOU WON'T BE A MONK.
SUCH A FOLLOWER WILL NEVER ATTAIN ENLIGHT-ENMENT...

LOOK WHO'S TALKING!
YOU HAVEN'T EVEN SHAVED YOUR HEAD!

YOU ARE RIGHT

ZIP
NO TIME LIKE NOW

OH OH
GIMME SWORD!
I'M GONNA
SH-SHAVE HEAD
TOO!
OWW
CUT MY HEAD!
DAMN D-DULL
BLADE!
HA HA
I-I'M
MONK
!
HE LOOKS
EVEN
SCARIER
NOW...

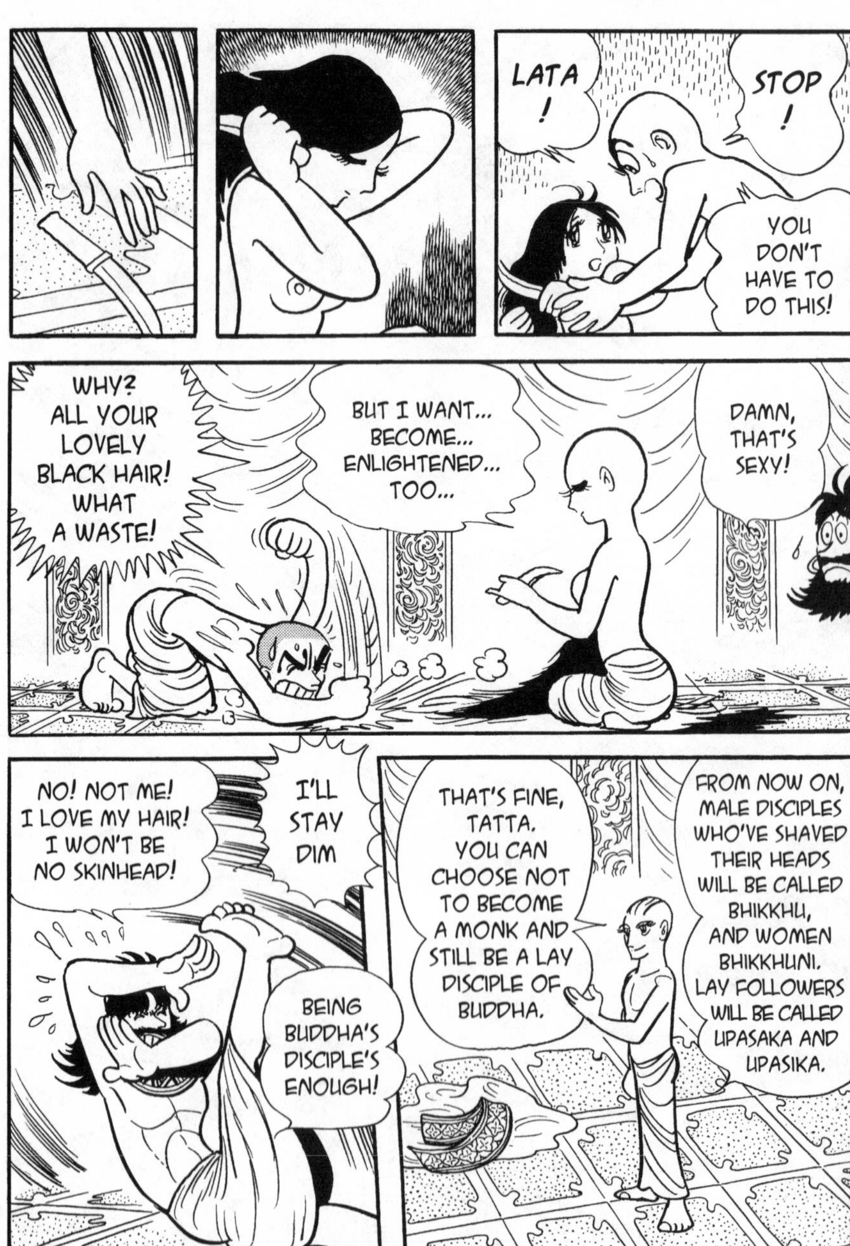
LATA
!
STOP
!
YOU DON'T HAVE TO DO THIS!
WHY? ALL YOUR LOVELY BLACK HAIR! WHAT A WASTE!
BUT I WANT... BECOME... ENLIGHTENED... TOO...
DAMN, THAT'S SEXY!
NO! NOT ME! I LOVE MY HAIR! I WON'T BE NO SKINHEAD!
I'LL STAY DIM
BEING BUDDHA'S DISCIPLE'S ENOUGH!
THAT'S FINE, TATTA. YOU CAN CHOOSE NOT TO BECOME A MONK AND STILL BE A LAY DISCIPLE OF BUDDHA.
FROM NOW ON, MALE DISCIPLES WHO'VE SHAVED THEIR HEADS WILL BE CALLED BHIKKHU, AND WOMEN BHIKKHUNI. LAY FOLLOWERS WILL BE CALLED UPASAKA AND UPASIKA.

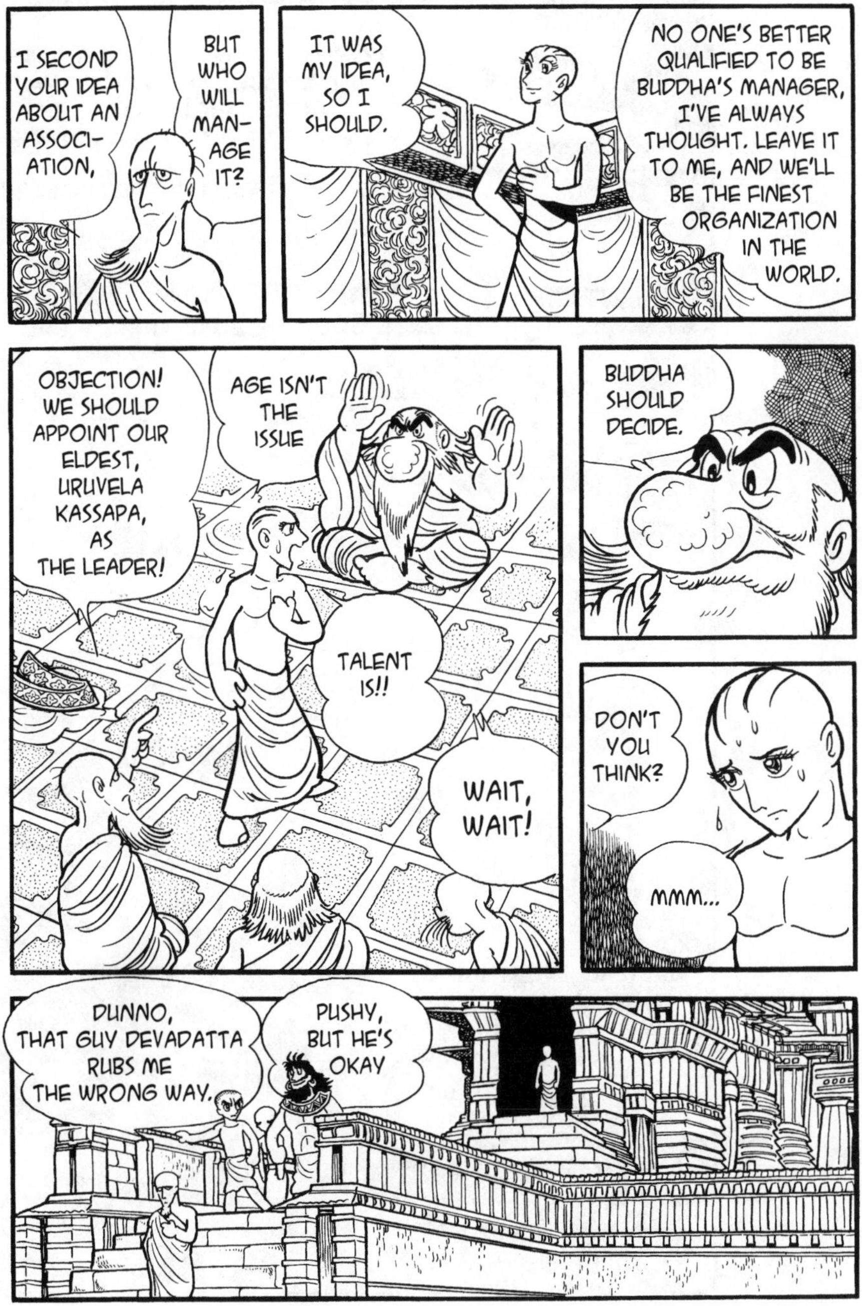

I SECOND YOUR IDEA ABOUT AN ASSOCIATION,

BUT WHO WILL MANAGE IT?

IT WAS MY IDEA, SO I SHOULD.

NO ONE'S BETTER QUALIFIED TO BE BUDDHA'S MANAGER, I'VE ALWAYS THOUGHT. LEAVE IT TO ME, AND WE'LL BE THE FINEST ORGANIZATION IN THE WORLD.

OBJECTION! WE SHOULD APPOINT OUR ELDEST, URUVELA KASSAPA, AS THE LEADER!

AGE ISN'T THE ISSUE

TALENT IS!!

WAIT, WAIT!

BUDDHA SHOULD DECIDE.

DON'T YOU THINK?

MMM...

DUNNO, THAT GUY DEVADATTA RUBS ME THE WRONG WAY.
PUSHY, BUT HE'S OKAY

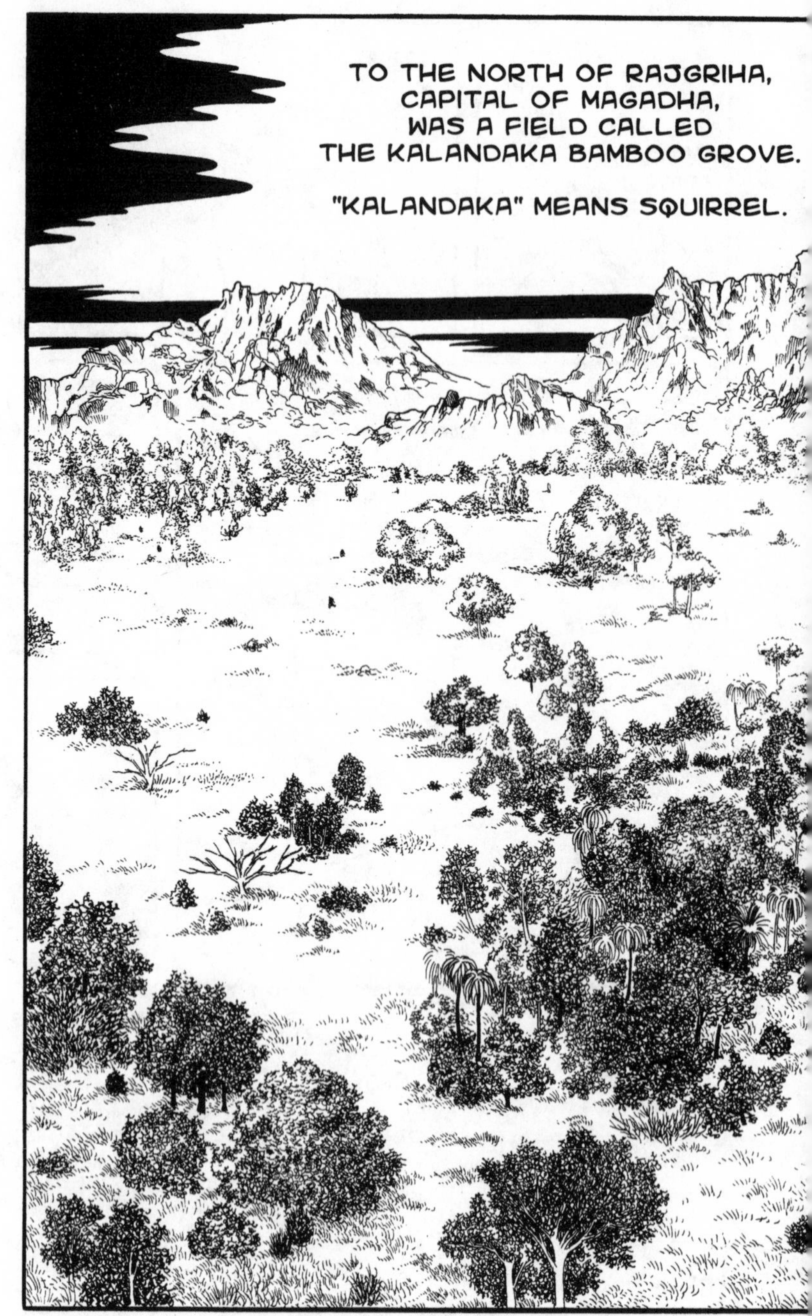
TO THE NORTH OF RAJGRIHA, CAPITAL OF MAGADHA, WAS A FIELD CALLED THE KALANDAKA BAMBOO GROVE.
"KALANDAKA" MEANS SQUIRREL.

ONCE, ACCORDING TO LEGEND, A KING WHO LAY ASLEEP THERE WAS SAVED BY A SQUIRREL, WHO WOKE HIM UP JUST BEFORE A VIPER COULD STRIKE HIM.

THIS WAS THE GROVE THAT KING BIMBISARA OFFERED TO BUDDHA. THE VENUVANA (BAMBOO) MONASTERY, AS IT CAME TO BE KNOWN, TURNED INTO A MAJOR BASE FOR SPREADING BUDDHA'S TEACHINGS.

HEY... ANANDA!

WHO'S THERE ?!
LONG TIME NO SEE!
HUH, AHIMSA ?

GET OUT OF HERE. I'VE CUT ALL TIES WITH YOU.
THANKS FOR THE WARM WELCOME.
SO HOW'D'YA LIKE THE MONK LIFESTYLE, EH?

YOU DON'T SEEM TO BE ENJOYING IT.
SHUT UP!

FOR YOUR OWN GOOD...
HEH HEH HEH...

GIVE UP THIS MONK CRAP AND WORK WITH ME.
I SAID GET LOST!

TOMORROW, BUDDHA WILL BE PREACHING ON THAT PLATFORM, YEAH? WELL, THOSE'LL BE HIS LAST WORDS.
CAN YOU KEEP A SECRET?
WHAT?!

GUESS WHAT, HEHEH... IT GETS BETTER. THE ASSASSIN IS AJATASATTU, KING BIMBISARA'S BRAT. WHAT A SHOCKER, EH?
PRINCE AJATASATTU?
THAT'S A LIE...

KA
KLOP
KLOP
KLOP
KLOP
KLOP

AJATASATTU! WAIT, NOW!

PLEASE TELL ME IT'S NOT TRUE YOU'RE PLANNING TO ATTACK BUDDHA!
WHO TOLD YOU THAT, MOTHER?
I HAD TO THREATEN ONE OF THE MAIDS UNTIL SHE FINALLY SPOKE.

THEN THERE'S NO USE DE-NYING IT...
IT'S TRUE

PRINCE!

DON'T TRY TO STOP ME
IT'S THE ONLY WAY TO RELEASE FATHER FROM HIS PAIN.

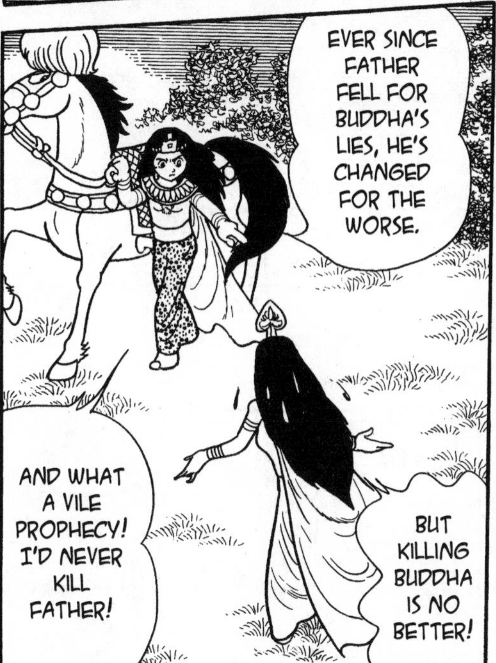
EVER SINCE FATHER FELL FOR BUDDHA'S LIES, HE'S CHANGED FOR THE WORSE.
AND WHAT A VILE PROPHECY! I'D NEVER KILL FATHER!
BUT KILLING BUDDHA IS NO BETTER!

ONCE HE'S GONE, ALL HIS LIES WILL EVAPORATE. IT'S NOT JUST FOR FATHER. THE WHOLE WORLD WILL BE BETTER OFF!
AND MY OWN PRIDE IS AT STAKE!

LISTEN TO ME !!
IMAGINE HOW SHOCKED YOUR FATHER WILL BE WHEN HE RETURNS FROM HIS ROUNDS!

I KNOW. I'M READY FOR ANY KIND OF PUNISHMENT... SOMEDAY, HE'LL UNDERSTAND.

YOU TOO, MOTHER, PLEASE UNDERSTAND MY FEELINGS

KLOP KLOP KLOP KLOP
OH... AJATASATTU ...

AFTER HIM! DO ANYTHING YOU CAN TO DISRUPT HIS PLAN.

YES'M

DAMN, THEY'RE PERSISTENT
YOU, DISTRACT THEM. LEAD THEM AS FAR AWAY FROM HERE AS POSSIBLE.
LIKE HOW FAR ?
SASKATCHEWAN, I DON'T CARE.
TRAVEL FEES

NO PERKS FOR YOU, FOOL! AND MAKE IT A DAY TRIP!
KLOP
KLOP

KLOP
KLOP
KLOP
KLOP

ONLY A FEW HOURS 'TIL DAWN

BUDDHA
MUST YOU GIVE A SERMON THIS MORNING? SOMEONE WANTS TO KILL YOU!
IS THAT TRUE? HOW DO YOU KNOW THIS, ANANDA?
UHM, I HAVE RELIABLE SOURCES.
THE KILLER'S HIDING NEAR THE STONE DAIS!!
I CAN'T CANCEL THE SERMON. EVERYBODY'S GATHERED ALREADY TO LISTEN TO ME.
NO, PLEASE! THE ONE WHO WANTS TO KILL YOU IS...

AJATASATTU!
THE PRINCE? DON'T BE A FOOL.
IT'S THE EXCUSE MANGA AUTHORS USE TO MISS AN ISSUE ...
WE COULD SAY YOU'VE FALLEN ILL.
NOT CANCEL, JUST POSTPONE
WHOEVER IT IS, WHEREVER IT IS, I SHAN'T BE FORCED TO CANCEL A SERMON.

I CAN CHEAT FEAR TODAY— BUT WON'T IT RETURN TOMORROW?

I AM. BUT WHAT IS THERE TO BE DONE ?
PLEASE DON'T GO! YOU'LL DIE! AREN'T YOU AFRAID?

AND FIND PEACE IN ITS BOSOM.
RATHER, I MUST EMBRACE THIS FEAR

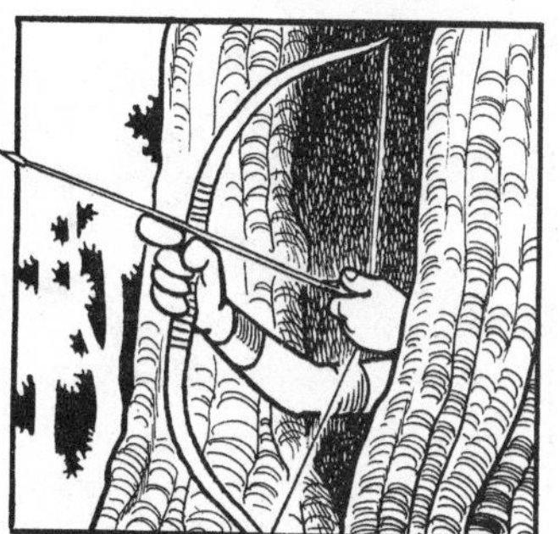

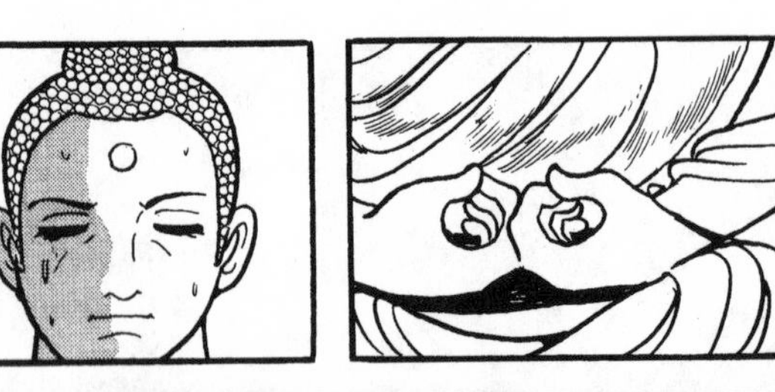

WHISH!

THUD!

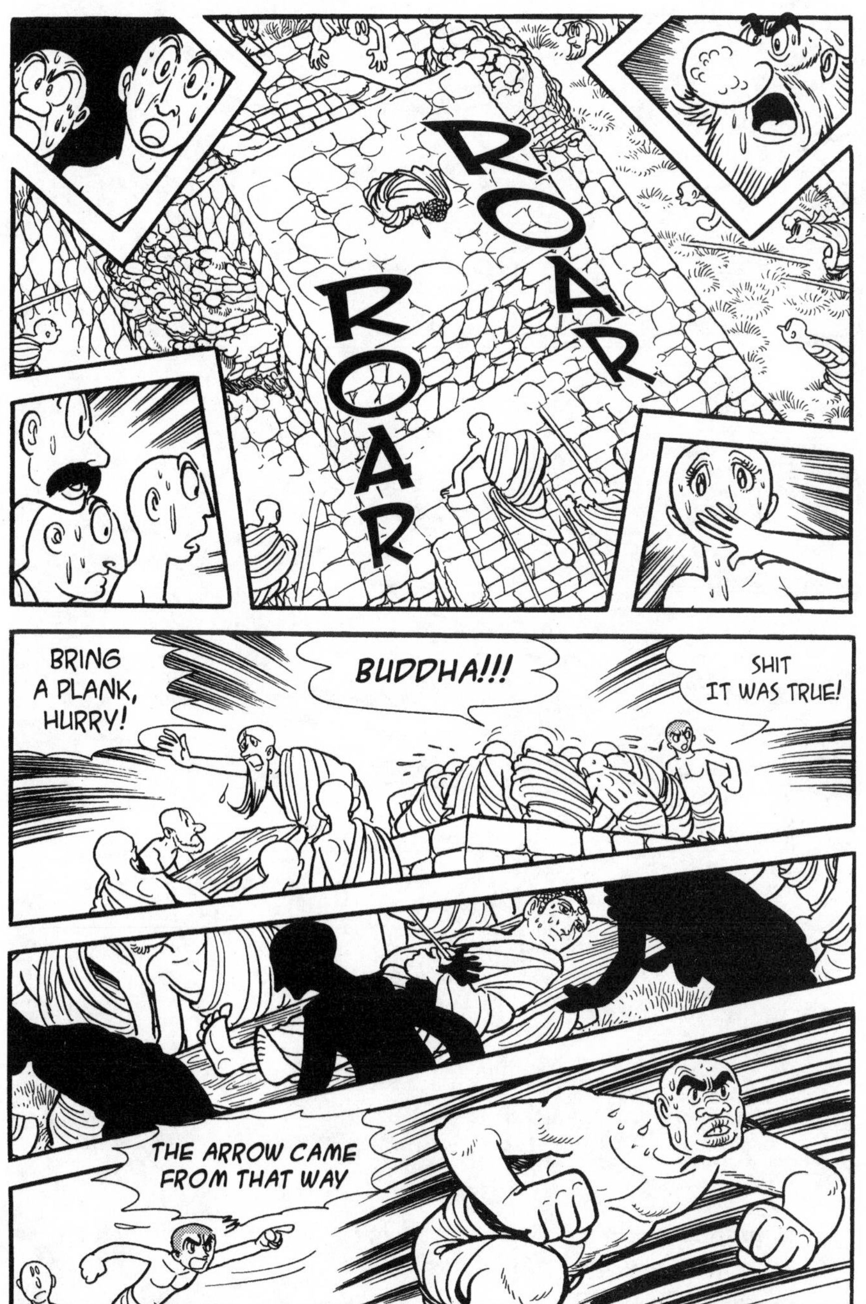
ROAR
ROAR
BRING A PLANK, HURRY!
BUDDHA!!!
SHIT IT WAS TRUE!
THE ARROW CAME FROM THAT WAY

RARRR
COME OUT
Y-YOU WHO SHOT BUDDHA !!
WUH-WHERE YOU HI-HIDING?! ARRRGHH!
THUMP

...

PHEW...

PULL IT OUT SLOWLY... SLOWLY... ...
SOMEBODY DO SOMETHING!!! BUDDHA'S GONNA DIE!!
BRING ME WINE! STRONG WINE!

BUDDHA SAVED MY LIFE ONCE. NOW IT'S MY TURN. I HAVE TO SAVE HIM!

CAUTERIZE THE WOUND WITH RED-HOT IRON!

WHEN THE ARMY OF KOSALA NEARLY TOOK MY LIFE, YOU SHARED YOUR BLOOD WITH ME.
YOU THEN SHIELDED ME FROM PRINCE CRYSTAL'S SWORD!

YOU MUST LET ME SAVE YOU NOW!

DHEPA, WILL HE BE ALL RIGHT?

CHANCES ARE SLIM...

IF THERE'S A ONE IN A MILLION CHANCE, I'LL SEIZE IT... HE WON'T DIE!

NEVER KILLED A MAN BEFORE...

MURDER.
IT'S GOT SUCH A TERRIBLE AFTERTASTE. THIS IRRITATION...
BUT I WAS TOTALLY RIGHT TO DO IT!
IN THE END, I HAD NO CHOICE REALLY... FOR THE SAKE OF JUSTICE...

AJATASATTU!

WHERE THE HELL ARE YOU?!

PRINCE!!

SMAK

YOU ROTTEN FOOL!
SLAP! SLAP!

YOU SHOT BUDDHA! WHY?!
AJATASATTU... WHAT IN THE WORLD HAVE YOU DONE?!

PUNISH ME IF YOU MUST!
BUT I KNOW... THERE WAS NO OTHER WAY...
YOU MAKE ME SICK!!
JUST NOW I SENT A DOCTOR TO VENUVANA...
IF IT'S TOO LATE AND BUDDHA DIES YOU'LL FEEL YOUR PUNISHMENT 'TIL YOUR DYING DAY!
IDIOT... HAVE YOU ANY IDEA WHAT YOU'VE DONE?
FATHER, PLEASE, LISTEN TO ME.
EVERYONE IN THE CASTLE, THE WHOLE CITY FANCIES THAT I WILL KILL YOU IN FIVE YEARS
AND I CAN'T STAND IT!
IT CAN'T POSSIBLY BE TRUE THAT I'M GOING TO KILL YOU!
BECAUSE THAT'S THE PROPHECY!
A PROPHECY SPREAD BY THAT BUDDHA!!

IT WAS BUDDHA WHO SPREAD THAT STUPID RUMOR. UNTIL HE DIES, HE'LL ALWAYS CONFUSE YOU!
SILENCE!!

GUARDS! LOCK THE PRINCE UP IN THE TOWER.

OH... MY SON...
I CAN'T BELIEVE THIS IS HAPPENING ...

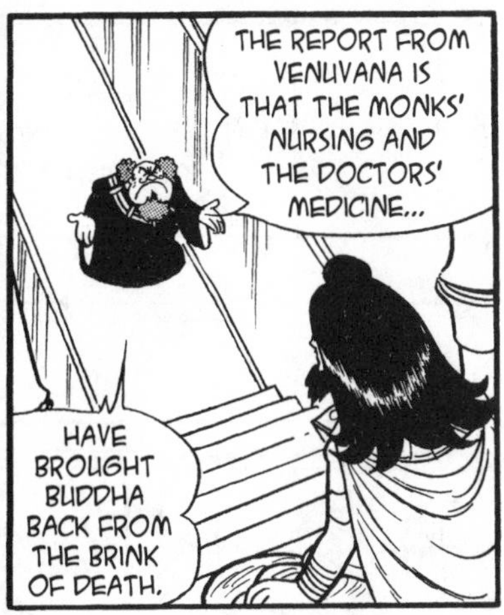
THE REPORT FROM VENUVANA IS THAT THE MONKS' NURSING AND THE DOCTORS' MEDICINE...
HAVE BROUGHT BUDDHA BACK FROM THE BRINK OF DEATH.

THANK GOODNESS ...

WHAT SHALL WE DO WITH THE PRINCE?

LET HIM SIT AND STEW FOR NOW! DON'T LET A WORD OF THIS WRETCHED EVENT LEAK TO THE PUBLIC. IF ANYONE'S CAUGHT BABBLING ABOUT THIS EXECUTE HIM ON THE SPOT!

PRINCE, MIGHT I BEG AUDIENCE WITH YOU?
DOOR'S OPEN.

DEVADATTA !!
I DIDN'T THINK IT WAS YOU!

HOW ARE YOU ?
NOT TOO BAD... BUT I'VE BEEN ALONE FOR THREE MONTHS.

POOR PRINCE...
OH... I'M SO HAPPY TO SEE YOU...

IS BUDDHA DEAD ?
ACTUALLY, HE'S RECOVERED NICELY. HE'LL SOON BE WALKING ON HIS OWN.

DAMN...
I THOUGHT I'D GOTTEN HIM... LUCKY BASTARD
PLEASE, PRINCE, DON'T TALK THAT WAY ABOUT LORD BUDDHA.

BUDDHA IS A GREAT MAN.
DON'T TELL ME YOU'RE ON HIS SIDE TOO?!

YOU'RE GREATER! YOU SHOULD BE IN THE GUINNESS BOOK OF RECORDS AS THE SMARTEST MAN EVER!
1
2
3

I COULD USE SOME OF THOSE SMARTS NOW...

I...CAN'T TAKE THIS ANYMORE.

I'M TREATED LIKE SOME DANGEROUS BEAST...
THEY ALL THINK I'M GONNA KILL FATHER

WHAT IS IT?

IF YOU COULD GET RID OF THAT PROPHECY, I'D BE IN YOUR DEBT FOREVER.
THERE IS ONLY ONE OPTION

IT'S A VERY DIFFICULT OPTION.

LET THE KING RETIRE.
WHAT ?!

MAKE HIM ABDICATE AND SET OUT ON A LONG JOURNEY.

WHAT DO YOU MEAN ?

HE MUST LEAVE SO THAT YOU WILL NEVER MEET HIM AGAIN.

THEN THE PROPHECY COULD NEVER BE FULFILLED.

BUT I DON'T THINK FATHER WOULD EVER RETIRE...
THAT DOES MAKE SENSE
WOW

THEN HE MUST BE FORCED TO DO SO.

SHIT... IT'S BEEN THREE MONTHS ALREADY.

WHEN WILL THAT BUDDHA CROAK?!

THAT WAS NO SLIGHT SCRATCH, AND YET... I'M STUCK HERE WAITING FOR HIM TO KICK THE BUCKET.

BUT THIS TIME MISTER SAINT'S PROSPECTS AREN'T TOO BRIGHT! HEHEH

?

?

UGH
BAM!
AAAAAHK!
L-LEMME GO! HELP ME! IT'S BIGFOOT!

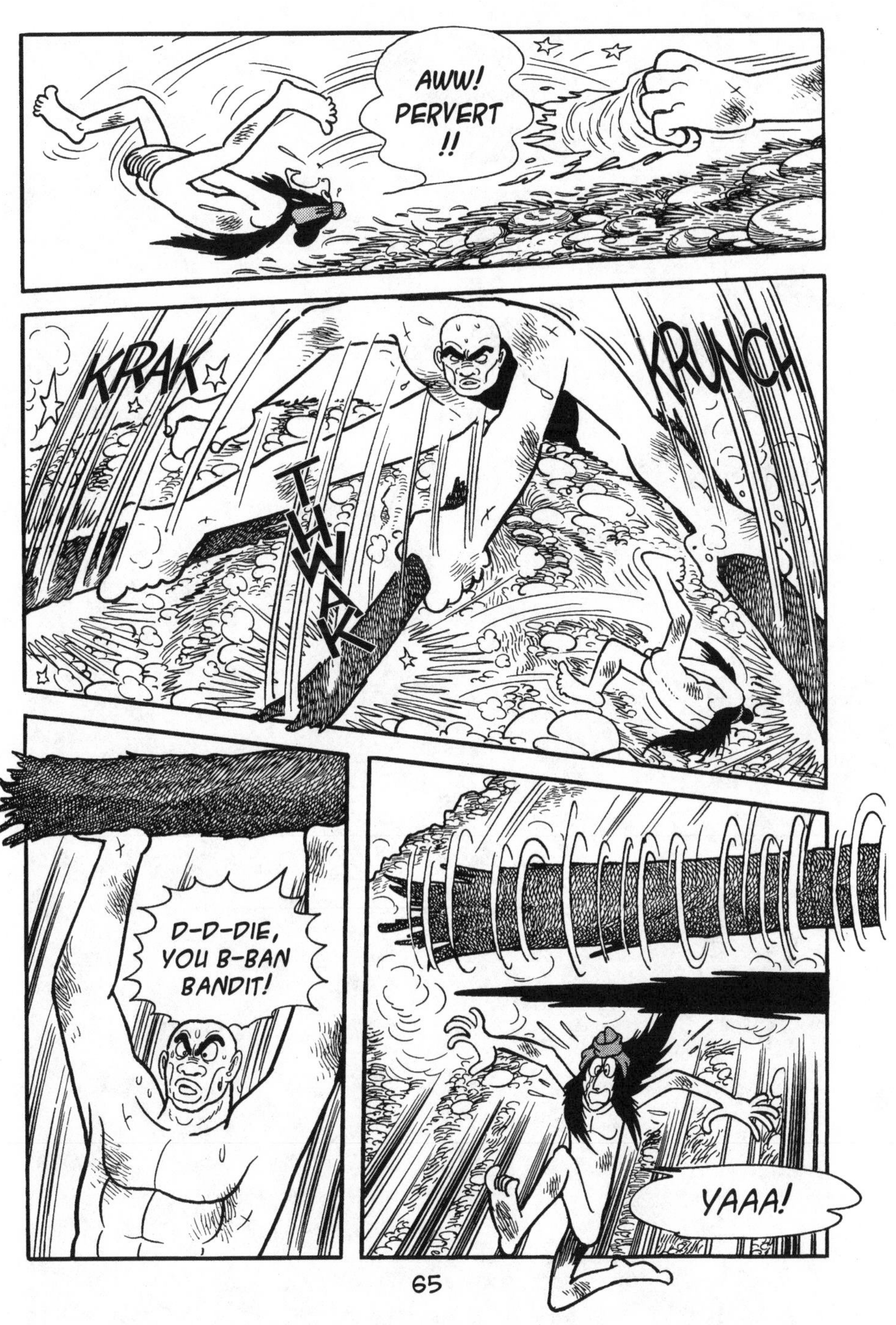
AWW! PERVERT !!
KRAK
KRUNCH
THWAK
D-D-DIE, YOU B-BAN BANDIT!
YAAA!

WHUMP
THUD
UNGH
THUD
ROLL
ROLL
BOOM
BOOM

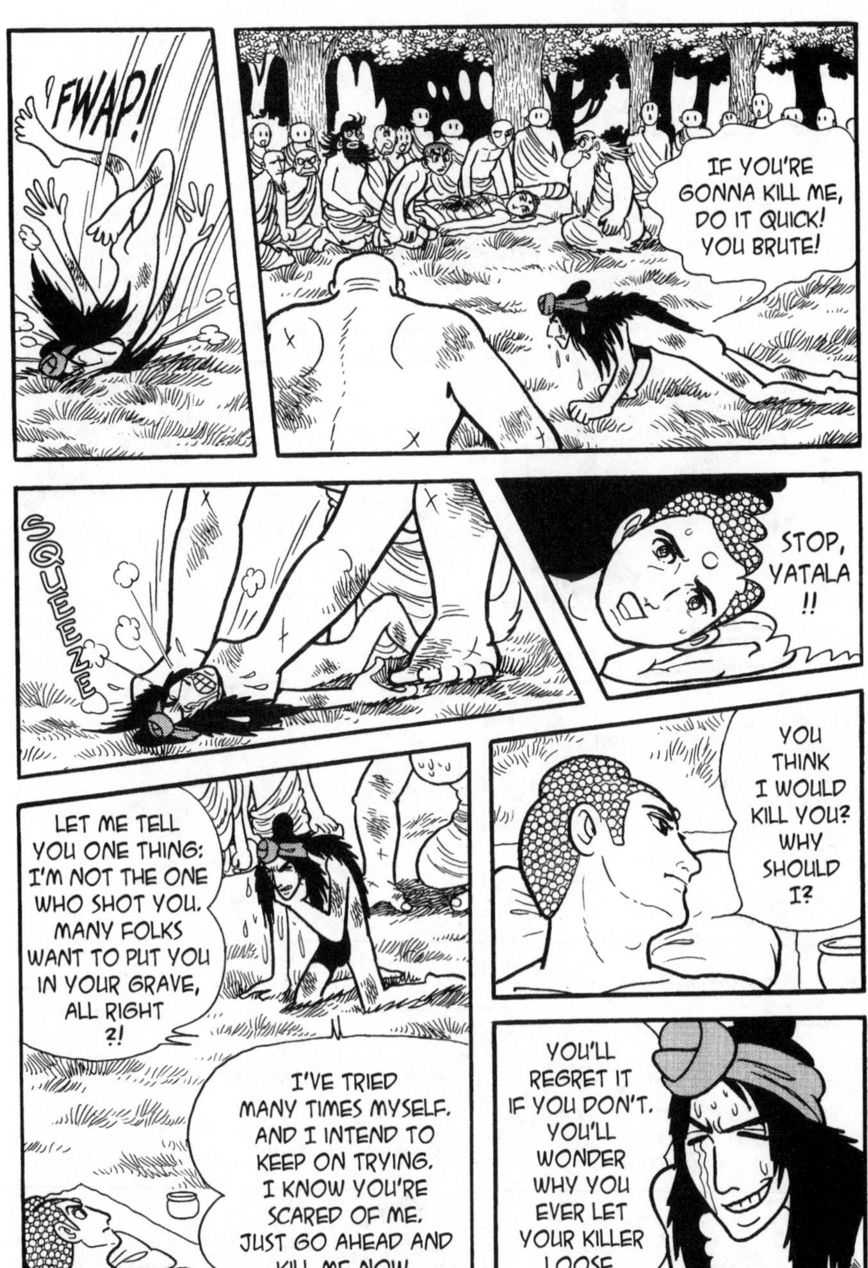
FWAP!
IF YOU'RE GONNA KILL ME, DO IT QUICK! YOU BRUTE!
SQUEEEZE
STOP, YATALA !!
YOU THINK I WOULD KILL YOU? WHY SHOULD I?
LET ME TELL YOU ONE THING: I'M NOT THE ONE WHO SHOT YOU. MANY FOLKS WANT TO PUT YOU IN YOUR GRAVE, ALL RIGHT ?!
YOU'LL REGRET IT IF YOU DON'T. YOU'LL WONDER WHY YOU EVER LET YOUR KILLER LOOSE.
I'VE TRIED MANY TIMES MYSELF. AND I INTEND TO KEEP ON TRYING. I KNOW YOU'RE SCARED OF ME. JUST GO AHEAD AND KILL ME NOW.

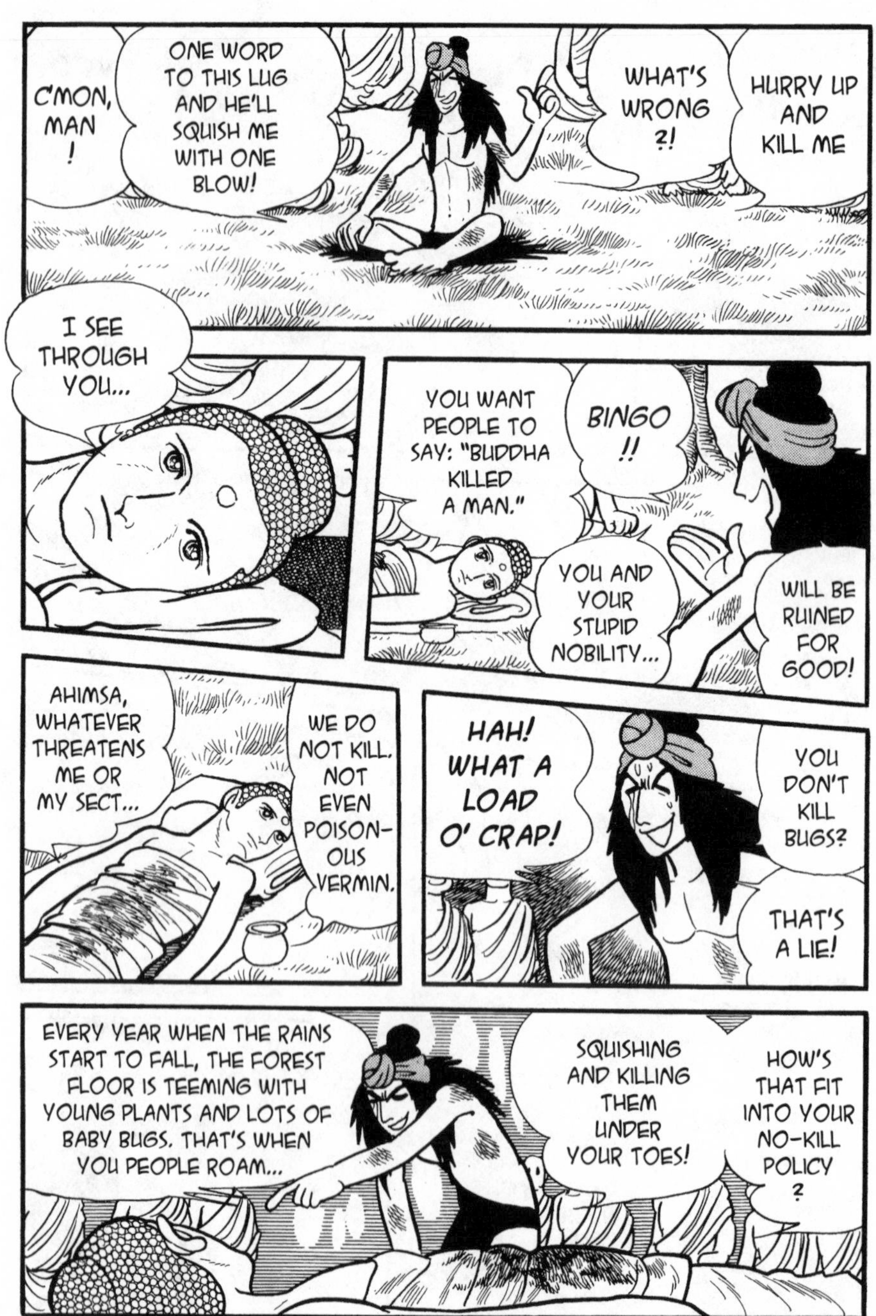
HURRY UP AND KILL ME
WHAT'S WRONG ?!
ONE WORD TO THIS LUG AND HE'LL SQUISH ME WITH ONE BLOW!
C'MON, MAN !
I SEE THROUGH YOU...
BINGO !!
YOU WANT PEOPLE TO SAY: "BUDDHA KILLED A MAN."
YOU AND YOUR STUPID NOBILITY...
WILL BE RUINED FOR GOOD!
WE DO NOT KILL. NOT EVEN POISON-OUS VERMIN.
AHIMSA, WHATEVER THREATENS ME OR MY SECT...
YOU DON'T KILL BUGS?
THAT'S A LIE!
HAH! WHAT A LOAD O' CRAP!
HOW'S THAT FIT INTO YOUR NO-KILL POLICY ?
SQUISHING AND KILLING THEM UNDER YOUR TOES!
EVERY YEAR WHEN THE RAINS START TO FALL, THE FOREST FLOOR IS TEEMING WITH YOUNG PLANTS AND LOTS OF BABY BUGS. THAT'S WHEN YOU PEOPLE ROAM...

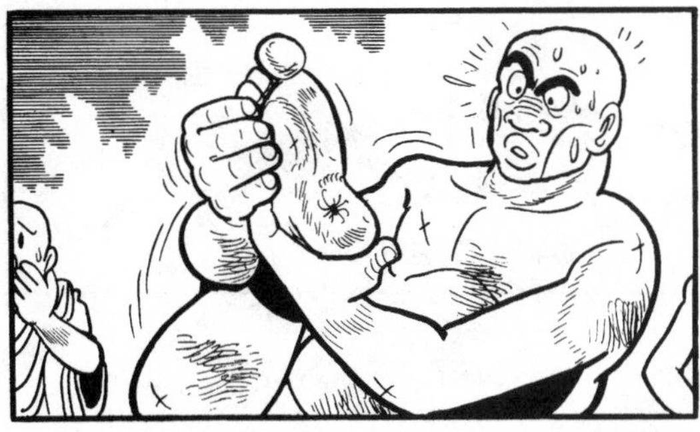

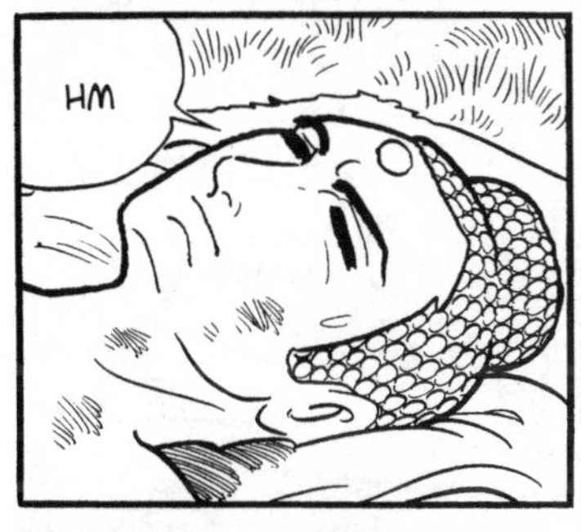
HM

AHIMSA, I THANK YOU FOR YOUR INSIGHT. YOU'VE MADE AN EXCELLENT POINT.
I TEACH MY DISCIPLES TO ABIDE BY FIVE PRECEPTS AT ALL TIMES. THE MOST IMPORTANT OF THOSE IS NON-VIOLENCE.

IF YOU CAN KILL BUGS AND SPROUTS
WHY NOT KILL A MAN?

IT MEANS NOT HARMING ANY FORM OF LIFE.
FROM NOW ON, WE WON'T WALK THROUGH THE FOREST DURING THE RAINS.
AND SO THAT WE WON'T FORGET YOUR CONTRIBUTION, I NAME THE PRECEPT "AHIMSA".
WHAT ?!

YOU BASTARD !! THANKS BUT NO THANKS !!
O WHAT A SAINT! THE NAIVE FOOL !!
CRAP! HE'S GONNA LET ME LOOSE ?!
AHIMSA, I TRUST YOU'LL OBSERVE THE PRECEPT NAMED AFTER YOU.
ANANDA, BE SO KIND AS TO SHOW OUR FRIEND TO THE EDGE OF THE GROVE.
THAT'S MORE THAN ENOUGH FOR THE DAY.
REST NOW.
YES
ALL RIGHT I WON'T KILL HIM THEN! LET HIM CROAK ON HIS OWN!
WHY DO YOU HATE BUDDHA SO MUCH ?
TELL ME FIRST, WHAT'S HE GOT THAT YOU WANTED TO BE HIS DISCIPLE?

DON'T TELL ME YOU FOLLOW THAT GUY'S "FIVE PRECEPTS" LIKE A GOOD BOY?
IT'S BULL!
WHEN YOU'RE GOING THROUGH A TRIAL, YOU HAVE TO OBEY 250 RULES!
YOU THINK FIVE IS BAD?
I'M GOING THROUGH SOMETHING WORSE THAN THAT...
BUT I...

THE DEVIL'S TRYING TO DRIVE ME INSANE! EVERY NIGHT, THE GHOSTS OF FOLKS I KILLED COME TO ME, IN LEAGUE WITH DEMONS, ATTACKING ME IN MY DREAMS...

THERE'S MORE: THOSE MONKS HATE ME CUZ I USED TO BE A KILLER.

SOME EVEN THROW STONES AT ME...
HUH

I WANT TO TEST MYSELF. TO SEE HOW MUCH I CAN TAKE. TO FIND OUT WHEN THE PAIN WILL GO AWAY.
YEAH? IF YOU GRIN AND BEAR IT YOU'LL BE ENLIGHTENED ?

NOT EVEN CLOSE... BUT AT THAT POINT I'LL BE A SOTAPANNA.

A SOTAPANNA IS — WELL, YOU COULD SAY A FRESHMAN SAINT.
ABOVE THAT YOU HAVE SAKADAGAMIN AND ANAGAMIN.
THE HIGHEST CLASS IS ARHAT. FOLLOWERS CAN PUT UP MEMORIALS TO SUCH A SAINT.

NONSENSE. "SAKADAGAMIN AND ANAGAMIN"! WHAT ARE YOU GUYS, A PHARMACY?
BUDDHA TOLD ME HE THINKS I CAN MAKE ARHAT ONE DAY.

LET'S BE PARTNERS AGAIN!! THERE'S SO MUCH TO LOOT, SO MUCH TO WIN! YOU DON'T WANT THAT?!
ANANDA!!

LEAVE ME ALONE...! GOODBYE

CHAPTER TEN

IMPRISONED PRINCE

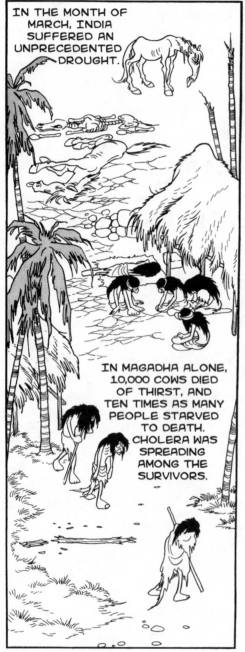

IN THE MONTH OF MARCH, INDIA SUFFERED AN UNPRECEDENTED DROUGHT.

IN MAGADHA ALONE, 10,000 COWS DIED OF THIRST, AND TEN TIMES AS MANY PEOPLE STARVED TO DEATH. CHOLERA WAS SPREADING AMONG THE SURVIVORS.

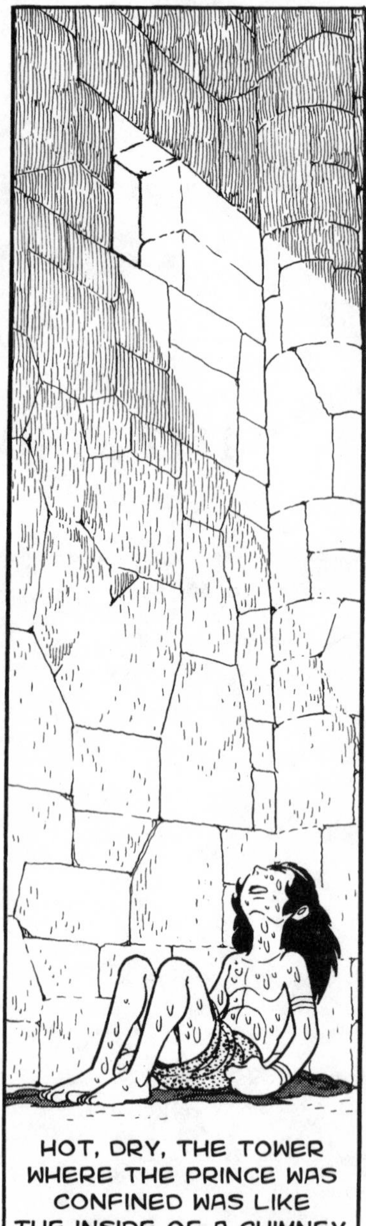

HOT, DRY, THE TOWER WHERE THE PRINCE WAS CONFINED WAS LIKE THE INSIDE OF A CHIMNEY, A DEATH CHAMBER.

PRINCE, I BRING TODAY'S RATION OF COOLED WATER.
GIMME!!
GLUG GLUG GLUG
GLUG
HOW IS IT OUTSIDE? PEOPLE STILL DROPPING LIKE FLIES?
MAYBE 50 OF OUR TROOPS DIE OF ILLNESS EVERY DAY. THE CITY STREETS ARE FLOODED WITH CORPSES.

I SEE

I SUPPOSE THIS IS BETTER THAN BEING OUTSIDE.

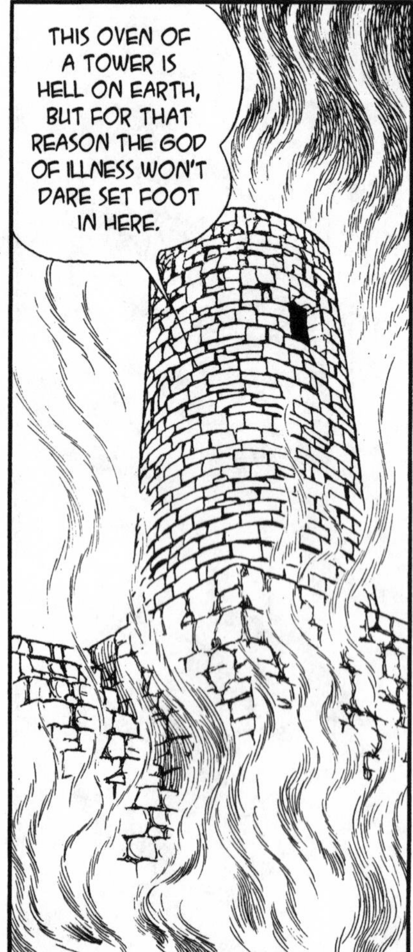
THIS OVEN OF A TOWER IS HELL ON EARTH, BUT FOR THAT REASON THE GOD OF ILLNESS WON'T DARE SET FOOT IN HERE.

HOW FARES MY FATHER ?

FROM WHAT I'VE HEARD, HE'S CONFINED HIMSELF IN VENUVANA, WHERE HE PRAYS.

HE'S WITH THAT MONK AGAIN? DAMN!
AS IF PRAYING WITH THAT FOOL WILL SCARE AWAY EVIL SPIRITS!
THAT'LL BE ALL!

...

IF YOU PERMIT ME...
I'D LIKE TO SHARE AN IDEA WITH YOU...

WHAT IS IT?

THIS PLACE WHERE YOU SIT IS ESPECIALLY HOT.
AT THE FOOT OF THE TOWER'S NORTH SIDE, ONE GETS A FAIR AMOUNT OF SHADE AND A COOL BREEZE. IF YOU WISH, I COULD LEAD YOU THERE ONCE A DAY.

THAT'S VERY THOUGHTFUL OF YOU...

AH... LEAD THE WAY
YOU'D BE ABLE TO NAP THERE.

...PLEASE KEEP THIS A SECRET, PRINCE...
UNDER-STOOD

HERE WE ARE
WOW! YESSS! HOW COOL IT IS HERE!!
JUST A THREE MINUTE WALK FROM HELL TO HEAVEN!
THIS IS WONDERFUL. THANK YOU, GUARD CAPTAIN!
I'LL RETURN FOR YOU IN AN HOUR, MILORD.
THIS IS WHAT THEY CALL BLISS...
?

BONK

THAT HOUSE PEOPLE ARE GOING IN AND OUT OF— WHAT IS IT?
HUH?
OH
W-WHAT'S THE MATTER, SIR?

SO WHY DON'T THEY BRING ME MY MEALS?

THEY'RE SLAVES...
THEY JUST BRING THE MEALS TO THE CELLS.

YOU MEAN THE ONE RIGHT AHEAD? IT'S THE KITCHEN WHERE MEALS ARE PREPARED FOR THE PRISONERS HERE, MILORD.
SO THOSE GIRLS ARE COOKS ?

THOSE ARE LOWLY WOMEN...
WE GUARDS HAVE THE HONOR OF BRINGING MEALS TO THE PRINCE.

LET THEM BRING ME MINE, YES?
UH-UH, MILORD.
I'D BE FLOGGED!

CAP'N, DO ME THIS FAVOR! I'LL TAKE THE BLAME!
PLEASE, I'M DEAD SERIOUS ABOUT THIS!

HER, THE GOLDEN-HAIRED ONE!

HEY
HALT

COME HERE

I'M NOT GONNA HURT YOU. COME AND SIT WITH ME.

SO...
HOW OLD'RE YOU?
FOURTEEN, YOUR HIGHNESS
HM!
WE'RE NEARLY THE SAME AGE

HM, YOU'RE SHAKING
ALL RIGHT, ENOUGH BOWING!
HERE, LOOK AT ME!

WHAT'S YOUR NAME?
YOUR HIGHNESS, THEY CALL ME YUDELKA.

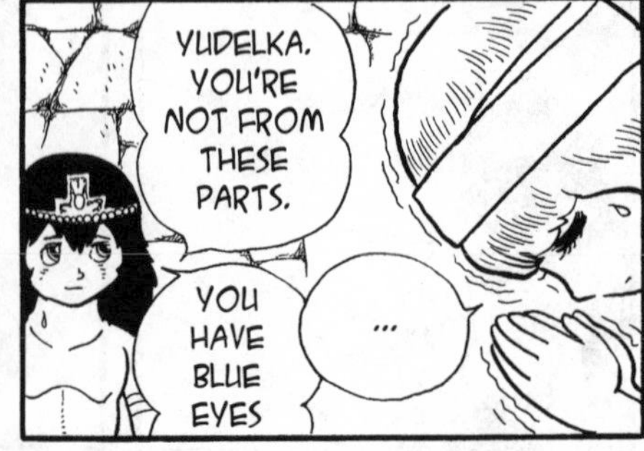
YUDELKA. YOU'RE NOT FROM THESE PARTS.
YOU HAVE BLUE EYES
...

WHY ARE YOU SILENT? ANSWER ME!!
AH, YOU'RE SCARED. AM I RIGHT? NEVER HAD TO TALK TO ROYALTY BEFORE, I TAKE IT.
FINE, YOU CAN GO NOW. BUT TOMORROW, BRING ME DINNER AGAIN. UNDERSTOOD?

PRINCE AJATASATTU IS TAKING HIS REST.
YES, WE SHOULD LET HIM REST.

DEVADATTA, YOU ARE THE BOY'S MOST TRUSTED CONFIDANT. MORE SO THAN HIS OWN PARENTS.
YOU KNOW WHAT'S BEEN WEIGHING ON HIS MIND. HOW MAY WE HELP HIM?
THIS IS NOT AN EASY MATTER...

MY QUEEN, YOUR UTMOST RESOLVE WOULD BE NEEDED

I'LL BEAR ANYTHING IF BY DOING SO THE PRINCE AND THE KING WILL FIND PEACE.
SPEAK THEN, I'M READY!

WELL THEN ...

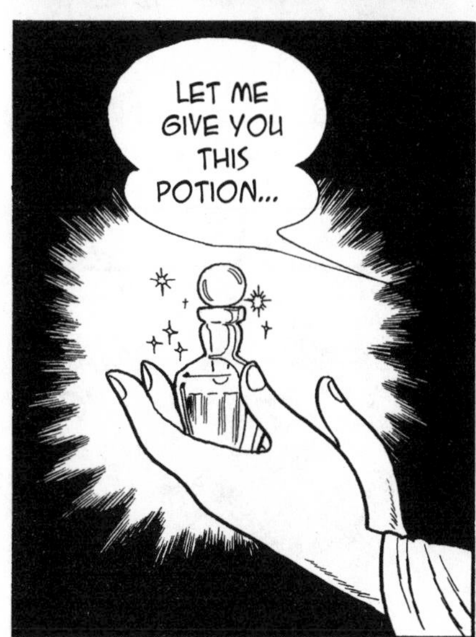
LET ME GIVE YOU THIS POTION...

IT IS A KIND OF DRUG. I ASSURE YOU, IT IS NOT POISONOUS. IT HAS THE EFFECT OF CALMING ONE'S SPIRIT SOMEWHAT.

GO ON...

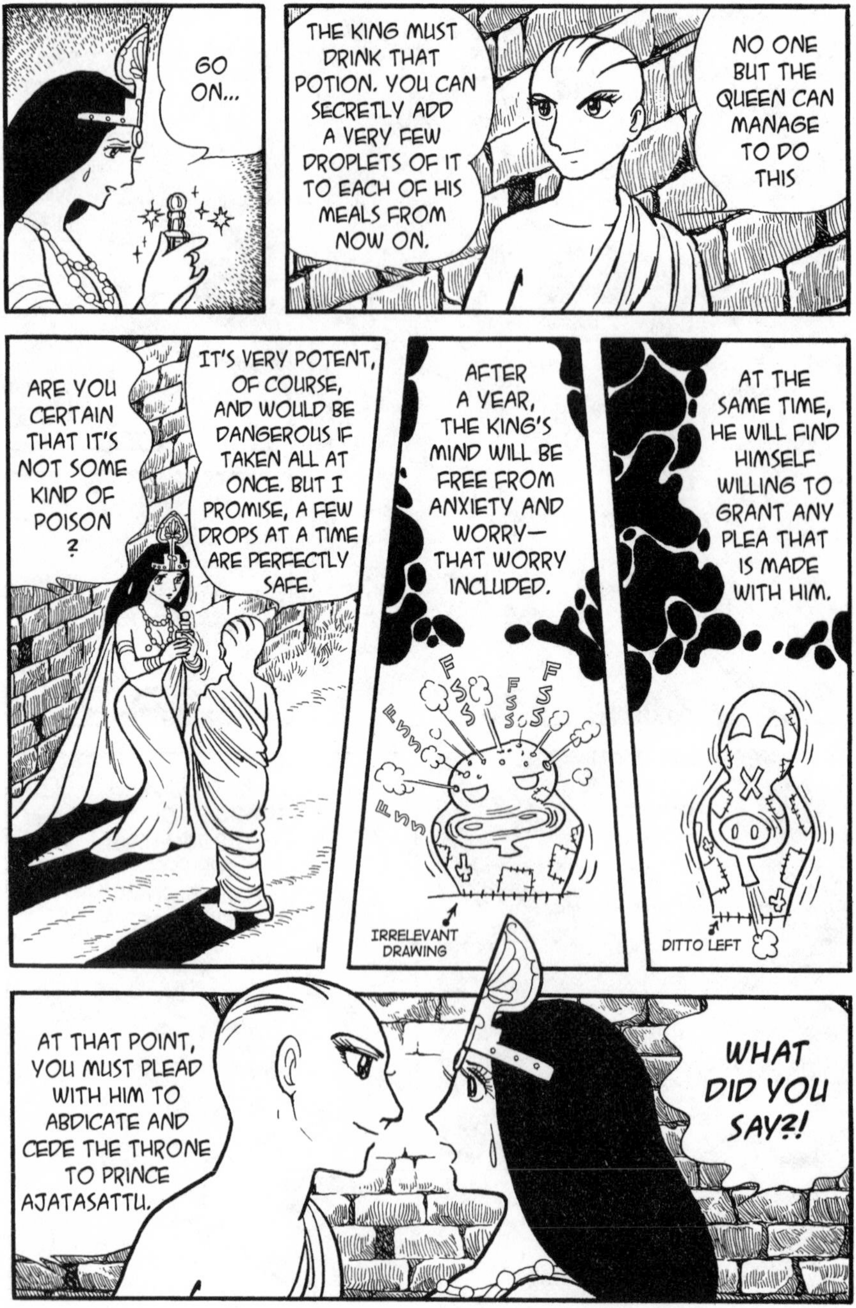

THE KING MUST DRINK THAT POTION. YOU CAN SECRETLY ADD A VERY FEW DROPLETS OF IT TO EACH OF HIS MEALS FROM NOW ON.
NO ONE BUT THE QUEEN CAN MANAGE TO DO THIS

ARE YOU CERTAIN THAT IT'S NOT SOME KIND OF POISON?

IT'S VERY POTENT, OF COURSE, AND WOULD BE DANGEROUS IF TAKEN ALL AT ONCE. BUT I PROMISE, A FEW DROPS AT A TIME ARE PERFECTLY SAFE.

AFTER A YEAR, THE KING'S MIND WILL BE FREE FROM ANXIETY AND WORRY—THAT WORRY INCLUDED.

FSSS

IRRELEVANT DRAWING

AT THE SAME TIME, HE WILL FIND HIMSELF WILLING TO GRANT ANY PLEA THAT IS MADE WITH HIM.

DITTO LEFT

AT THAT POINT, YOU MUST PLEAD WITH HIM TO ABDICATE AND CEDE THE THRONE TO PRINCE AJATASATTU.

WHAT DID YOU SAY?!

I'M SURE HIS MAJESTY WILL GRACIOUSLY STEP DOWN. IN THE FIRST PLACE HIS HARD WORK OVER THE YEARS MUST HAVE CONSUMED HIS BODY. HE LOOKS TIRED.

THE POINT IS THAT YOU MUST ASK HIM TO RETIRE.
H-HOW DARE YOU ...

AND WHEN HE DOES RETIRE, SET OFF, YOU WITH HIM, ON A LONG JOURNEY TO SOME FARAWAY LAND. MY QUEEN, THERE IS NOTHING LIKE TRAVEL.
HOW DARE YOU SPEAK THUS... TO MY FACE...! SHAMELESS!

YOU THINK I'D LEND A HAND TO YOUR WRETCHED SCHEME ?!
WATCH ME SMASH THIS VIAL

CAREFUL
THIS DOESN'T COME CHEAP!

YOU'RE GOING TOO FAR EVEN IF YOU'RE BUDDHA'S DISCIPLE!
WHAT NASTY, IMPUDENT PLOYS YOU HATCH WITH YOUR DEVIOUS MIND!
MAY I PROVE TO YOU JUST HOW SAFE THIS DRUG IS?
AS YOU CAN SEE, IN SMALL AMOUNTS THE DRUG IS HARMLESS.
DEVADATTA... ...YOU ARE A HORRIBLE MAN !!
SOONER OR LATER, THE KING WILL RETIRE ANYWAY, OF HIS OWN ACCORD.
DROP THIS, I HAVE HEARD MORE THAN ENOUGH !!
MY QUEEN, I HAVE NOTHING BUT THE HAPPINESS OF THE ROYAL FAMILY IN MIND.
MY PLAN MAKES SURE THAT THE ROYAL LINE HOLDS AND DESCENDS THROUGH YOU.

I HAVEN'T SPOKEN TO ANY WOMAN EXCEPT MY MOTHER FOR OVER A YEAR, YOU KNOW.
YES

BEING COOPED UP IN THIS KILN FOR SO LONG... YOU'VE NO IDEA HOW MUCH I MISS OUTSIDE SCENERY.
JUST ONCE, A BIRD LANDED ON THE SILL UP THERE.
A PRETTY BLUE BIRD...
YES

IS THAT ALL YOU'RE EVER GONNA SAY TO ME, "YES, YES"?

...

OKAY, LET'S TRY THIS, THEN.
TELL ME ABOUT YOUR-SELF!
YOUR HOMELAND, IT'S FAR AWAY TO THE WEST?

ARE YOU FROM THE KINGDOM OF KUSHANA? FURTHER WEST, FROM PARTHIA?
HOW DID YOU BECOME A SLAVE? DID FATHER'S TROOPS INVADE YOUR COUNTRY?
...YES
SO YOU WERE CAP-TURED.
YOUR FOLKS ?
THEY WERE KILLED...
BROTHERS AND SISTERS?
THEY WERE KILLED...
ALL OF THEM ?
...
YOU'RE CRYING. I'M SORRY.
YOU'RE ALL ALONE THEN...
...
FORGIVE MY FATHER, PLEASE.
THAT'S WHAT WAR IS LIKE...
YES

I'LL HAVE FATHER SET YOU FREE.
YOU CAN GO BACK HOME!
WHEN I'M OUT OF THIS PLACE, I'LL TRY TO MAKE AMENDS.

YUDELKA, PLEASE! PLEASE DON'T HATE ME.

I'M SO LONELY HERE

COME AGAIN TOMORROW!
TOMORROW...
IF I'M LEFT ALONE LIKE THIS ANY LONGER
I'LL GO CRAZY!

HOW MANY MORE YEARS MUST I SIT HERE?
AAH! I'M LOSING MY MIND!!

YUDELKA! WITHOUT YOU, I'M ALL BUT LOST! HELP ME!

YOU BROUGHT THESE FOR ME?
THEY WERE BLOOMING EVEN IN THIS HEAT.

YOU ACTUALLY PICKED THEM FOR ME?
I KNEW YOU COULD NOT SEE ANY FROM HERE.

YUDELKA ...
YOU'RE SUCH A SWEET GIRL!

YOU SMILED !!
MORE! SMILE! HA HA!
SHOW ME MORE OF THAT SMILE!

THESE FLOWERS ARE PRETTY, BUT YOUR SMILE PUTS THEM TO SHAME!

THEY SHOULD LAST A DAY EVEN IN THIS FURNACE
I'LL KEEP THEM IN THIS WATER BOWL
WHEN I SEE THEM I'LL THINK OF YOUR LOVELY SMILE.

YUDELKA
WHERE IS YUDELKA ?!
IT'S BEEN FIVE DAYS ALREADY SINCE HER LAST VISIT!
WHY ARE YOU GUARDS BRINGING MY MEALS AGAIN? WHERE IS SHE ?
WHAT?!
THAT SLAVE GIRL CAUGHT THE DISEASE

WHEN? WHEN DID SHE GET SICK? HOW IS SHE?
I DON'T KNOW, SIR! SHE'S JUST A SLAVE!
WHY WASN'T I TOLD? LET ME OUT! I'M GOING TO SEE HER!
WAIT, YOU CAN'T DO THAT, MILORD!
OUT OF MY WAY
OMPH!
PRINCE, NO ONE'S ALLOWED INTO THE HUT! IT'S OFF LIMITS DUE TO DISEASE!

WHY DIDN'T THEY TELL ME?
HOW COULD THEY NOT TELL ME! BECAUSE SHE'S A SLAVE?!
NOW I KNOW...
THIS IS HOW IT FEELS LIKE TO BE IN LOVE!
ATTENTION! THE PRINCE HAS GONE MAD!
GUARDS, SCRAMBLE!
GONG GONG GONG GONG
I SEE HIM
STOP, YOUR HIGHNESS! YOU'LL GET SICK!
ARGH! HE'S HEADING FOR THE SLAVE QUARTERS!

WHERE IS YUDELKA?
THAT'S PRINCE AJATASATTU! PAY YOUR RESPECTS, SLAVES!
LORD ...
ENOUGH, JUST TELL ME WHERE THE BLUE-EYED BLONDE IS!
DON'T! THE PLAGUE GOD WILL GET YOU!
DAMN! YUDELKA'S IN HERE?!

PRINCE, YOU MUST NOT!
KARC
YUDELKA...
WE'LL HAVE THE COURT DOCTOR TREAT YOU!
YOU...M-MUST NOT... COME HERE, PRINCE

YOU JUST SHOVED THEM ALL IN THERE AND NAILED THE DOORS SHUT?

OGRES, ALL OF YOU! STAND DOWN! THIS GIRL I WILL SAVE!

WHAT ?!

HE DID WHAT ?!

HE BROKE OUT OF THE TOWER, AND RESCUED A SICK GIRL FROM THE SLAVE QUARTERS

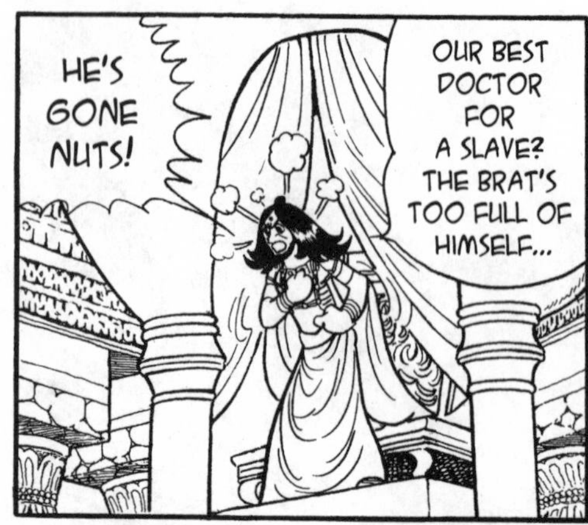
HE'S GONE NUTS!
OUR BEST DOCTOR FOR A SLAVE? THE BRAT'S TOO FULL OF HIMSELF...

DRAG THE GIRL AWAY FROM HIM, AND KILL HER.
WELL, YOU SEE...

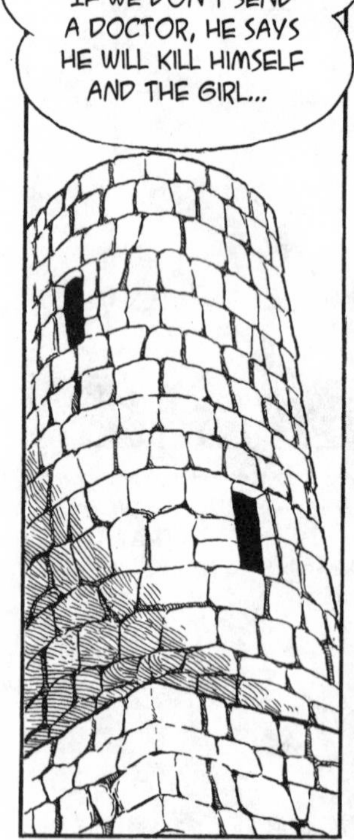
THE PRINCE HAS LOCKED HIMSELF INTO THE TOWER. IF WE DON'T SEND A DOCTOR, HE SAYS HE WILL KILL HIMSELF AND THE GIRL...

HE'S GOT A LOT OF NERVE, PESTERING US FROM PRISON.
LET US FETCH THE DOCTOR, BUT WE'LL HAVE HIM TREAT THE SLAVE IN HER OWN HUT.
I BELIEVE OUR ONLY CHOICE IS TO COMPLY...

GET IT DONE!

PRINCE AJATASATTU !!
MY LORD, PLEASE OPEN THE DOOR!
IT'S ME, THE DOCTOR ZIWAKA!

AH! WHO ELSE IS WITH YOU, GOOD DOCTOR ?
JUST THE MINISTER AND A FEW GUARDS
ALL RIGHT
YOU CAN COME IN...
BEFORE I DO SO, I HAVE A REQUEST. THE INVALID MUST BE SEQUESTERED, LEST THE DEMON POSSESS YOU TOO!
SEND HER BACK TO HER QUARTERS
NO WAY
NO !!
IT MUST BE HOT AND HUMID IN THAT CELL. THE INVALID HAS NO HOPE OF RECOVERY THERE.
THE SLAVES' HUT IS THE BETTER PLACE
...
FINE ...
YOU CAN CARRY HER THERE
BUT I'M GOING TOO!

PRINCE, THIS IS AS FAR AS YOU GO
YONDER PREMISE IS HOME TO FILTHY SHUDRA
PLEASE RETURN TO YOUR CELL

MOVE

PRINCE, YOU'RE STILL UNDER ARREST. WE CAN'T ALLOW YOU TO WANDER ABOUT AS YOU PLEASE!

DOCTOR, TAKE A LOOK AT THIS PLACE!

WITHOUT WATER OR MEDICINE, LEFT TO DIE A DOG'S DEATH! AREN'T THEY HUMAN, TOO?
ALL OF THEM FORCED TO LIE HERE IN THIS DUMP

IT CANNOT BE HELPED. THESE WERE BORN INTO SUCH LIVES.

BUT WHY AREN'T SHUDRA TREATED LIKE HUMANS? THEY LOOK JUST AS HUMAN AS WE DO!
...

LAY HER THERE

THIS IS NOT GOOD. SHE'S UN-CONSCIOUS AND CAN'T TAKE HER MEDICINE.

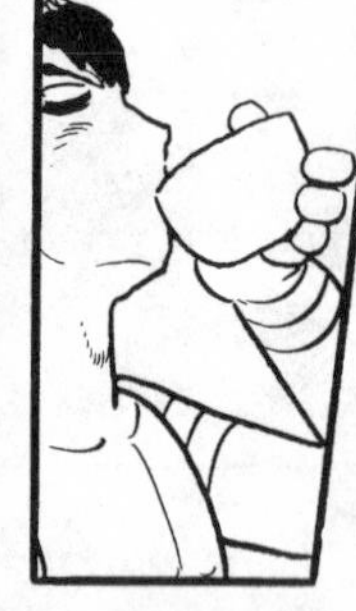
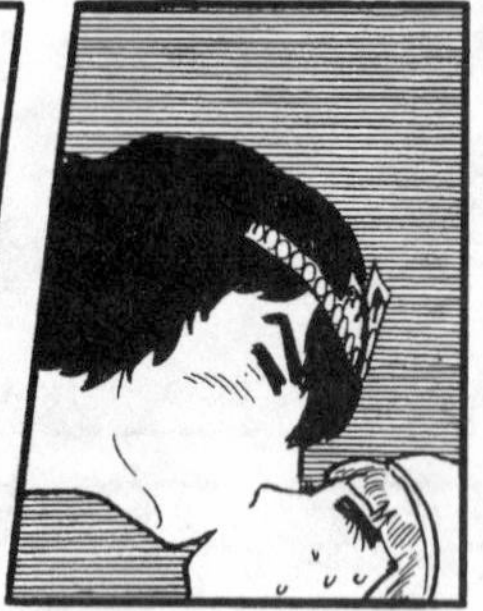

WH-WHAT ARE YOU DOING?!
MOUTH-FEEDING A SHUDRA WOMAN...
IT ISN'T PROPER !!

YOUNG PRINCE, DON'T TELL ME...

YOU'VE TAKEN A LIKING TO THIS GIRL? THAT IS WHY YOU CARE FOR HER!
YOU'RE RIGHT, MINISTER UNDERBELLY. HER NAME'S YUDELKA.
SHE'S BEEN MY SOLE COMFORT THIS PAST MONTH, MY ONLY FRIEND, WHO'S KEPT ME HUMAN!

IN THAT CASE, WE CAN ASSIGN HER AS YOUR PERSONAL SLAVE. BUT YOU MUST STOP WITH THE MOUTH-FEEDING!

IF THE KING HEARS OF THIS...
GO TELL HIM IF THAT'S WHAT YOU WANT.

AS IF I WOULD DARE TO SPEAK OF IT!
IT WAS ON MY ADVICE THAT THE KING ORDERED A DOCTOR TO TEND TO A SLAVE! I'D HAVE TO TAKE THE BLAME FOR WHAT YOU DID!

MINISTER UNDERBELLY, PLEASE...

GET YUDELKA RELEASED FROM HER BONDAGE. WHEN SHE GETS BETTER, I WANT HER TO BE FREE!

HER COUNTRY WAS RANSACKED BY FATHER'S ARMY. SHE WASN'T BORN INTO SLAVERY LIKE OTHER SHUDRA. I WANT TO RETURN HER TO HER TRUE STATION AND LET HER GO HOME!
PRINCE, I HAVE SERVED SINCE YOUR FATHER'S FATHER WAS KING...
AS PRIME MINISTER, YOU CAN DO ANYTHING, CAN'T YOU?
AND I LOOK FORWARD TO SERVING YOU, SOMEDAY. AND THAT IS BECAUSE I TRUST YOU WILL GROW UP TO BECOME A GREAT MAN, SPLENDID, WORTHY OF THE THRONE!
UNTIL THAT DAY, DON'T FLOUT COMMON SENSE SO. IT'S NOT IN YOUR INTEREST!

WHO PUT ME IN THAT TOWER?
IS THAT SUPPOSED TO BE COMMON SENSE?!
I'M IN LOVE WITH THIS GIRL. I LOVE HER FROM THE BOTTOM OF MY HEART!
ONCE SHE'S FREE, I WANT TO START SEEING HER
AND THEN ?
I MIGHT MARRY HER
YOU WILL NOT
PLEASE. THINK AGAIN, PRINCE.
YOU ARE THE FUTURE KING!
PUT HER IN YOUR HAREM OR SOMETHING, BUT

MINISTER UNDERBELLY! HAVE YOU NEVER BEEN IN LOVE WITH A WOMAN?

OH, I'VE HAD A DOZEN LOVERS IN MY TIME, YOUNG SIR!
I'VE BEEN MARRIED 8 TIMES!

THEY WERE ALL WOMEN OF FINE BREEDING.
I NEVER ONCE HANKERED AFTER ANY SLAVE. OR FORMER SLAVE!

THE MEDICINE SEEMS TO BE WORKING. SHE BREATHES STEADY.

DOCTOR ZIWAKA, PLEASE TAKE GOOD CARE OF HER.
I'M GOING BACK TO THE TOWER, BUT I'D LIKE YOU TO COME REPORT ON HER CONDITION TOMORROW. BY THE GODS, DOCTOR, BRING HER BACK TO HEALTH!

SO THAT MOUTH-TO-MOUTH WORKED, RIGHT? RIGHT?

SPIRIT OF THE MOON
I BEG YOU
I BEG YOU TO PROTECT THAT GIRL

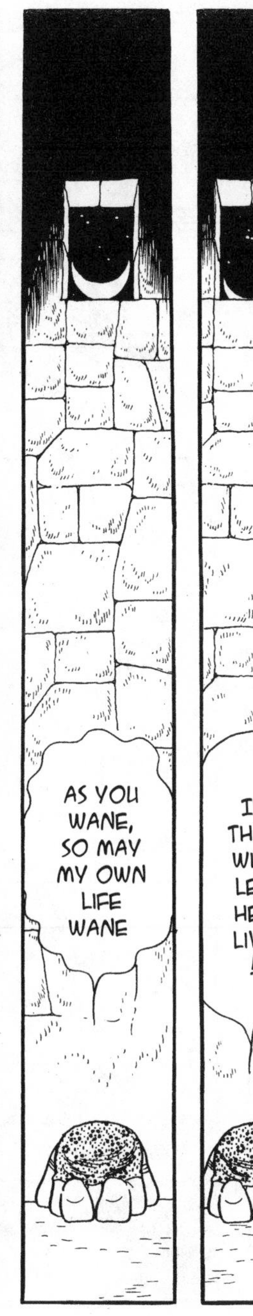
AS YOU WANE, SO MAY MY OWN LIFE WANE

IF THAT WILL LET HER LIVE !

YUDELKA !!

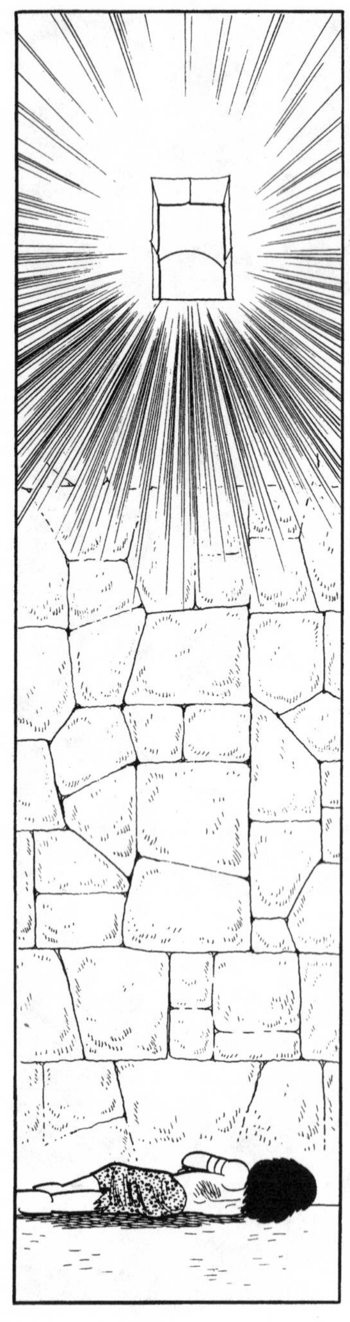

DOCTOR ZIWAKA

AH, DEAR PRINCE, YOU ARE AWAKE?

HA HA HA. SET YOUR HEART AT REST. HER FEVER'S GONE;
SHE CAN EVEN TALK.
DOCTOR !!
HOW IS SHE?

REALLY ?!

TELL ME THE TRUTH. YOU'RE NOT JUST TRYING TO CONSOLE ME?
IF YOU DON'T BELIEVE ME, LOOK OUT THE DOOR.

YUDELKA!
P... PRINCE...
A FEW OF THE OTHER SLAVES SHOULD ALSO BE GETTING BETTER.
DOCTOR! YOU ATTENDED TO THEM, TOO?
EH, THERE WAS A BIT OF MEDICINE LEFT OVER
YUDELKA, THIS DOCTOR SAVED YOU!
NO NO, IT WAS ALL YOUR DOING, PRINCE.

DO YOU REMEMBER THE STRANGE THING YOU SAID TO ME YESTERDAY?
WHY WE DON'T TREAT SHUDRA LIKE HUMANS, WHEN THEY HAVE FACES AND BODIES LIKE OURS?

BUT IT IS STRANGE, COME TO THINK OF IT, JUST AS YOU SAY.
I'VE NEVER BEEN TROUBLED BY SUCH AN IDEA BEFORE

PERHAPS IT'S A QUESTION OF SOME IMPORT. ESPECIALLY FOR DOCTORS.

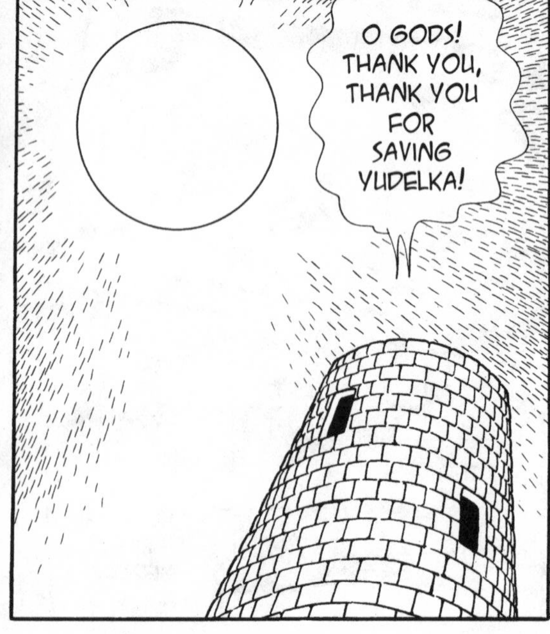
O GODS! THANK YOU, THANK YOU FOR SAVING YUDELKA!

I BET YOUR COUNTRY IS MUCH LESS HOT THAN OURS, WITH GRASS AND FRUIT TREES EVERYWHERE
AND CLEAR COOL SPRINGS, WHERE GIRLS FROLIC WITH WATERFOWL
DID I GUESS RIGHT?
YES, PRINCE. IT WAS SUCH A PLACE, WHEN I WAS LITTLE. I DON'T KNOW IF IT'S STILL THE WAY I REMEMBER IT, THOUGH...

WANT TO GO HOME ?

I ASKED THE MINISTER ABOUT GETTING YOU FREED. IT DOESN'T SEEM LIKELY.

EVEN IF YOU GET BETTER, YOU'LL STILL BE A SLAVE
AND I'M A SQUIRREL IN A CAGE!

YUDELKA, I HAVE AN IDEA
LET'S ESCAPE TOGETHER!
WHAT ?!

WE'LL RUN AWAY TO YOUR COUNTRY!
BUT... THAT'S...

I'M SCARED

WE'LL BE FINE! I'VE GOT A GREAT PLAN!

WE'LL SNEAK OUT PAST YOUR HUT. THEY DON'T PUT MANY GUARDS OVER THERE. THEN WE'LL TAKE TO THE FOREST, WHICH WILL COVER US UNTIL WE REACH THE BORDER.

WE'LL USE THESE GEMS TO BUY A HORSE FROM A MERCHANT.

BUT YOU'RE SUPPOSED TO INHERIT THE THRONE! YOU CAN'T JUST GO AHEAD AND DO SUCH A THING!
HA HA YOU SOUND SO MATURE

I DON'T CARE ABOUT THE THRONE, OKAY?
I'D GLADLY GIVE UP BEING ROYALTY!

I'LL LIVE IN YOUR COUNTRY AS A COMMONER, WITH YOU!

DON'T YOU SEE? I'D GIVE MY LIFE FOR YOU!
YUDELKA, I LOVE YOU

I'D EVEN BECOME A SLAVE. I DON'T EVER WANT TO LOSE YOU AGAIN!
I'D DO ANYTHING, FACE ANY DANGER, IF ONLY I COULD BE WITH YOU!

SLEEP ON IT, ALL RIGHT?
DON'T WORRY

I'LL WORK OUT THE WHOLE PLAN

!

YUDELKA, OH YUDELKA!
TOMORROW, WE WILL FLY AWAY
LIKE TWO BIRDS,
TO FIND OUR TRUE FREE
HEAVEN AND EARTH.

YOUR WATER, PRINCE
THANKS... WHERE'S THE SLAVE GIRL, YUDELKA?

SIR, SHE WAS PUT TO DEATH JUST THIS MORNING.
D... DEATH ?

YUDELKA?! DEAD?
H-HOW CAN THAT BE?!

N-NO!!
THAT WAS MY IDEA! IT WAS MY PLAN TO BREAK OUT!
IT WAS FOUND OUT THAT SHE WAS PREVAILING UPON YOU TO ESCAPE.

...I'M NOT PARTY TO HIGH-LEVEL DECISIONS, PRINCE...
WHY DIDN'T ANYONE INTERROGATE ME? HUH? WHY DIDN'T I HEAR A WORD OF THIS?

UM, MILORD ...I'VE BROUGHT HER HAIR FOR YOU.

IT'S A LIE! YUDELKA CAN'T BE DEAD!
THIS MUST BE SOME TRICK! SHE'S GOT TO BE ALIVE!

WHAT?! YUDELKA'S HAIR?

Y-
YUDELKA... SO YOU...

AH
AAAAH!

YUDELKA!
AH! AH! AH! AH!
UHH
WHO DID IT? WHO ON EARTH GAVE SUCH A CRUEL ORDER...?
YUDELKA AAH!
NO! NO
OHHH
AAAAH
OOHH

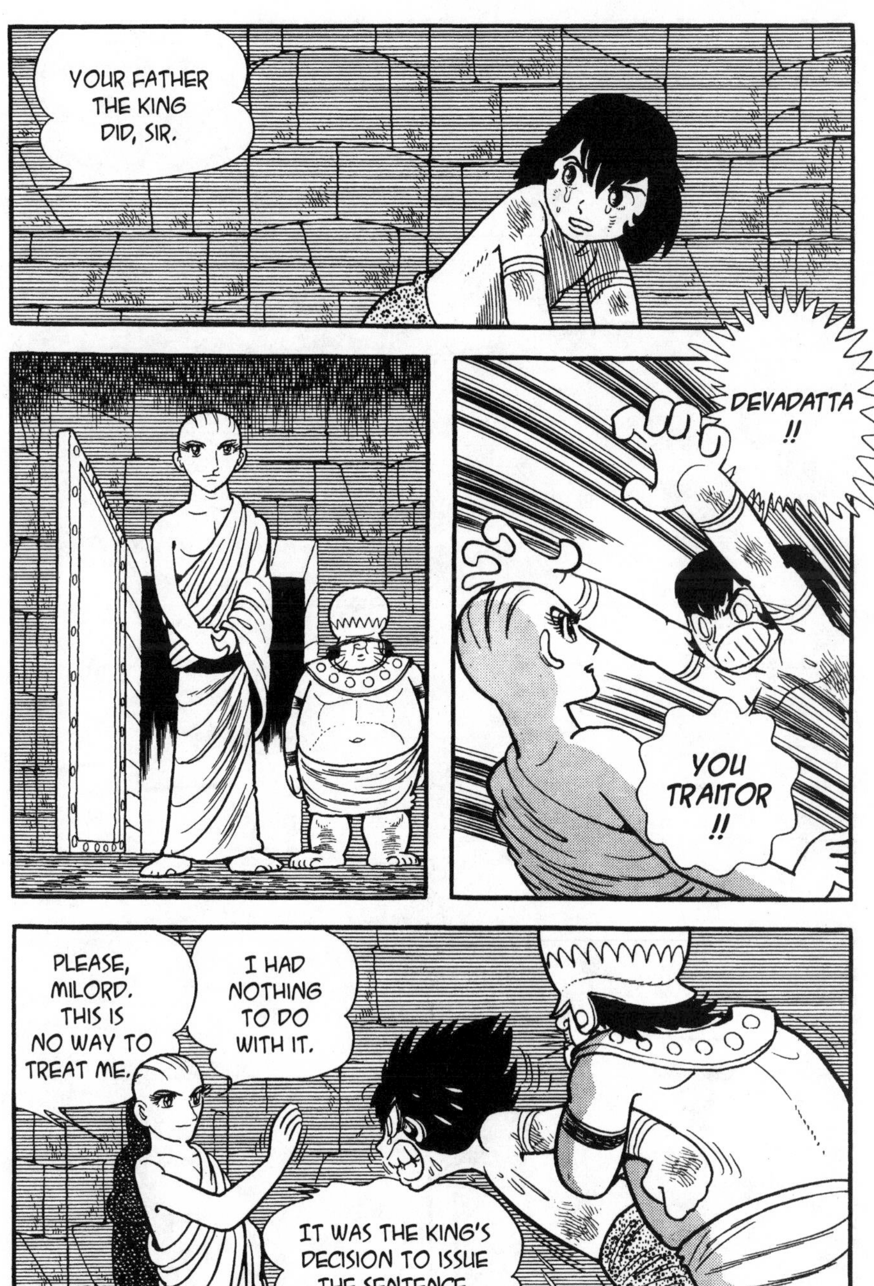
YOUR FATHER THE KING DID, SIR.
DEVADATTA !!
YOU TRAITOR !!
PLEASE, MILORD. THIS IS NO WAY TO TREAT ME.
I HAD NOTHING TO DO WITH IT.
IT WAS THE KING'S DECISION TO ISSUE THE SENTENCE.

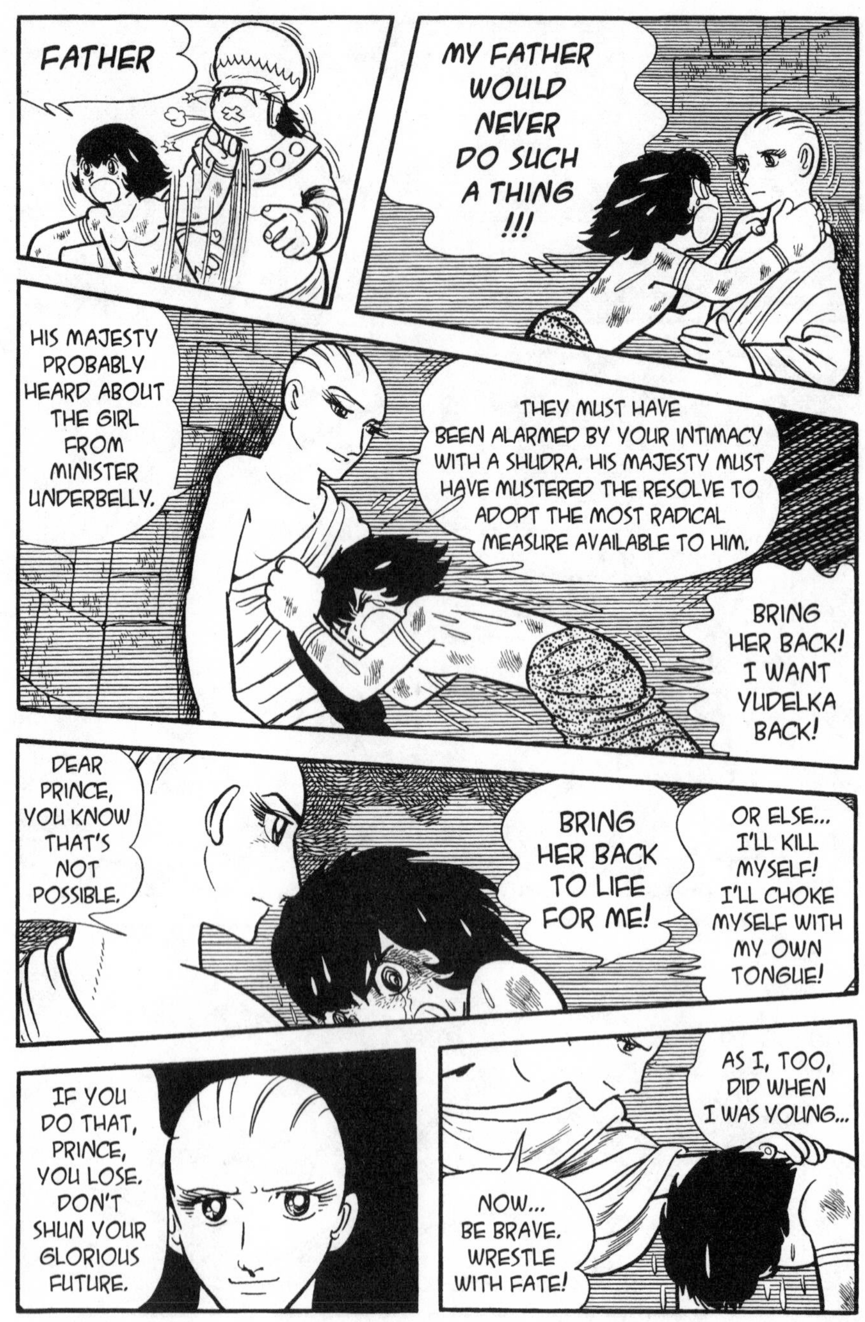
FATHER
MY FATHER WOULD NEVER DO SUCH A THING !!!
HIS MAJESTY PROBABLY HEARD ABOUT THE GIRL FROM MINISTER UNDERBELLY.
THEY MUST HAVE BEEN ALARMED BY YOUR INTIMACY WITH A SHUDRA. HIS MAJESTY MUST HAVE MUSTERED THE RESOLVE TO ADOPT THE MOST RADICAL MEASURE AVAILABLE TO HIM.
BRING HER BACK! I WANT YUDELKA BACK!
DEAR PRINCE, YOU KNOW THAT'S NOT POSSIBLE.
BRING HER BACK TO LIFE FOR ME!
OR ELSE... I'LL KILL MYSELF! I'LL CHOKE MYSELF WITH MY OWN TONGUE!
IF YOU DO THAT, PRINCE, YOU LOSE. DON'T SHUN YOUR GLORIOUS FUTURE.
AS I, TOO, DID WHEN I WAS YOUNG...
NOW... BE BRAVE. WRESTLE WITH FATE!

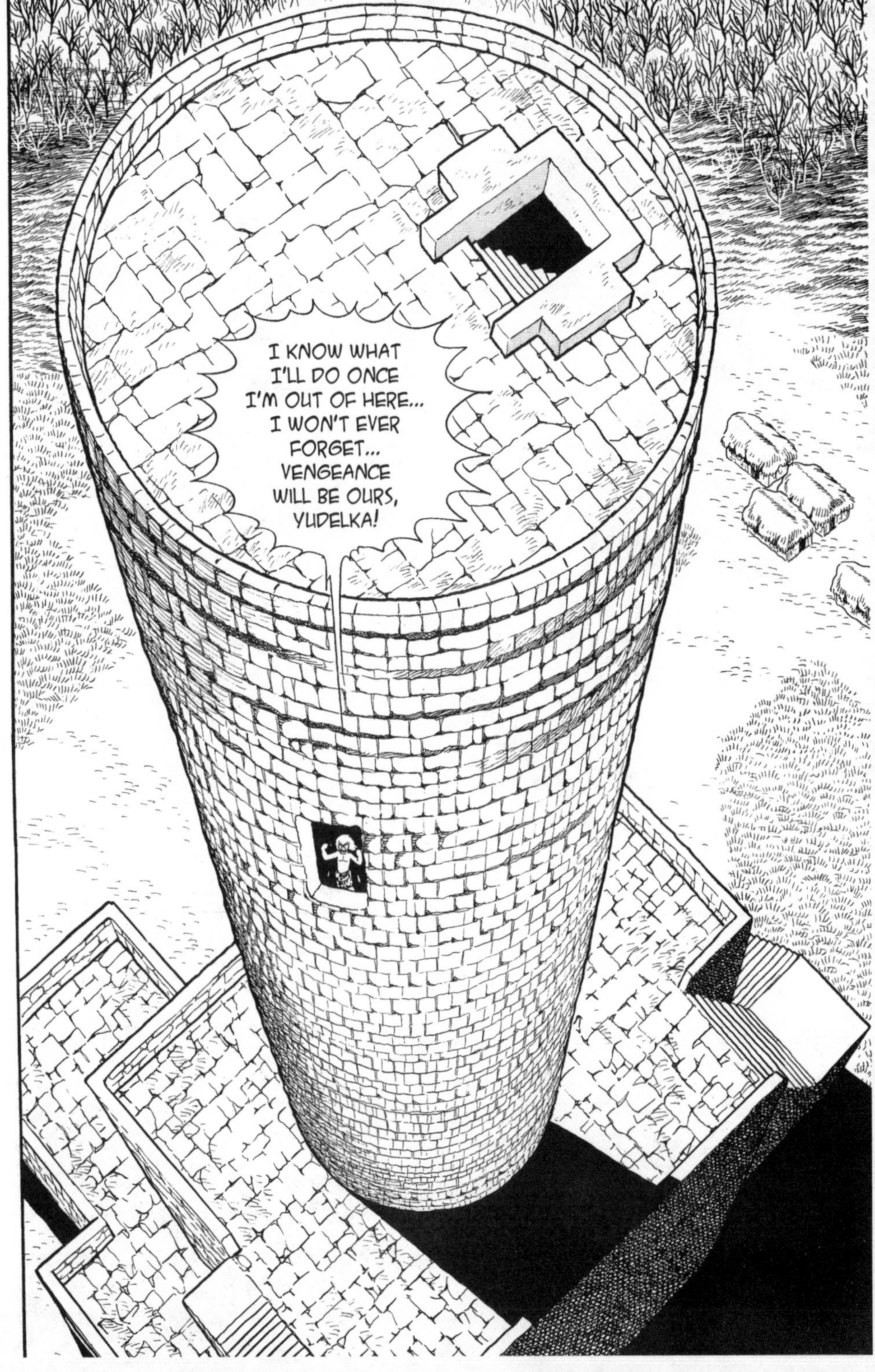
I KNOW WHAT I'LL DO ONCE I'M OUT OF HERE... I WON'T EVER FORGET... VENGEANCE WILL BE OURS, YUDELKA!

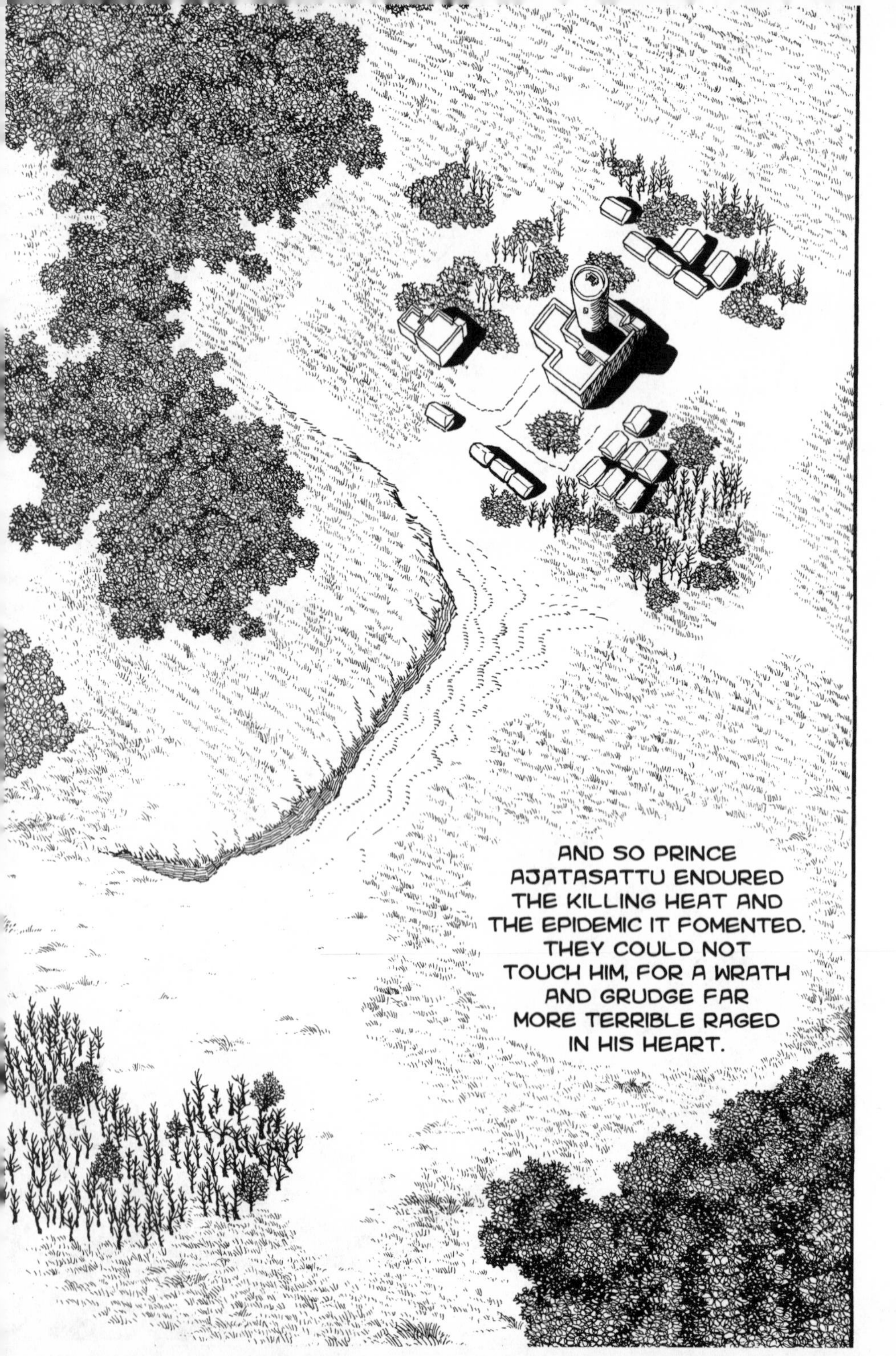
AND SO PRINCE AJATASATTU ENDURED THE KILLING HEAT AND THE EPIDEMIC IT FOMENTED. THEY COULD NOT TOUCH HIM, FOR A WRATH AND GRUDGE FAR MORE TERRIBLE RAGED IN HIS HEART.

PART SIX

CHAPTER ONE

Sariputta and Moggallana

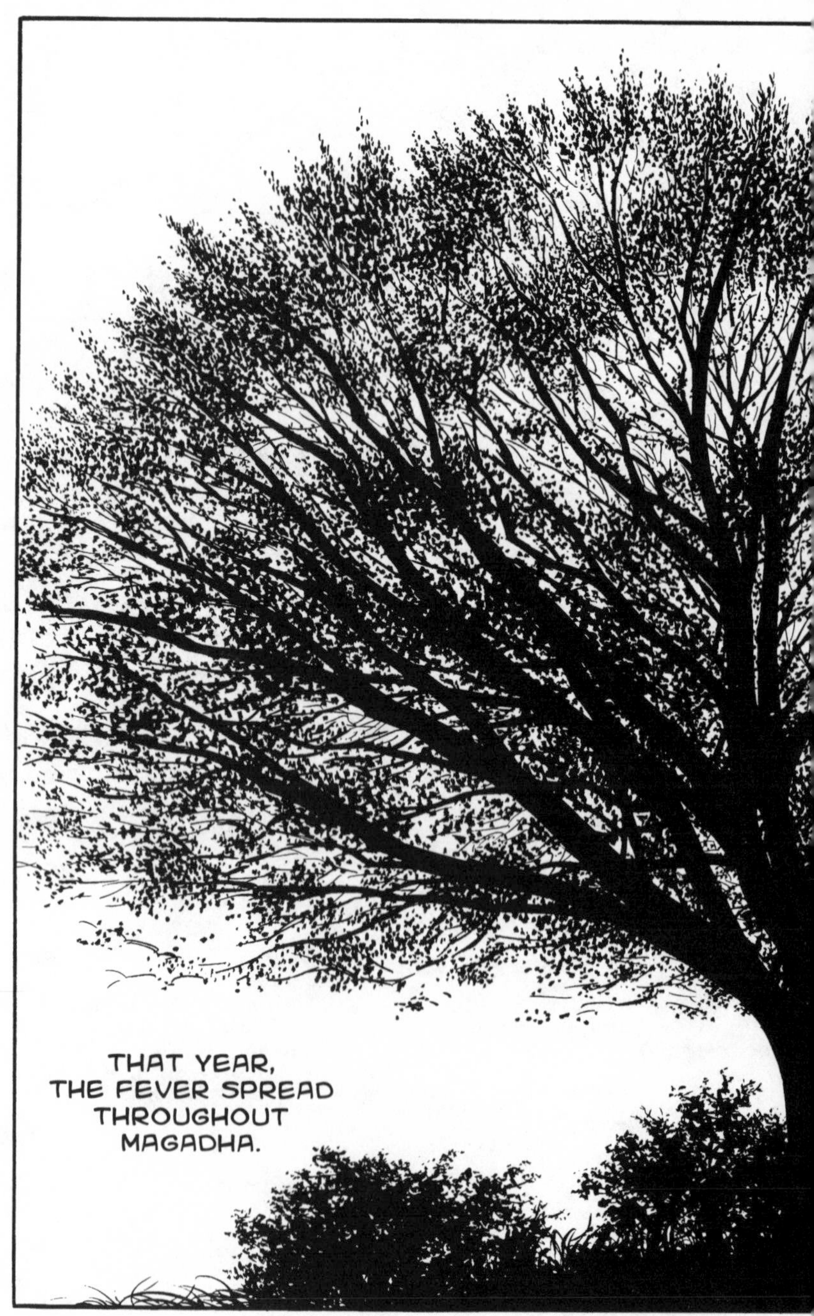
THAT YEAR, THE FEVER SPREAD THROUGHOUT MAGADHA.

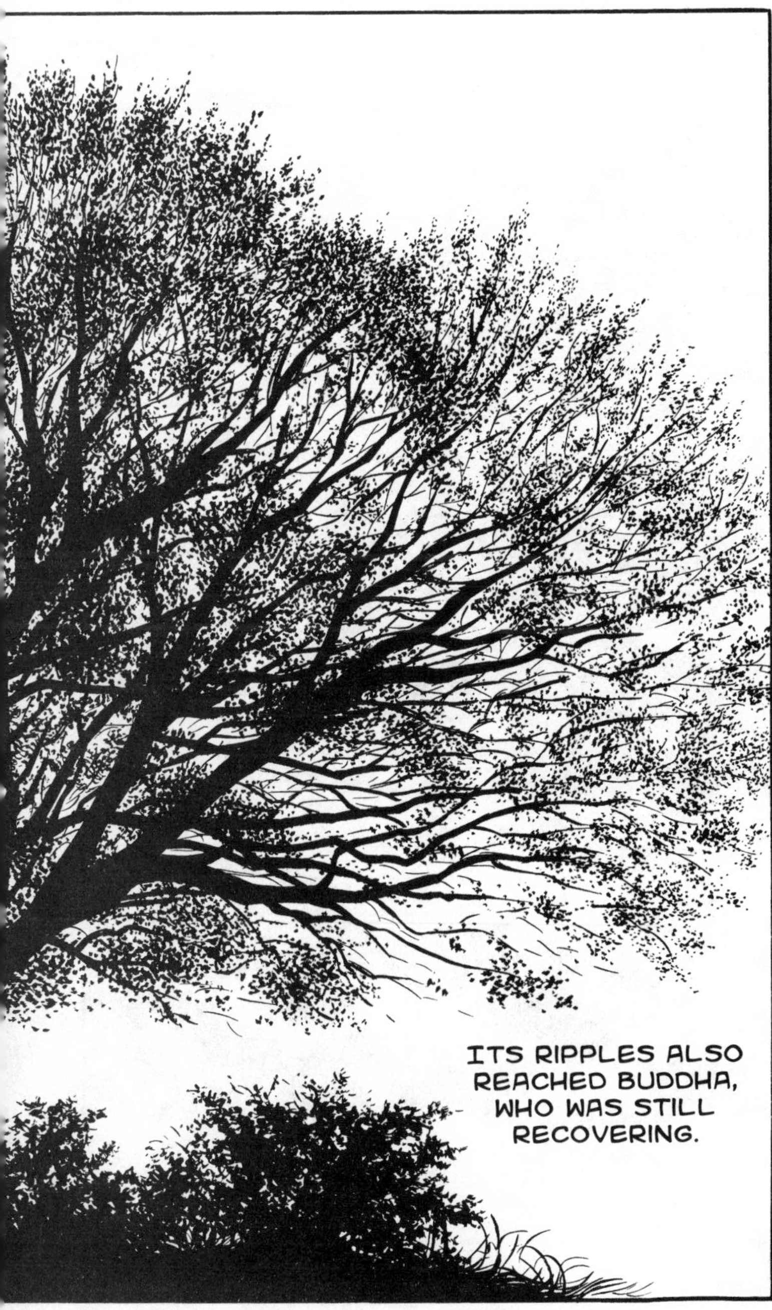
ITS RIPPLES ALSO REACHED BUDDHA, WHO WAS STILL RECOVERING.

VENUVANA

STILL STARING OUT AT NOTHING, TATTA?
I'M CHECKING TO SEE IF THEY DON'T HAVE LESS CORPSES TO BURN.

DOESN'T LOOK LIKE THEY'LL BE RUNNING OUT ANYTIME SOON. I'M AFRAID THIS FEVER PLANS ON STICKING AROUND A COUPLE MORE YEARS.
BUMMER

I'D HOPED BUDDHA HADN'T BEEN HIT TOO HARD, BUT HE'S STILL GOT DIARRHEA AND THE SWELLING...
GOD'S WATCHING OVER BUDDHA. HE'LL BE FINE.

BUT HE NEVER FULLY RECOVERED HIS HEALTH SINCE THAT INCIDENT, YOU KNOW.

HIS FACE HAS AGED SO IN THE PAST FEW MONTHS...

IT'S AS THOUGH, ALL OF A SUDDEN, HE HAS BECOME A MAN IN HIS FIFTIES, OR EVEN SIXTIES...

I'M WORRIED FOR THE SAKE OF ALL OF US... WHEN I FIRST MET HIM, HE WAS OVERFLOWING WITH VITALITY.

ACTUALLY, BUDDHA WAS NEVER IN GREAT HEALTH EVEN AS A YOUTH.
HE NEVER EXERCISED MUCH, AND HE DIDN'T LIKE TO PARTAKE IN BOUTS.

IF THE WORST WERE TO HAPPEN,
WHAT WOULD BECOME OF US?

HEY GUYS, QUIT BEING SO MORBID!
BUDDHA'S PROBABLY JUST TRYING TO TEACH YOU INSOMNIACS HOW REFRESHING A NAP CAN BE!

OKAY, THEN MAYBE HE'S TRYING TO REMEMBER SOME KIND OF CURE WHILE HE'S SLEEPING, RECOVERING OLD MEMORIES FROM THE PAST...
WHY WOULD HE TEACH SUCH A THING, FOOL!

CUT THE CRAP, TATTA!

BUDDHA, HE HEALED MY WIFE'S SORES AND BROUGHT BACK HER VOICE! HECK, HE EVEN SAVED YOU ONCE! SO STOP FRETTING!
I'M SAYIN' NO FEVER WILL EVER GET HIM!

I MEAN...

YOU THINK I'M NOT WORRIED SICK TOO?
I'M LOSING SLEEP OVER IT, OKAY?

ANANDA...
YES?

MIGHT I BEG A FAVOR ?

ANYTHING
I NEED YOU TO LOOK FOR A MAN.

WHO AND WHERE IS THIS MAN ?
I DO NOT KNOW. ONE WHO CAN SEE INTO THE FUTURE.

?

I'VE TOLD YOU ABOUT ASSAJI, HAVE I NOT?

YES, YOU TOLD ME.
I WANT SOMEONE JUST LIKE HIM, A MAN WHO CAN SEE INTO THE FUTURE LIKE ASSAJI!

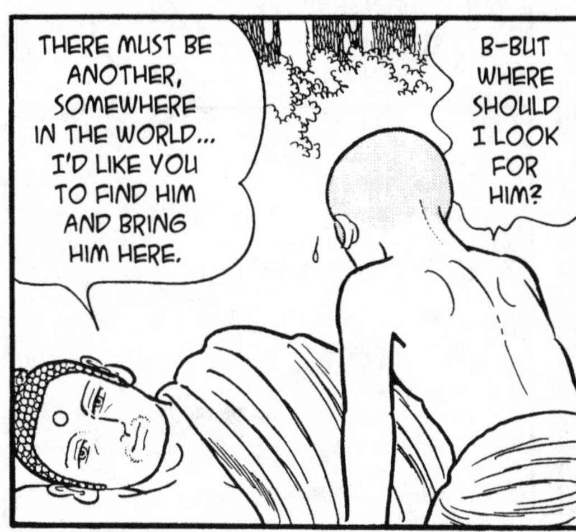
THERE MUST BE ANOTHER, SOMEWHERE IN THE WORLD... I'D LIKE YOU TO FIND HIM AND BRING HIM HERE.
B-BUT WHERE SHOULD I LOOK FOR HIM?

BUDDHA
I'LL HAVE MY MEN COMB MY KINGDOM FOR SUCH A ONE.

NO, SENIYA, THIS TASK ISN'T FOR YOU.
ANANDA WILL FIND HIM. ONLY ANANDA CAN FIND HIM.
BUT BUDDHA, IF I LEAVE THIS SANCTUARY... THERE ARE MEN WHO WILL RECOGNIZE MY FACE... THEY WILL HOUND ME OUT AND GIVE ME CHASE...
I MIGHT NOT LIVE TO FIND THE MAN!
ANANDA! THIS TASK IS CRUCIAL TRAINING FOR YOU.
I DON'T CARE HOW LONG IT TAKES. FIND HIM.
ACHIEVE THIS AND BECOME A SOTAPANNA.
GO.
...
WORRY NOT.

LATA...
I NEED TO DO A FAVOR FOR BUDDHA. I MUST LEAVE.

... WHEN?
NOW. AND I DON'T KNOW HOW MANY YEARS IT'LL TAKE.

BUDDHA SAVED US. IF HE HAS ASKED A FAVOR OF YOU, MAY YOU SERVE HIM WELL.
RIGHT... WHILE I'M AWAY, WORK HARD AND BECOME A FINE BHIKKHUNI, YES?

ANANDA, HERE
BUDDHA WANTED YOU TO HAVE THIS.

IT'S A REAL MONK'S ROBE!
BUDDHA... HAS A LOT OF FAITH IN YOU.

ME? WHY?

THAT'S A GOOD QUES-TION, I MUST SAY.
NOW TRY IT ON.

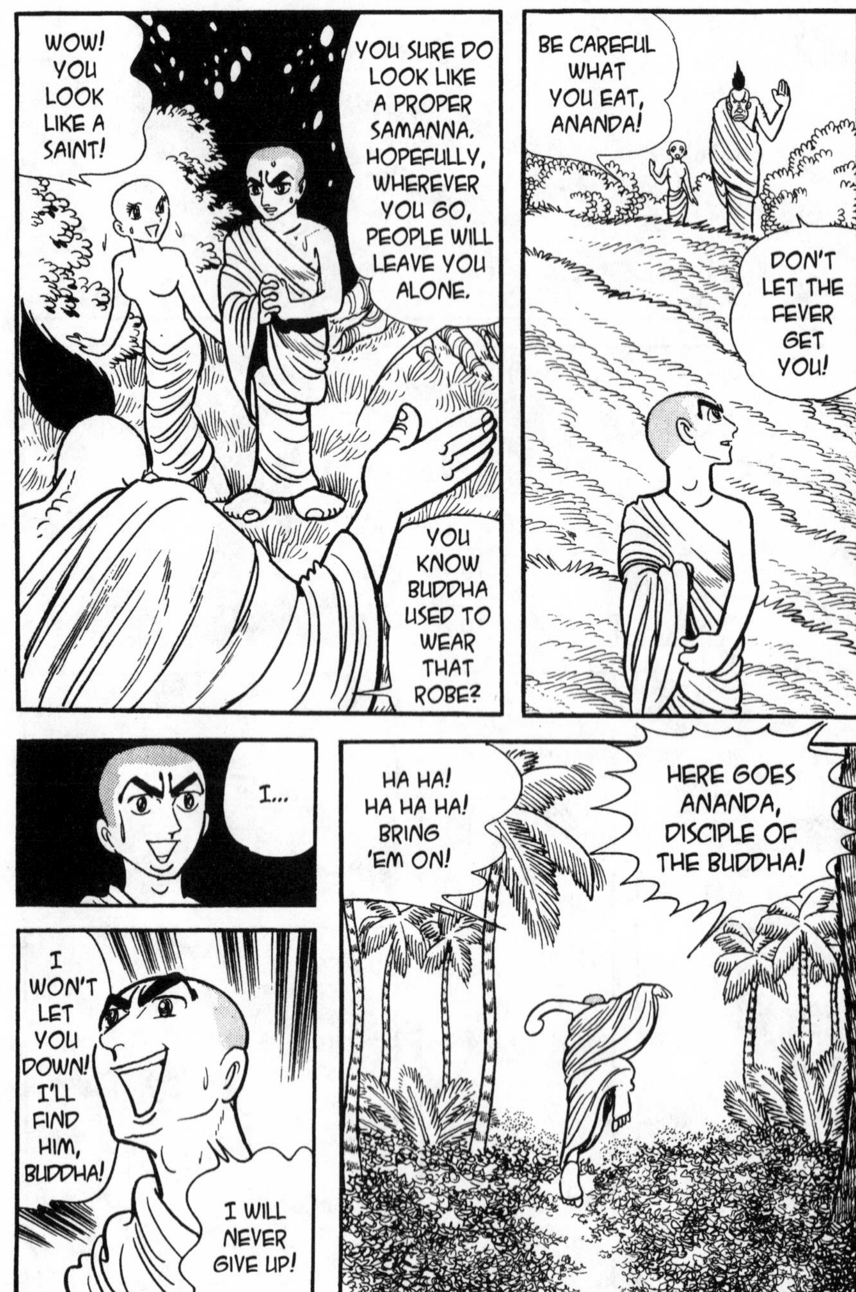
WOW! YOU LOOK LIKE A SAINT!
YOU SURE DO LOOK LIKE A PROPER SAMANNA. HOPEFULLY, WHEREVER YOU GO, PEOPLE WILL LEAVE YOU ALONE.
YOU KNOW BUDDHA USED TO WEAR THAT ROBE?
BE CAREFUL WHAT YOU EAT, ANANDA!
DON'T LET THE FEVER GET YOU!
I...
I WON'T LET YOU DOWN! I'LL FIND HIM, BUDDHA!
I WILL NEVER GIVE UP!
HA HA! HA HA HA! BRING 'EM ON!
HERE GOES ANANDA, DISCIPLE OF THE BUDDHA!

WHAT IS THE IDEA?! WHY ANOTHER PROPHET?! I'LL BE TOLD AGAIN THAT I'LL BE KILLED IN FOUR YEARS! IT'LL BE JUST LIKE SIXTEEN YEARS AGO!

...SENIYA, LET ME ASK YOU SOMETHING. WHY IS YOUR SON IN PRISON?

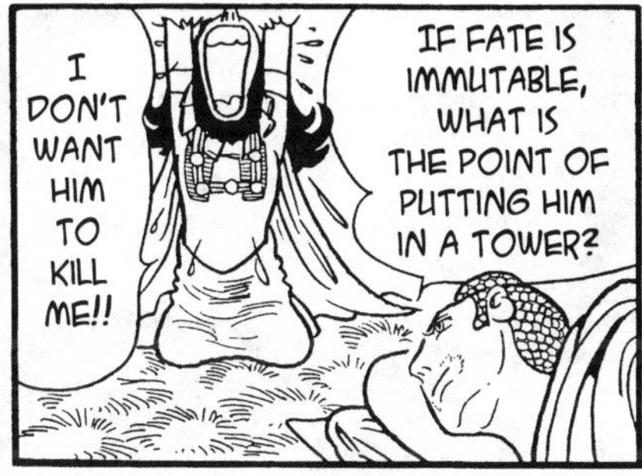
I DON'T WANT HIM TO KILL ME!!
IF FATE IS IMMUTABLE, WHAT IS THE POINT OF PUTTING HIM IN A TOWER?

HM...?

YOU HAVE DONE ...
A TERRIBLE THING !

YOU'VE SET UP A BAD PRECEDENT.
EXPECT TO PAY FOR IT IN KIND SOMEDAY...

I KNOW HOW YOU FEEL. YOU SAY TO YOURSELF,
"CURRENT ILLS I CAN DO NOTHING TO AVERT...
BUT THERE MUST BE SOME WAY TO THWART FUTURE ILLS."

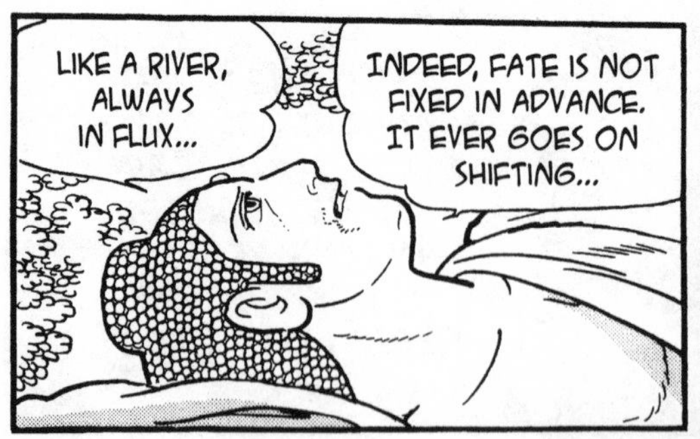
LIKE A RIVER, ALWAYS IN FLUX...
INDEED, FATE IS NOT FIXED IN ADVANCE. IT EVER GOES ON SHIFTING...

YOU HAVE FOUR YEARS LEFT, AND IT SHOULD BE POSSIBLE TO CHANGE YOUR FATE.
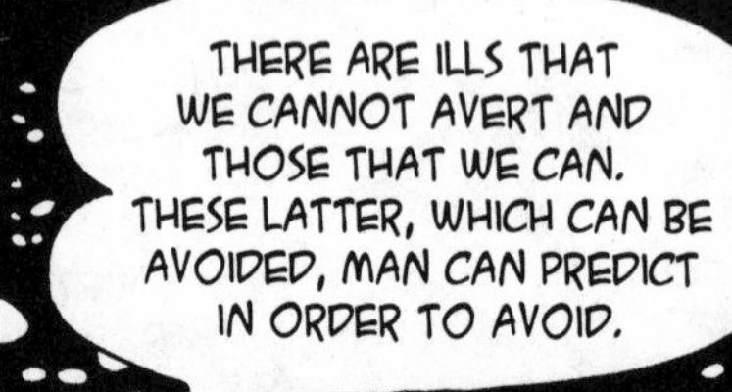
THERE ARE ILLS THAT WE CANNOT AVERT AND THOSE THAT WE CAN. THESE LATTER, WHICH CAN BE AVOIDED, MAN CAN PREDICT IN ORDER TO AVOID.
HE WHO CAN SEE THINGS COMING. THE WORLD IN OUR AGE NEEDS HIM.

IF ONE WITH SUCH A GIFT WERE TO APPEAR HERE AND NOW, I WOULD PAY HIM THE GREATEST HONOR AND HUMBLY ASK FOR HIS HELP.
HAVE HIM SEE INTO YOUR FUTURE, AND MAKE EFFORTS TO ALTER YOUR FATE.

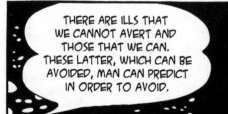

WEATHER'S SO NICE, MAYBE I'LL TAKE A PEE.

?

HEY
UH OH...

MURDER!!

HUSH

ANYONE HOME?
SLAM

SPLAT!
SPLUSH
SPAT
SPAT
SPAT
SPAT
SPLAT!

SHOPKEEP WAS RIGHT.
YEAH, IT'S HIM.

THE DEVIL ANANDA!
HOW MANY HAVE YOU KILLED ALREADY? WHAT DO YOU PLAN ON DOING TO US?

LIKE WE'RE GONNA FALL FOR YOUR SORRY DISGUISE!
CUT THAT SHIT OUT!
THUD
THWACK
BONK

...

SWAT
SWAT
SWAT

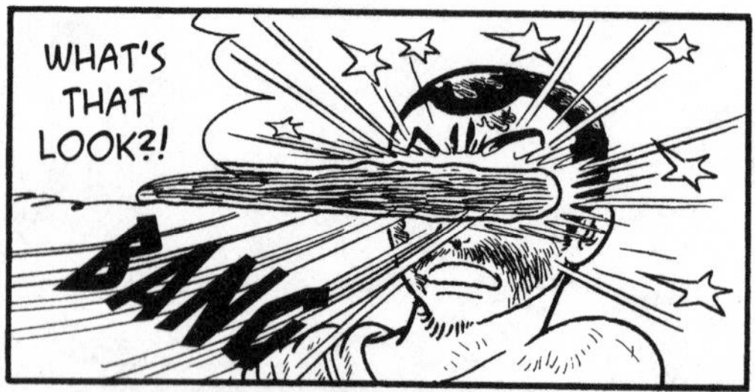
WHAT'S THAT LOOK?!
BANG

HERE, HAVE SOME ROTTEN SOUP! BEG FOR IT!
SLUCH

NOW GET LOST!

LOSER LOSER
THIEF!

WHO ARE YOU? YOU WHO WATCH ME?

WHY DO YOU FOLLOW ME?
YOU ALWAYS APPEAR WHEN I GET CHASED OUT OF A VILLAGE. WHO ARE YOU?!

IF YOU WERE SENT TO KEEP AN EYE ON ME, ANSWER ME!!

HOW MUCH LONGER MUST I SUFFER LIKE THIS?!

YET EVERYWHERE I GO, I AM THE KILLER ANANDA, CHASED OUT LIKE SOME POISONOUS SNAKE!
I WAS GIVEN BUDDHA'S OWN ROBES TO SHIELD ME FROM HARM
BUT WHAT REALLY KILLS ME IS THAT THEY AREN'T ACCEPTING ME AS BUDDHA'S DISCIPLE!
ALMS THEY WON'T GIVE ME. I'M SCRAPED RAW AND STARVING

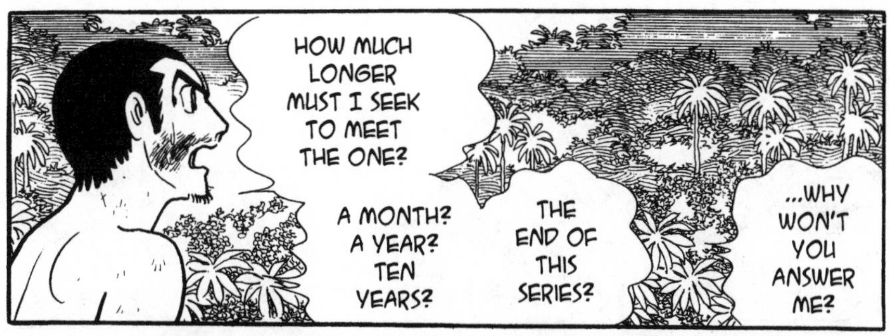
HOW MUCH LONGER MUST I SEEK TO MEET THE ONE?
A MONTH? A YEAR? TEN YEARS?
THE END OF THIS SERIES?
...WHY WON'T YOU ANSWER ME?

YOU NEVER DO...

BUT LET ME TELL YOU, I WON'T GIVE UP...

BUDDHA SAID THIS WAS CRUCIAL TRAINING FOR ME...

EXCUSE ME, SIR!

WHY DO YOU GO WITH A SPIRIT ?

A... SPIRIT... ?
I SEE A FIGURE RIGHT NEXT TO YOU. IT DOES NOT APPEAR TO BE FLESH AND BLOOD. IT MUST BE A GHOST.
YES, I SEE IT. SIR, HAVE YOU NOT NOTICED ?

AH, I SEE IT OVERLAPPING WITH YOU! THIS IS VERY STRANGE... YOUR BODY MUST BE UNDER THE SPIRIT'S PROTECTION!

ACTUALLY
EVERY NOW AND THEN I SENSE THAT I'M NOT ALONE ...

WHAT DOES THIS SPIRIT LOOK LIKE ?
IT LOOKS LIKE A BOY WITH A BANDAGE ON HIS FOREHEAD AND A TERRIBLE RUNNY NOSE.
HE'S THE MAN BUDDHA USED TO TELL ME ABOUT !
ASSAJI... YOU SEE HIM?!
PERHAPS THANKS TO IT, YOUR FACE IS SAINTLY, YOUR EYES BRIGHT AND CLEAR.
YOU SPOKE JUST NOW OF A BUDDHA. THAT MEANS "ENLIGHTENED."
YES. HE WAS BORN TO THE SHAKYA. A TRULY GREAT MAN, WHO HAS ACHIEVED SATORI.
WHAT IS HIS TEACHING?
IS THIS BUDDHA YOUR TEACHER, THEN ?
UHM
I'VE ONLY JUST STARTED LEARNING FROM HIM...
SO DON'T ASK ME...

IN THAT CASE, COULD YOU JUST GO OVER THE MAIN TENETS ?
UHM...

ALL SUFFERING HAS A CAUSE. BUDDHA TEACHES WHAT THOSE CAUSES ARE.
ALL SUFFERING CAN BE ENDED. BUDDHA TEACHES THE WAYS TO END THEM.

THE CAUSES OF ALL SUFFERING...
THE WAYS TO END SUFFERING...
OH... SUCH TRUTH!
YOU HAVE STUNNED ME...
SINCE YOU KNOW THIS TRUTH...
YOU MUST BE ENLIGHTENED, TOO!
OH NO, PLEASE... NOT AT ALL!
I-I'M STILL STRUGGLING WITH MY OWN PAIN...

YOU SAID YOU FELT A PRESENCE TO THE EAST, SO I SENT HIM OFF TO INVESTIGATE.

HE'S TAKING HIS SWEET TIME COMING BACK, NOW, ISN'T HE? OGLING AT GIRLS, I BET.

I SENSE HIM. HE'S JUST A MILE AWAY AND WILL ARRIVE SOON.

OH, GREAT, FINALLY!
HMM, WHAT DID HE FIND?

THERE'S SOMEONE WITH HIM.

WHAT DID I TELL YA? IT'S SOME GIRL!
I KNEW HE WAS GETTING RESTLESS THESE DAYS. HE'S GONE AND FOUND A GIRL! CHEATER!
MASTER, WHY DO YOU DOUBT HIM SO MUCH?
HE'S A MAN OF RARE DECENCY

MY DOCTRINE IS NOT TO BELIEVE!
THE WORLD IS TEEMING WITH DOUBTFUL THINGS. YOU'D BE IN REAL TROUBLE IF YOU JUST WENT AHEAD AND BELIEVED ANYTHING!

GO FETCH SARIPUTTA. AND CHASE AWAY THE WENCH!

WELCOME BACK, SARIPUTTA
HI, MOGGALLANA

LET ME INTRODUCE YOU TO THIS MAN, WHO—

HOLD IT RIGHT THERE!

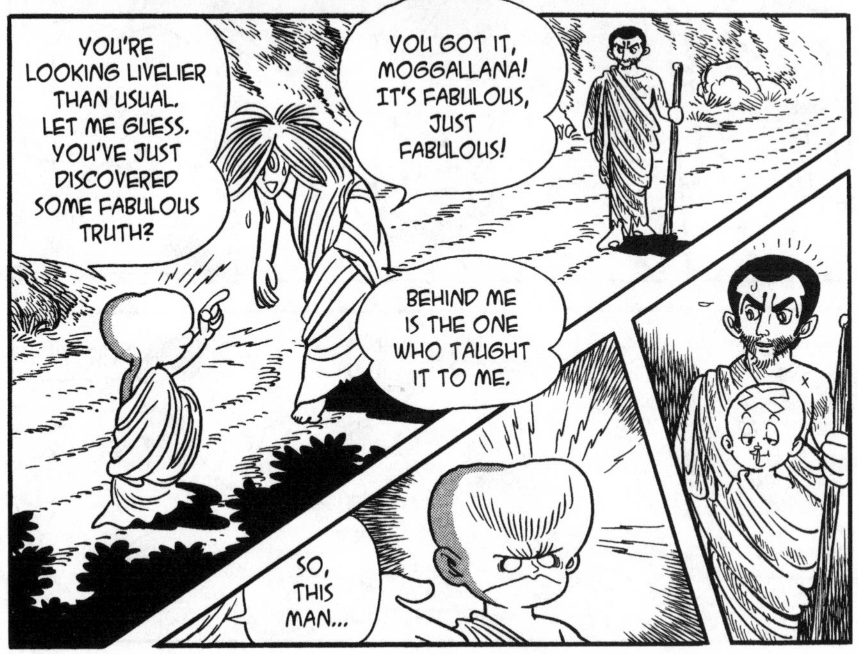
YOU'RE LOOKING LIVELIER THAN USUAL. LET ME GUESS. YOU'VE JUST DISCOVERED SOME FABULOUS TRUTH?
YOU GOT IT, MOGGALLANA! IT'S FABULOUS, JUST FABULOUS!
BEHIND ME IS THE ONE WHO TAUGHT IT TO ME.
SO, THIS MAN...

THAT MAN IS ANANDA, WHO USED TO BE A GREAT BANDIT, A WANTED MAN. BUT NOW HE IS TRAINING AS THE DISCIPLE OF A GREAT ONE.
ALSO, A SPIRIT WATCHES OVER HIM. THE SPIRIT'S NAME IS ASSAJI, THE ASCETIC.
HOW DO YOU KNOW ?!
TEN YEARS AGO, ASSAJI FED HIMSELF TO A FAMILY OF STARVING WOLVES.
YOUR TEACHER WAS PROFOUNDLY MOVED BY HIS DEED,
AND SOON AFTER FOUND ENLIGHTEN-MENT.
WHO ARE YOU? HOW CAN YOU SEE ALL THAT?
ANANDA, SIR, MOGGALLANA IS GIFTED WITH A STRANGE POWER...
HE CAN SEE DEEP INTO THE SOUL. WHAT'S MORE...
HE HAS THE POWER TO SEE INTO THE PAST, AND ALSO THE FUTURE.
HE CAN PREDICT THE FUTURE ?

NOW MOGGALLANA HAS GONE MISSING TOO!

...

WHAT A FARCE! HE WENT TO FETCH SARIPUTTA ...
AND NOW THEY'RE BOTH SCREWING AROUND! URRGH...
OUR SECT IS GETTING LAX!

I BET THEY GOT ALMS AND WENT ON A PICNIC!
THOSE LAZY BUMS !!
MAYBE THEY'RE GETTING BOOZED UP...
WITH SOME EXTRA BUCKS THEY MADE TELLING FORTUNES ON A STREET CORNER!

THOSE TWO ARE THE VERY PILLARS OF OUR SECT. WHEN YOU DOUBT THEM SO, IT SADDENS US.
DOUBT IS A GOOD THING. THAT IS THE GIST OF WHAT I, SANJAYA, PREACH.

DO NOT BELIEVE PEOPLE. DO NOT BELIEVE SOCIETY. DO NOT BELIEVE NATURE. DO NOT BELIEVE IN TIME. DO NOT BELIEVE IN LIFE OR DEATH. DO NOT BELIEVE THE WEATHER REPORTS. DO NOT BELIEVE THE YANKEES WILL WIN THE PLAYOFFS.

IF YOU NAIVELY BELIEVE SOMETHING BUT TURN OUT TO BE WRONG, IT'S DEPRESSING!
YOU'LL BE ASHAMED AND BE THE BUTT OF JOKES!

IS THE SUN YELLOW? IT MIGHT BE GREEN. IS IT DAYTIME? IT MIGHT BE THE MIDDLE OF THE NIGHT. DO TIGERS EAT RABBITS? MAYBE RABBITS EAT TIGERS. DO BIRDS FLY THE SKY? MAYBE THE SKY IS FLYING THE BIRDS! THE ONLY TRUTH IS THAT YOU CAN'T BE CERTAIN ABOUT ANYTHING! GET IT?

AH, DEAR SIRS!!

LOOK WELL, PLEASE. WE ARE THE REAL THING.
DAMMIT! I DON'T BELIEVE IN LOOKING, EITHER.

SIR,
THIS MAN IS A FOL-LOWER OF THE BUDDHA ...

WHAT BUDDHA ?
YOU THOUGHT I'D BELIEVE THAT ?!

MASTER, THE ONE CALLED BUDDHA HAS BEEN TEACHING WONDERFUL TRUTHS.

"ALL SUFFERING ALWAYS HAS A CAUSE. BY LEARNING THE CAUSES, WE CAN KNOW HOW TO END SUFFERING. WE CAN FIND PEACE OF MIND AND SAVE OURSELVES."

WHAT A PELLUCID AND EYE-OPENING TEACHING! MASTER SANJAYA, WHAT DO YOU THINK?
WHAT SUFFERING? I DON'T BELIEVE IN IT. NOR DO I BELIEVE IN CAUSES. YOU JUST CAN'T TRUST WHAT OTHER PEOPLE SAY.
TO BEGIN WITH, I DON'T BELIEVE A WORD OF THIS STUPID MANGA!
EXCUSE ME?!
WHO KNOWS, THE AUTHOR MIGHT BE A ROTTEN PUMPKIN.
HE'S RIGHT... SORRY, FOLKS. I DIDN'T MEAN TO FOOL YOU. I AM A ROTTEN PUMPKIN.
WHAT DID I TELL YOU? ALWAYS DOUBT!
THIS IS HOPE-LESS!
YEAH
MASTER, THEN ALLOW ME NOT TO BELIEVE YOU.

I WILL NEVER AGAIN BELIEVE YOU OR A WORD OF YOUR TEACHINGS.
I DON'T BELIEVE IN THIS SECT.
AND NOW, WE SHALL LEAVE.
WHAT ?!
WE'LL GO WITH THIS MAN TO BUDDHA. WE BELIEVE BUDDHA IS THE MASTER WE'VE ALWAYS WANTED.
BULL!
I DON'T BELIEVE HE EXISTS!
SO WHY SHOULD I BELIEVE THAT YOU'RE REALLY LEAVING?
I'M GOING IF SARIPUTTA IS.
SAME HERE
ME TOO...

LET'S GO.
I'M OFF, TOO.
IF THOSE TWO THINK BUDDHA IS WORTHY, THEN SO DO I.
WAIT!!
DOUBTFUL
YOU'RE LIKE A SON TO ME! HOW CAN YOU BE SO COLD? DON'T DO THIS TO ME... HAVE YOU NO HEART?
AREN'T WE RUNNING THIS SECT TOGETHER?
RIP
IT'S NOT TOO LATE TO RECONSIDER!
FAREWELL, MASTER
THIEVES! THOSE ARE MY DISCIPLES!

P-PLEASE DON'T GO!
IF YOU HAVE COMPLAINTS, YOU CAN TELL ME!
PLEASE, STAY FOR JUST ANOTHER YEAR!

DAMMIT... ALL GONE!! WHAT TREACHERY! BACKSTABBERS! AH... DAMN BUDDHA!

WHAT A SURPRISE. HOW MANY ARE SAINT SANJAYA'S DISCIPLES?
TWO HUN-DRED AND FIFTY

SO MANY?! I'M ABOUT TO BRING 250 PEOPLE TO BUDDHA'S SIDE?

YES. YOU KILLED 250 PEOPLE, ANANDA... AND WE NUMBER THE SAME!

WHAT?!

THE EXACT SAME NUMBER. IT IS NO COINCIDENCE.

DO YOU KNOW EVERYTHING ABOUT MY PAST?

LIKE I SAID, MOGGALLANA CAN SEE A MAN'S FATE IN ITS ENTIRETY AND READ THE DEEPEST PARTS OF THE MIND.
HE'S HAD THE GIFT SINCE HE WAS A LITTLE BABY.

THEN TELL ME!! WHAT IS MY FUTURE?! WILL I EVER SEE MY GUILT ABSOLVED AND ATTAIN ENLIGHTENMENT?

SURE, I CAN TELL YOU. YOU'LL BE YOUR MASTER'S AIDE.

AIDE?!

BUDDHA IS A MAN OF GREAT SPIRIT, BUT POOR HEALTH. HE'S BEEN SICKLY SINCE CHILDHOOD AND NOW, ESPECIALLY, HE HAS TO COPE WITH DISEASE...
YOU WILL BE THE ONE AT HIS SIDE, ALWAYS LOOKING AFTER HIM.

WHEREVER HE GOES, HE'LL RELY ON YOUR SUPPORT.
MY SUPPORT? HE'D PUT FAITH IN AN EX-CON LIKE ME?
YES. YOU'LL BE RIGHT BY HIS SIDE WHEN HE BREATHES HIS LAST.

BUT HIS TEACHINGS WILL NEVER DIE. OVER THE COURSE OF **2,000** YEARS, HIS TEACHINGS WILL SPREAD ACROSS THE WORLD. HIS TRUTHS WILL SAVE BILLIONS OF PEOPLE.

2,000 YEARS?! AND AFTER THAT?
I CAN'T SEE QUITE THAT FAR...
MY POWER HAS ITS LIMITS.

MAYBE THE WORLD WILL END. MANKIND COULD DIE OUT. CALL IT THE "LATTER DAYS."

YOU ARE THE MAN BUDDHA ASKED FOR...

BUT DOESN'T KNOWING THE FUTURE TAKE THE JOY OUT OF LIVING?
NOT AT ALL. THE FUTURE I SEE NOW IS THE FUTURE OF THINGS AS THEY ARE. THE FUTURE CHANGES, LIKE SO MANY SWIRLS IN A RIVER.

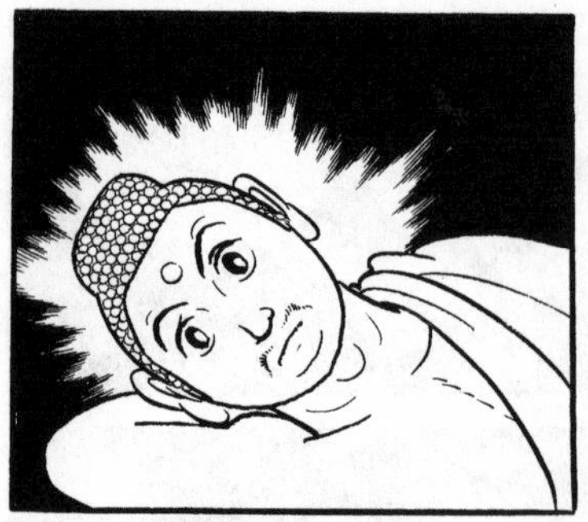

DHEPA, ANANDA'S ALMOST HERE!

ASSAJI JUST WHISPERED TO ME THAT ANANDA IS BRINGING A GREAT NUMBER OF NEW DISCIPLES TO US!
WHAT? HE IS?

ANANDA'S BACK SO SOON? HE ONLY LEFT HALF A YEAR AGO

ALL OF YOU, GO GREET ANANDA!
ASSAJI WOULD NOT BE WRONG ABOUT THIS.

APPARENTLY, HE'S ALMOST HERE.
ANANDA? HMM, HARD TO BELIEVE.

IT'S TRUE! I SEE A WHOLE CROWD!

AND THAT'S ANANDA AT THEIR HEAD. WOW!
NO JOKE. HOW MANY DOZENS...

HEY~!
HEY, ANANDA! WHO ARE THOSE PEOPLE?

HEY, I'M BACK!! I DID IT!
I'VE BROUGHT BACK A REAL PROPHET!!

GOOD JOB, ANANDA!
MAN...!

AH..!!

I HAVE RETURNED
WELL DONE, ANANDA
WAS IT A TRIAL FOR YOU?

THESE ARE THE DISCIPLES OF SAINT SANJAYA. ALL 250 OF THEM!
AMAZING...

ALLOW ME TO INTRODUCE YOU TO SARIPUTTA AND MOGGALLANA

I'VE WAITED FOR YOU TWO...
FOR A VERY LONG TIME!

WE HAVE BEEN TIED TO YOU BY FATE ITSELF.
IT IS THE SAME WITH US. TO SERVE YOU AND TO SPREAD YOUR TEACHINGS,

NOW, LEAD THESE TWO TO THE PIPAL!
BUT BUDDHA, THAT'S WHERE YOU TAKE YOUR REST...

NO MATTER. I HAVE JUST MET MY FUTURE SUCCESSORS!

CHAPTER TWO

A Crowd of Critics

WHAT THE HECK IS BUDDHA THINKING?
HE'S GIVEN SEATS OF HONOR TO THOSE NEWBIES OVER SENIOR DISCIPLES!

IF I MAY SAY SO MYSELF, I'M THE TOP MONK HERE IN TERMS OF RANK.

RELAX

I'M SURE HE HAS HIS REA-SONS.
HE DOESN'T NEED TO EXPLAIN HIS MOTIVES FOR ACCORDING THEM SENIORITY, YOU KNOW.
BUT HE SAID THEY WERE TO BE HIS SUCCESSORS!

DOES THAT MEAN HE'S THINKING ABOUT RETIRING?
IS HE PLANNING TO LEAVE OUR SECT?

I DUNNO, BUT I DON'T LIKE IT...
PLAYING FAVORITES ...

BUDDHA NAMED HIS HEIRS ?!
WHO ?
OVER MY DEAD BODY !!
THESE NEW FACES CALLED MOGGALLANA AND SARIPUTTA.
I GUESS I NEED TO TALK TO BUDDHA!!
I, DEVADATTA, AM THE SECT'S TRUE HEIR!

BUDDHA!
I HEAR YOU'VE CHOSEN WHO WILL BE LEADING AFTER YOU.

INDEED. LET ME INTRODUCE SARIPUTTA AND MOGGALLANA.

YOU CAN'T DECIDE JUST LIKE THAT!!

BUDDHA... WE'VE BECOME A VERY LARGE GROUP, WITH MANY EXECUTIVE STAFF.
MAJOR ISSUES, LIKE WHO TO NOMINATE AS OUR NEXT LEADER...
...MUST BE RESOLVED DULY BY A COUNCIL.

WHAT ARE YOU TRYING TO SAY?

WE ARE AN ORGAN-IZATION...

WHEREIN WE HAVE VARYING VIEWS AND STAND-POINTS.
THE LEADER MUST BE CHOSEN FROM AMONG THE WHOLE BODY OF DISCIPLES!
AND THE ONE WE FINALLY CHOOSE MUST BE AN ABLE MANAGER WHO CAN RUN THIS SECT EFFICIENTLY.
I'D RATHER CHOOSE A LEADER WHO WILL BE DEVOTED TO HELPING PEOPLE FIND PEACE AND HAPPINESS.
THAT'S SECONDARY! MANAGEMENT SKILLS ARE TOP PRIORITY!!
I'M SORRY BUDDHA, I KNOW I'M BEING TOO FORWARD. BUT PLEASE HEAR ME OUT!
WHAT DO YOU KNOW ABOUT WHAT'S SECONDARY?

AS WE GAIN FOLLOWERS, WE'LL RECEIVE MORE ALMS AND DONATIONS. SOON, WE'LL HAVE NEED FOR COLLECTIONS AND ACCOUNTING IN OUR SECT.

IF PEOPLE DONATE LAND AND BUILDINGS, SOMEONE HAS TO BE IN CHARGE OF THEIR ADMINISTRATION.

EVENTUALLY, A SECT HAS TO HAVE A LARGE TEMPLE. BECAUSE FOLLOWERS NEED SUCH SUSTENANCE!

TELL ME, WHOSE IDEA IS ALL THIS?

MINE! I ALREADY HAVE A PROPOSAL AND THE BLUEPRINTS!

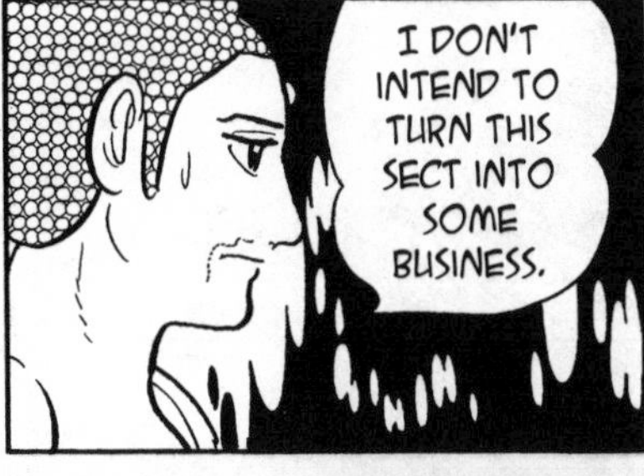

I DON'T INTEND TO TURN THIS SECT INTO SOME BUSINESS.

T-THAT'S WHY YOU NEED SOMEONE WHO CAN!

NO ONE IN OUR SECT IS BETTER SUITED TO ASSUME THE MANTLE OF LEADERSHIP!

AS YOUR MOST CAPABLE MANAGER, I'VE LED EFFORTS TO STREAMLINE AND MODERNIZE THIS SECT.

FURTHERMORE, EXCEPTING YOURSELF, I'M THE ONLY ONE WITH STRONG CONNECTIONS TO THE ROYAL FAMILY OF MAGADHA. I KNOW I HAVE THE COMPLETE TRUST OF PRINCE AJATASATTU, BIMBISARA'S SON!
ONCE THE PRINCE ASCENDS TO THE THRONE, HE'LL BECOME OUR BIGGEST SUPPORTER!
BUDDHA, PLEASE SAY YOU'LL LEAVE THE SECT TO ME!
BUDDHA, I SIMPLY ADORE YOU...
YOU JUST CHARM ME... YOU AND I ARE FAMILY!

I LOVE YOU, BUDDHA...
MORE THAN ANYONE ELSE ON EARTH
HONEY, PLEASE?
THAT'S ENOUGH!!

I'D NEVER LEAVE THE SECT IN YOUR HANDS!

YOU'VE BARELY BEGUN YOUR TRAINING. YOU'RE NOT YET A WHOLE MAN!

OUR ONLY PURPOSE IS TO SPREAD THE WAY THAT THE GODS HAVE TAUGHT US. WHAT MANAGING TEMPLES AND OFFERINGS? YOUR MATERIALISTIC THINKING IS JUST VULGAR!

WOW, WHAT A SHOCKER. I'VE KNOWN BUDDHA FOR 30 YEARS, AND I'VE NEVER SEEN HIM SO PISSED!

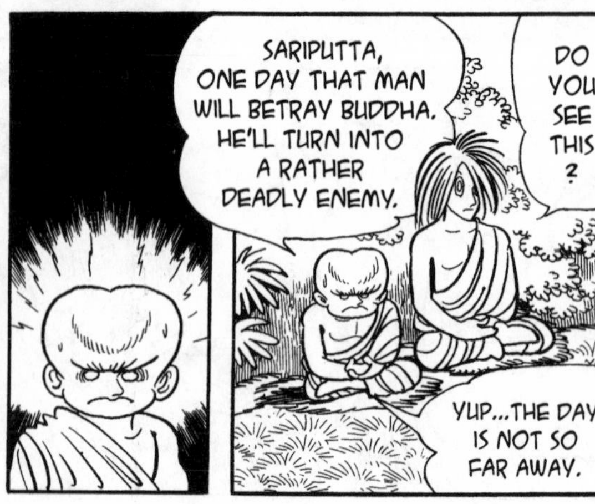
DO YOU SEE THIS ?
SARIPUTTA, ONE DAY THAT MAN WILL BETRAY BUDDHA. HE'LL TURN INTO A RATHER DEADLY ENEMY.
YUP...THE DAY IS NOT SO FAR AWAY.

THUS MASTER SANJAYA'S TWO MOST TRUSTED AIDES...
AND ALL 250 DISCIPLES WERE STOLEN BY BUDDHA! SANJAYA'S JUST ACHING FOR A CHANCE TO RETALIATE!

LOOK, A VISITOR
A WOMAN, NO LESS
MAYBE SHE WANTS TO BECOME A NUN?

I'M HERE TO SEE SIDDHAR-THA
SIDDHARTHA? ...OH, YOU MEAN BUDDHA.

I DON'T CARE WHAT HE CALLS HIMSELF. I NEED TO SEE HIM. THERE'S SOME THINGS I GOTTA SAY TO HIM!!

WAIT, LADY! MISSUS! MA'AM !
YOU CAN'T JUST BARGE IN...

EVERYONE, HEAR ME! MY NAME IS CHINTHA... I'VE GOT SOME BIG NEWS FOR YOU, SO LISTEN UP! THE CHILD IN MY BELLY IS SIDDHARTHA'S!
SIDDHARTHA'S BEEN MY LOVER FOR MORE THAN TEN YEARS! YOU MONKS ARE A HAPPY-GO-LUCKY LOT NOT TO KNOW HIS TRUE NATURE!
HE SLIPS AWAY FROM THIS GROVE TO COME DRINK WINE AND CAROUSE WITH ME UNTIL THE WEE HOURS OF THE MORNING! THAT'S HIS ROUTINE!

HEY... IS THIS TRUE?

HALF A YEAR AGO I WAS SICK.

SICK? NO WONDER YOU GOT SICK!

ALL THAT BOOZE GOT TO YOU!

HERE'S PROOF THAT THE CHILD IS YOURS. IT'S A LOVE LETTER YOU WROTE TO ME!

YOU PROMISED YOU'D BUILD ME A NICE BIG HOUSE ONCE YOU WERE SWIMMING IN ALMS MONEY!

LET ALONE MAKE SUCH A PROMISE, I'VE NEVER MET YOU BEFORE.

THAT CAN'T BE MY WRITING. I BELIEVE THIS IS SOME MISTAKE.

QUIT PLAYING DUMB!

STOP IT!

LET GO OF ME!
BROTHER, BUDDHA LOOKS ALL PANICKY...
SHE CAN'T BE RIGHT. BUT WE'LL WATCH...
BUDDHA HAD A LOVER? NO WAY...
CONFESS, YOU! TELL YOUR PRECIOUS DISCIPLES THAT THIS IS YOUR BABY!
WHAT, LOST YOUR BALLS?
...
MADAM!
AIEE!

FLOP

BUDDHA...
YOU NUTTY SWINDLING BITCH! WHORE!!
TAKE THAT!
DO NOT HURT HER !!
YES... M-MASTER SANJAYA TOLD ME TO TRY AND EMBARRASS BUDDHA...
WHO ASKED YOU TO PUT ON THIS CHARADE, LADY?

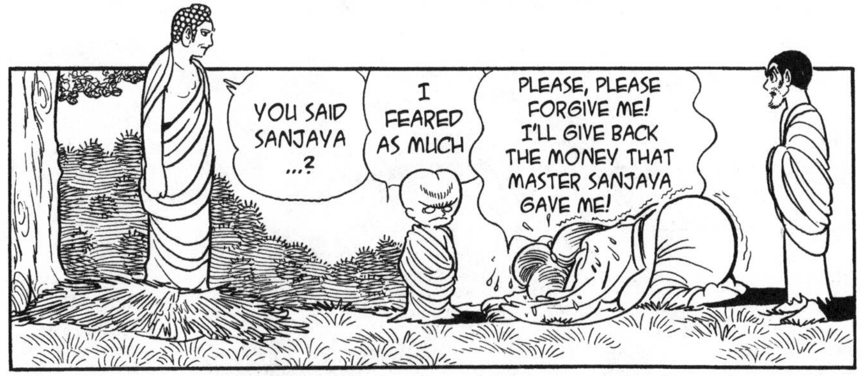
PLEASE, PLEASE FORGIVE ME! I'LL GIVE BACK THE MONEY THAT MASTER SANJAYA GAVE ME!
I FEARED AS MUCH
YOU SAID SANJAYA ...?

ANANDA
GIVE THIS LADY A DECENT MEAL, THEN SHOW HER OUT OF THE GROVE. DON'T EVEN THINK OF HARMING HER.
Y-YES, SIR

SANJAYA IS A SMALL MAN, RATHER NARROW-MINDED, YOU SEE. ALL OF HIS STUDENTS LEAVING TO FOLLOW BUDDHA HAS PROBABLY GIVEN HIM A THIRST FOR REVENGE.
THEN THAT WASN'T THE END OF IT?

MOGGALLANA PREDICTED TRULY. SINCE THAT INCIDENT, UNSAVORY RUMORS ABOUT BUDDHA SPREAD THROUGH RAJGRIHA LIKE WILDFIRE.
THEY WERE FUELED BY THE ANGRY FAMILIES OF THOSE WHO'D LEFT TO JOIN BUDDHA MOVED BY HIS TEACHINGS.

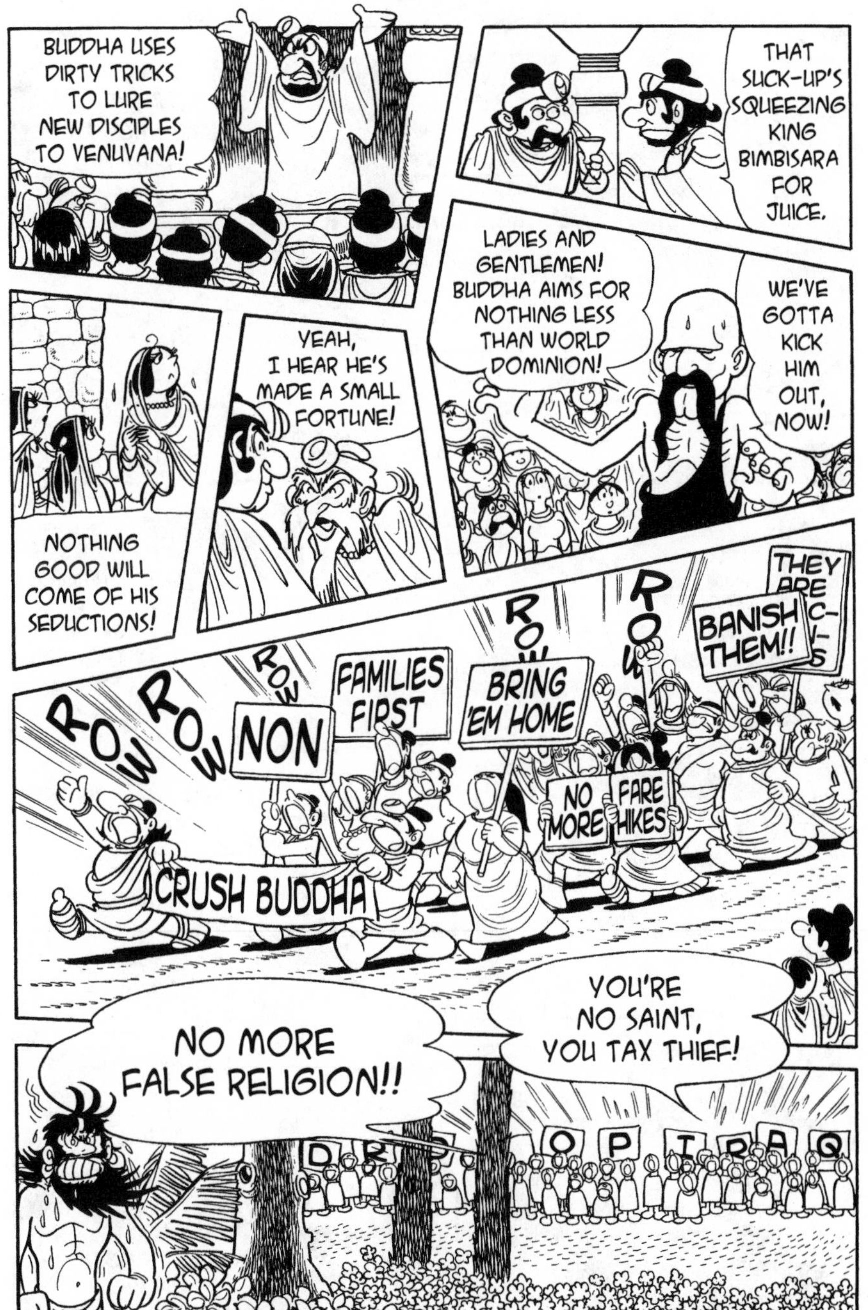

BUDDHA USES DIRTY TRICKS TO LURE NEW DISCIPLES TO VENUVANA!
THAT SUCK-UP'S SQUEEZING KING BIMBISARA FOR JUICE.
LADIES AND GENTLEMEN! BUDDHA AIMS FOR NOTHING LESS THAN WORLD DOMINION!
WE'VE GOTTA KICK HIM OUT, NOW!
YEAH, I HEAR HE'S MADE A SMALL FORTUNE!
NOTHING GOOD WILL COME OF HIS SEDUCTIONS!
ROW ROW ROW ROW ROW
NON
FAMILIES FIRST
BRING 'EM HOME
BANISH THEM!!
THEY ARE
NO MORE
FARE HIKES
CRUSH BUDDHA
NO MORE FALSE RELIGION!!
YOU'RE NO SAINT, YOU TAX THIEF!

SH-SHU-SHUDDUP !!

YOU NOT... YOU NOT GONNA B-BAD-MOUTH B-BUDDHA!

FESS UP

WE WERE JUST TRYIN' TO BEAT SOME SENSE INTO THEM!

DON'T BOTHER. LET THEM BE.

SINCE THE RUMORS ARE BASELESS, THEY WILL DIE OUT SOON.

WHERE DOES HE GET OFF BEING COCKY?
DIDN'T HE USE TO BE A BANDIT HIMSELF ?

YEAH. WHY'D ANYONE WANNA CRITICIZE SUCH A GREAT GUY?
POOR BUDDHA

HEY, LATA... I SHOULD TELL YOU...

MOGGAL-LANA SAID TO ME,

BUDDHA'S GONNA DEPEND ON ME WHEREVER HE GOES...
FOR THE REST OF HIS LIFE!

LATA!! BUDDHA'LL GRACIOUSLY PUT HIS FAITH IN A MAN LIKE ME !
THAT MOGGALLANA'S A REAL PSYCHIC, SO IT'S GOTTA BE TRUE.

A-ANANDA!

LATA YOU REALLY SAID THAT?

YOU CAN TALK NOW?

I'LL NEVER FORGET THAT DAY!

I'M GLAD TO SERVE HIM.

IF WE HADN'T DONNED OUR ROBES, WE'D BE MAN AND WIFE.

YES

WE'RE MONK AND NUN, SO IT'S FOOLISH TO TALK ABOUT MARRIAGE ...

WHAT A STRANGE FATE OURS HAS BEEN...

YES

YOU'RE RIGHT
BUT OUR HEARTS WERE JOINED FOR LIFE!
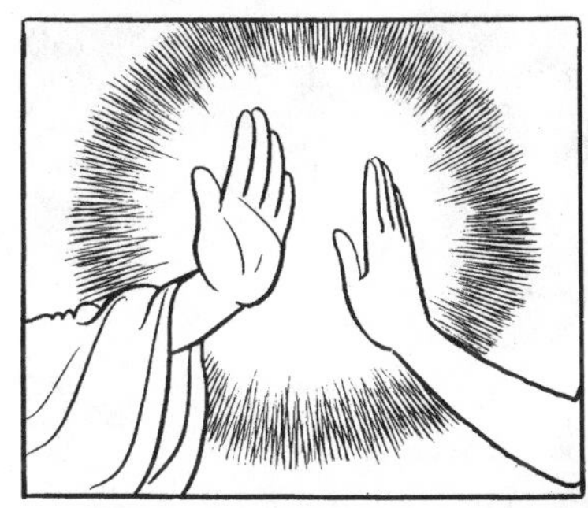
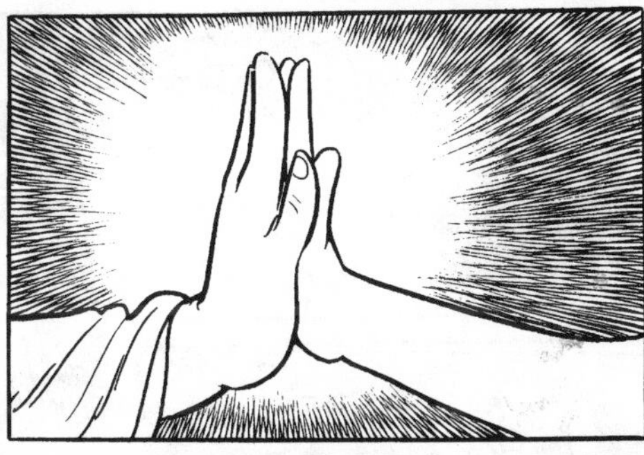

LATA, YOU REST FIRST.
WE'LL TAKE TURNS STANDING WATCH.

Nod
Nod

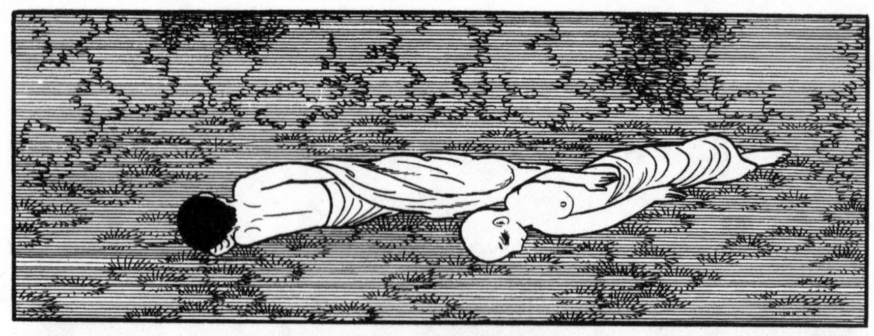

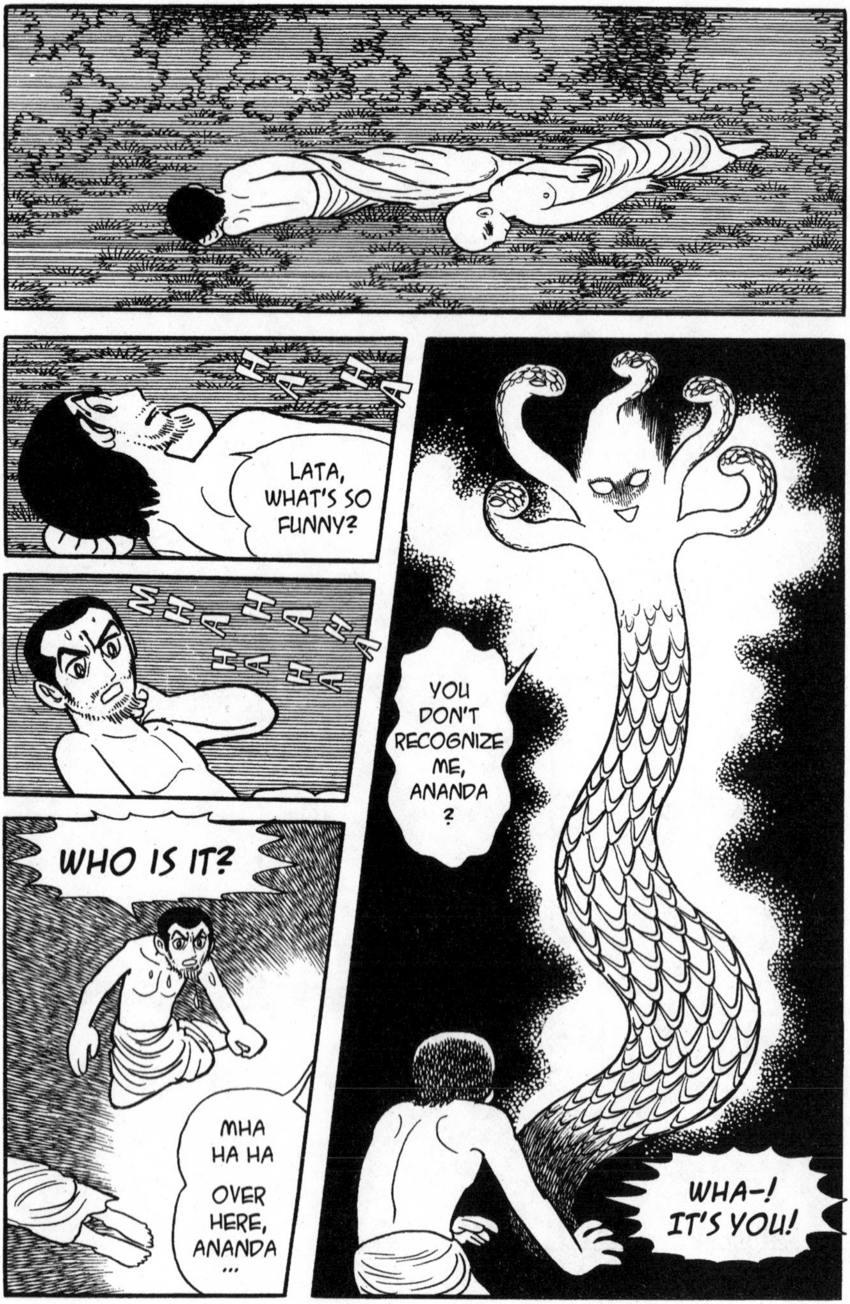

LATA, WHAT'S SO FUNNY?

WHO IS IT?

MHA HA HA

OVER HERE, ANANDA ...

YOU DON'T RECOGNIZE ME, ANANDA?

WHA-! IT'S YOU!

I NEVER STOPPED WATCHING OVER YOU. I WENT ON PROTECTING YOU.

I CUT ALL TIES WITH YOU. I NEVER WANTED TO SEE YOUR FACE AGAIN!

SO, AREN'T YOU IN LOVE WITH THIS PRETTY GIRL? AREN'T YOU ACHING TO MARRY HER?
JUST SAY IT, MY CHILD
AND IN A FLASH ...
I'LL GIVE YOU WHAT YOU DESIRE. OH! YOU WILL KNOW SUCH HAPPINESS!
BUT YOU MUST FORSAKE BUDDHA !
BUDDHA MEANS EVERYTHING TO ME!

BUDDHA'S TEACHINGS ARE MORE PRECIOUS THAN ANY TREASURE ON EARTH!
I DON'T WANT ANYTHING FOR MYSELF. I JUST WANT BUDDHA TO BE IN GOOD HEALTH!

TALKING IN YOUR SLEEP? A DREAM?

HM?

NO!
YOU FOOL !!
WHY DID YOU CHOOSE BUDDHA?
I WAS SO SURE LATA WAS MORE IMPORTANT TO YOU!
MY HEART SPOKE...

IT'S TOO LATE NOW... YOU'VE RUINED MY PLAN!
LATA WILL DIE! ANANDA... IT'S TOO LATE NOW...
BUDDHA ...
?

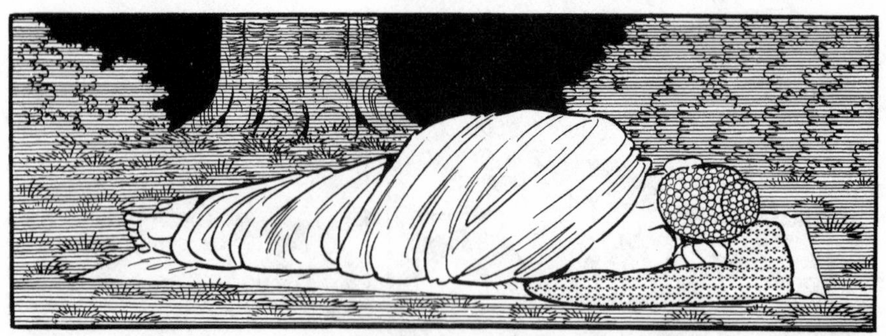

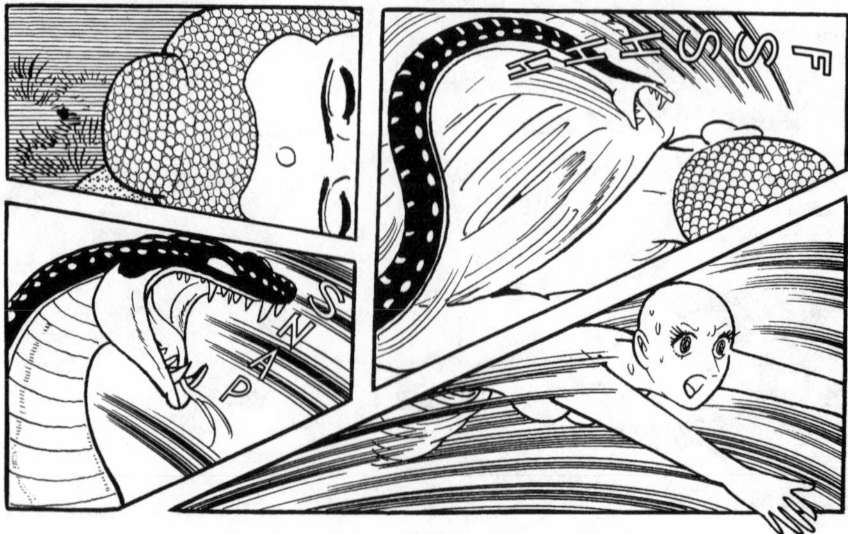
FSSHHH
SNAP

LATA

LA-TAA!!
BLECH

BEH

LATA
...L-LATA...

UH...
UH UH
HUUH...!

...

ANANDA, I'M SORRY... LATA SAVED MY LIFE, AND YET...
I COULD DO NOTHING TO HELP HER!

ANANDA WASHED
LATA'S BODY IN THE RIVER
AND PLACED HER ON
A WOODEN BIER ADORNED WITH
WILD GRASSES AND FLOWERS.
IT WAS ALL HE COULD DO,
THIS TOKEN OF LOVE.

IN INDIA IN THOSE DAYS, RITES FOR THE DECEASED AMOUNTED TO "AERIAL SEPULTURE," WHERE THE BODY WOULD BE LEFT OUTSIDE UNTIL NOTHING WAS LEFT BUT BONES, OR A "PLATFORM BURIAL," WHERE BIRDS WOULD BE ALLOWED TO PICK AT THE REMAINS. AERIAL SEPULTURE WAS PRACTICED AS RECENTLY AS 200 YEARS AGO IN OKINAWA AND OTHER REGIONS OF JAPAN.
ANANDA. AS LONG AS I LIVE, I'LL REMEMBER LATA, WHO PROTECTED ME FROM THE SNAKE. SHE SACRIFICED HER LIFE TO SAVE MINE
WE WILL BE DOING HER PART TOO AS WE TRY TO SAVE PEOPLE.
FOR HER SAKE, THEN, I MUST BE ABOUT MORE OFTEN, TO DELIVER SERMONS.

UM, BUDDHA? WHERE DO YOU THINK LATA WENT WHEN SHE DIED?
AH, YES... I BELIEVE SHE IS NOW ONE WITH NATURE'S ESSENCE.

WHAT DOES THAT MEAN?

SHE SCATTERED INTO THE GREAT SKY.
DISSOLVED INTO TINY LITTLE BITS INVISIBLE TO OUR EYES,

SOMEDAY WE SHALL GO, TOO...
AND THERE INTERMINGLE WITH LATA

SERIOUSLY?!

SUCH ARE THE LAWS OF THE UNIVERSE.

THEN I'LL MEET HER AGAIN?!
I THINK SO

RUMBLE
ROLLROLL

HUH ?
HOW MANY YEARS HAS IT BEEN?
Y-YOU ARE...
BRAHMAN ?!
TRUE. WE SPOKE AFTER YOU FOUND ENLIGHTENMENT, SIDDHARTHA.
I'VE MISSED YOU SO...
IT'S BEEN TEN YEARS SINCE WE LAST MET!!
BRAHMAN, I BELIEVE I'VE BEEN GIVING EVERYTHING TO MY WORK.
I HAVE MORE THAN 1,000 DISCIPLES ...
YOU HAVEN'T BOTHERED KEEPING THE PROMISE I HAD YOU MAKE BACK THEN.

YOUR DISCIPLES WAIT UPON YOU HAND AND FOOT AS YOU LOLL ABOUT IN YOUR SPACIOUS RESTING GROUND. YOU CALL THAT YOUR LIFEWORK?
AS YOU GLADLY ENJOY YOUR COZY LIFE IN THIS BAMBOO GROVE,
PEOPLE ARE STRUGGLING, SUFFERING, AND DYING IN MISERY, IN EVER GREATER NUMBERS.
RUMMBLE
ZSHHH

ZSHHHH
ZSHHHH
ZSHHH
RUMBLE
RUMBLE ROLL
SHHHH
SHHH
SHHHH
"AWAKENED ONE," IT IS FOR YOU TO SAVE THOSE PEOPLE.
DO NOT WASTE ANOTHER MOMENT !

KEEP YOUR PROMISE
NOW I REMEMBER, BRAHMAN, AND I HAVE BEEN IDLE...
WHAT THE...
ZSSSH
ZSSSH
ZSSSH
BUDDHA! YOU'RE SOAKED!
WHY DID YOU SLEEP OUT HERE? YOU'LL GET SICK ALL OVER AGAIN!

CHAPTER THREE

DEATH SWAMP

ANANDA...

I'VE BEEN THINKING ABOUT GOING TO KOSALA.

T-TO KOSALA ?!
WHY? IT'S SO FAR AWAY!

KOSALA IS ALMOST AS BIG A KINGDOM AS MAGADHA. I'M SURE THERE ARE MANY PEOPLE WHO SUFFER THERE, AS WELL.
BEFORE I DIE, I MUST HELP AS MANY PEOPLE AS POSSIBLE...
IN MEMORY OF LATA.

BUT YOUR HEALTH ...

OH, I DON'T PLAN ON DYING ANYTIME SOON.

?

I MUST HAVE AT LEAST ANOTHER 40 YEARS OR SO BEFORE I PASS ON.
I MUST USE THAT TIME WELL...

SO, ANANDA,

WOULD YOU BE WILLING TO HELP ?

O-OF COURSE I'LL HELP YOU!
ANYTHING FOR YOU !

WILL YOU COME WITH ME ON THIS JOURNEY ?
YESSIR! MY PLEASURE !

WHAT? BUDDHA'S GOING AWAY?
ARE YOU SERIOUS?

I SURE HOPE IT'S JUST A RUMOR
WE SHOULD GO ASK HIM
RIGHT

REALLY ?!
YOU'RE GOING ?
BUDDHA, THAT'S SO MEAN!
WE FORMED THIS SECT FOR THE SOLE PURPOSE OF HEARING YOUR SERMONS!
EVERYTHING WILL FALL APART IF YOU, OUR LEADER, WERE TO LEAVE!

THAT'S RIGHT!
A SECT WITHOUT BUDDHA IS LIKE COFFEE WITHOUT CREAM!
TRULY

PLEASE RECONSIDER! THIS JOURNEY COULD BE THE DEATH OF YOU!

PLEASE UNDER-STAND ...
I CAN'T JUST SPEND THE REST OF MY DAYS IN THIS PEACEFUL HAVEN...
I MUST TRAVEL AND SAVE SOULS!

THEN WE'LL SPLIT UP AND GO GIVE SERMONS ON YOUR BEHALF.
WE NEED YOU TO STAY HERE IN VENUVANA!

I AM THE ONLY ONE WHO CAN DO THIS WORK!

THE HEAVENS THEMSELVES GAVE ME THIS TASK.
BUT STILL...

TRUE. IT IS AS YOU SAY, BUT...
DAMMIT! YOU CAN'T JUST GO DO WHATEVER THE HELL YOU WANT!
WE'RE FINISHED IF YOU GO! THERE WON'T EVEN BE A "WE" ANYMORE. WE'LL DISBAND!
BUDDHA, WHEREVER YOU GO, I'LL BE THERE, TOO.
ME, TOO !!
US TOO !
LET US WALK WITH YOU!

PLEASE TAKE US WITH YOU!

THANK YOU, BUT I CAN'T HAVE SO MANY COME WITH ME.
WE'D BE TOO GREAT A BURDEN ON THOSE WHO WOULD HOUSE OR FEED US.

I WILL BRING ANANDA AND HIM ONLY.
I PROMISE I WILL RETURN. STAY HERE IN VENUVANA.

LUCKY BASTARD!

COMPARED TO THE REST OF YOU, ANANDA'S STILL A WEAK MAN. THIS WILL BE A TRIAL.
HE'LL HAVE TO LEARN NOT TO SLIP INTO OLD HABITS.

AW, HELL

DAMMIT!

...
DEAR, BUDDHA'S LEAVING NOW!

SO WHAT?!

DON'T YOU WANT TO SAY GOODBYE? HE ASKED ME WHERE YOU WERE.
OH YEAH, DID HE?

I AIN'T SPECIAL ENOUGH FOR BUDDHA!
HE'S GOT PLENTY OF DISCIPLES BETTER THAN ME!
BUT BUDDHA SAID HE'S COUNTING ON YOU TO PROTECT THE SECT FROM HARM, DEAR...
OH REALLY? WELL THANKS SO FRIGGIN' MUCH, PAL!
WHY'D HE LEAVE SARIPUTTA AND MOGGALLANA IN CHARGE, THEN?

WHAT DOES HE SEE IN THOSE TWO THAT WE DON'T GOT?

WELL, THEY DO SEEM TO BE PSYCHICS
RIGHT?
I WISH I WERE TOOOO!

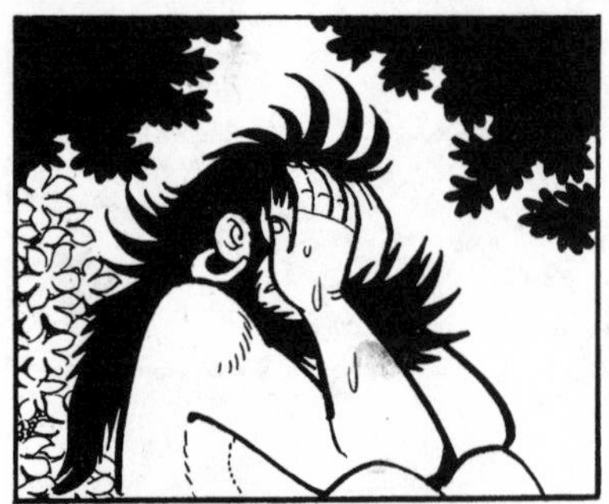

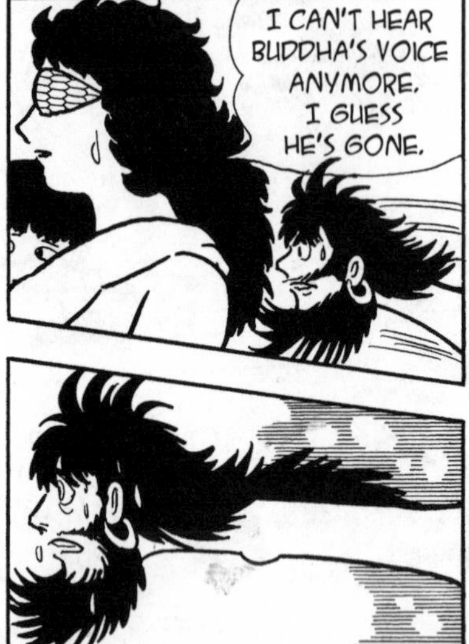

I CAN'T HEAR BUDDHA'S VOICE ANYMORE. I GUESS HE'S GONE.

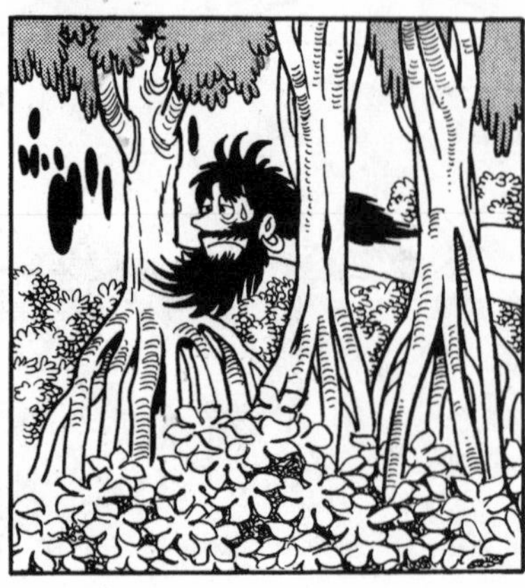

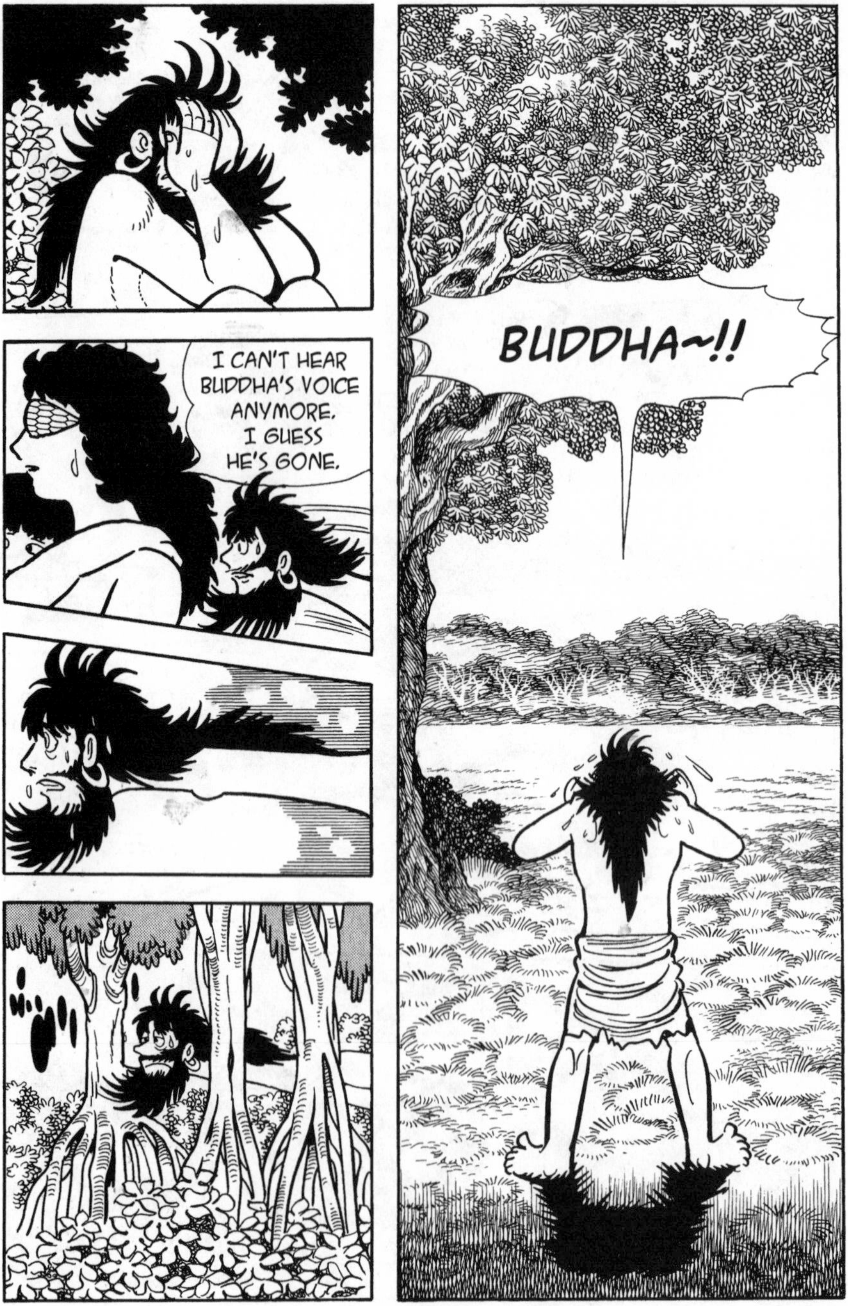

BUDDHA~!!

DAMMIT!
DAMN IT TO HELL!!!
THUMP THUMP
TATTA! WHAT BRINGS YOU HERE AT THIS HOUR? I'M BUSY WITH PRAYERS.
PRAYERS SHMARES! BUDDHA'S GONE AWAY. THE WHOLE SECT'S DEPRESSED!

HE'S GONE, YOU SAY?

YEAH, OFF TO KOSALA! HE WON'T BE BACK FOR A WHILE.

SO WHO'S STILL IN THE BAMBOO GROVE?

A THOUSAND DISCIPLES! BUDDHA LEFT SARIPUTTA AND MOGGALLANA IN CHARGE, BUT EVERYONE'S UNHAPPY. THE SMALLEST UPSET COULD DESTROY THE SECT!

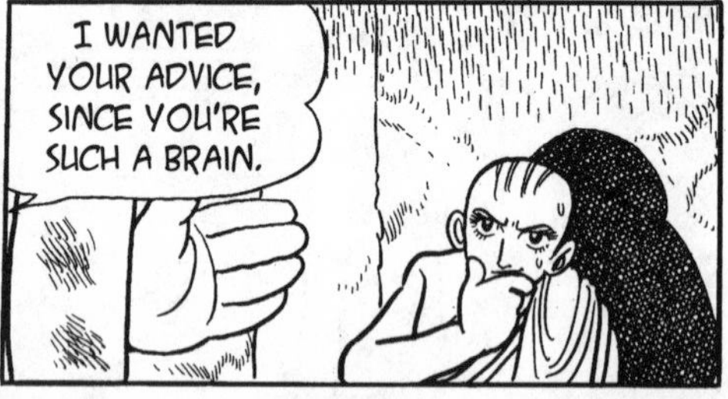

I WANTED YOUR ADVICE, SINCE YOU'RE SUCH A BRAIN.

BUDDHA'S GONE, AND THE MONKS ARE UNHAPPY?
INTERESTING. THIS COULD BE MY CHANCE TO SEIZE CONTROL!

UNAWARE OF DEVADATTA'S SECRET MUSINGS
BUDDHA AND ANANDA JOURNEYED EVER NORTHWARD.

WHOOOOOSH
WHEE
WHOOSH

I REMEMBER THIS SWAMP...

TWENTY YEARS AGO
DHEPA AND I WADED THROUGH THIS SWAMP
ON THE WAY TO MAGADHA.

HOW FAR DOES IT GO?

I THINK IT TOOK US FIVE DAYS TO CROSS IT.

FIVE DAYS ?!

OOPS!
SPLASH!

BUDDHA!

ARE YOU ALL RIGHT ?
PLEASE, PULL YOURSELF TOGETHER

THIS IS ONE SERIOUS SWAMP. ISN'T THERE AT LEAST SOME SHOAL OR BANK TO REST ON?
IT'S LIKE THIS THE WHOLE WAY. AND LAST TIME, IT RAINED.
ASSAJI, WHOM YOU KNOW, WAS ALSO WITH US. HE GOT VERY SICK AND NEARLY DIED.
WE NURSED HIM IN A TOWN UP AHEAD
THERE'S A TOWN?!
INDEED. IF WE CAN MAKE IT THAT FAR...
SUN'S ABOUT TO SET. WE SLEEP STANDING IN THIS MUCK?
YES, ANANDA.

WE CAN TAKE TURNS SLEEPING. THE ONE WHO IS AWAKE HOLDS UP THE OTHER. THAT'S HOW WE MADE IT THE LAST TIME.
WELL, THAT WAS THEN! YOU'RE NOT STRONG ENOUGH FOR IT NOW.
AH... IT'S NO-THING ...
BUDDHA! WHAT'S THAT UP AHEAD ?
THERE'S SOMETHING FLOATING ...
BUDDHA, I THINK IT'S A LOG!
WHAT LUCK! WITH THAT, WE CAN BOTH GET SOME REST.
HUH ?

OFF THE LOG, YOU BUM DEVILS!
AHH, I'LL CRUSH YOU ALL!

ANANDA
YOU MUST NOT !!
DO NOT KILL THEM.
BUT...

THEY MAY BE SPIDERS, BUT THEY, TOO, ARE STRUGGLING TO SURVIVE IN THIS HELLISH SWAMP...
THANKS TO THEM, YOU AND I CAN'T USE THE LOG!
WE OUGHT TO GET SOME REST!

ANANDA !!
WHAT IF ONE OF THESE SPIDERS IS LATA REBORN?
THAT'S...

COULD THAT BE...?

THE SPIRITS OF LIVING THINGS ARE ALL CONNECTED IN ANOTHER WORLD.
THESE ARE OUR BRETHREN. LET THEM BE.
YES

FSSSHHHH

WHEN IT RAINS ...

FSSSH
FSSSH
FSSSH
FSSSH
IT POURS! MERCY!

FSSHHH
FZSHHH
FSHH

LET'S TURN BACK!

YOUR BODY CAN'T TAKE THIS... WE MUST WAIT FOR A BETTER SEASON!
NO...

I'M BEING TESTED BY THE HEAVENS. THE IDLE MAN OF VENUVANA IS BEING FORCED TO REMEMBER HIS DAYS AS AN ASCETIC.

I'LL KEEP GOING. I MUST.

JUST THINK OF IT AS AN EXCELLENT TRIAL FOR YOURSELF AS WELL.

OKAY

M-MY FEET CAN'T REACH THE BOTTOM ANYMORE!
TIME TO SWIM, THEN.

AH! I SEE SOMETHING IN THE DISTANCE. LOOKS LIKE A WALL...
THAT COULD BE IT! THE TOWN WALL OF PANDAWA!

YES! A TOWN! WE'RE SAVED!
THE TOWN OF PANDAWA... THIS IS WHERE WE FOUND SHELTER, DHEPA, ASSAJI, AND I.
I CAN'T BELIEVE WE MADE IT.
DOES ANYONE LIVE HERE?
NO, IT'S JUST RUINS NOW. BACK THEN AN EPIDEMIC HAD SWEPT THROUGH THE TOWN.
THESE ARE THE GRAVES FROM THEN.
AH, AND THAT'S WHERE
WE SPENT THE NIGHT.

LOOKS LIKE THERE WAS A PRETTY BAD FIRE.
YES, I ALMOST FORGOT. BANDITS CAME AND SET THE TOWN ON FIRE, BURNING IT DOWN.

IT'S DRY OVER HERE!
PLEASE REST

AND GUESS WHO THE BANDIT WAS?
OUR VERY OWN TATTA!

HA
WHAT A TANGLED WEB WE WEAVE

IN THAT MANSION RIGHT ACROSS THE STREET LIVED A WOMAN, ALL ALONE. A WEALTHY HEIRESS,

HER NAME WAS VISAKHA.

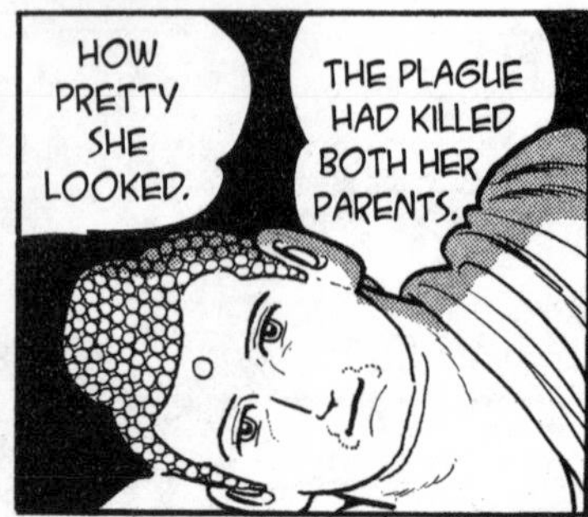
HOW PRETTY SHE LOOKED.
THE PLAGUE HAD KILLED BOTH HER PARENTS.

SHE WAS LONELY AND WOULD NOT LET ME LEAVE.

TRIED TO GET ME TO MARRY HER.
HA HA HA... MEMORIES...
I WONDER HOW SHE IS DOING.

I CAN'T VOUCH FOR THE TASTE ...
BUT HERE'S SOME SUPPER.
OH... THANK YOU.

DO YOU THINK SHE'S STILL HERE, IN THIS TOWN ?

NO... NO, I DOUBT IT. SHE MUST HAVE MOVED AWAY.
THE FIRE RAZED THE WHOLE TOWN.

LYING HERE NOW, I FEEL LIKE IT WAS ONLY YESTERDAY.

HM, VISAKHA. HOW I'D LOVE TO SEE HER AGAIN.

WHERE ARE YOU?
ANANDA?!

ANANDA

HE MUST HAVE FOUND ANOTHER PLACE TO SLEEP.

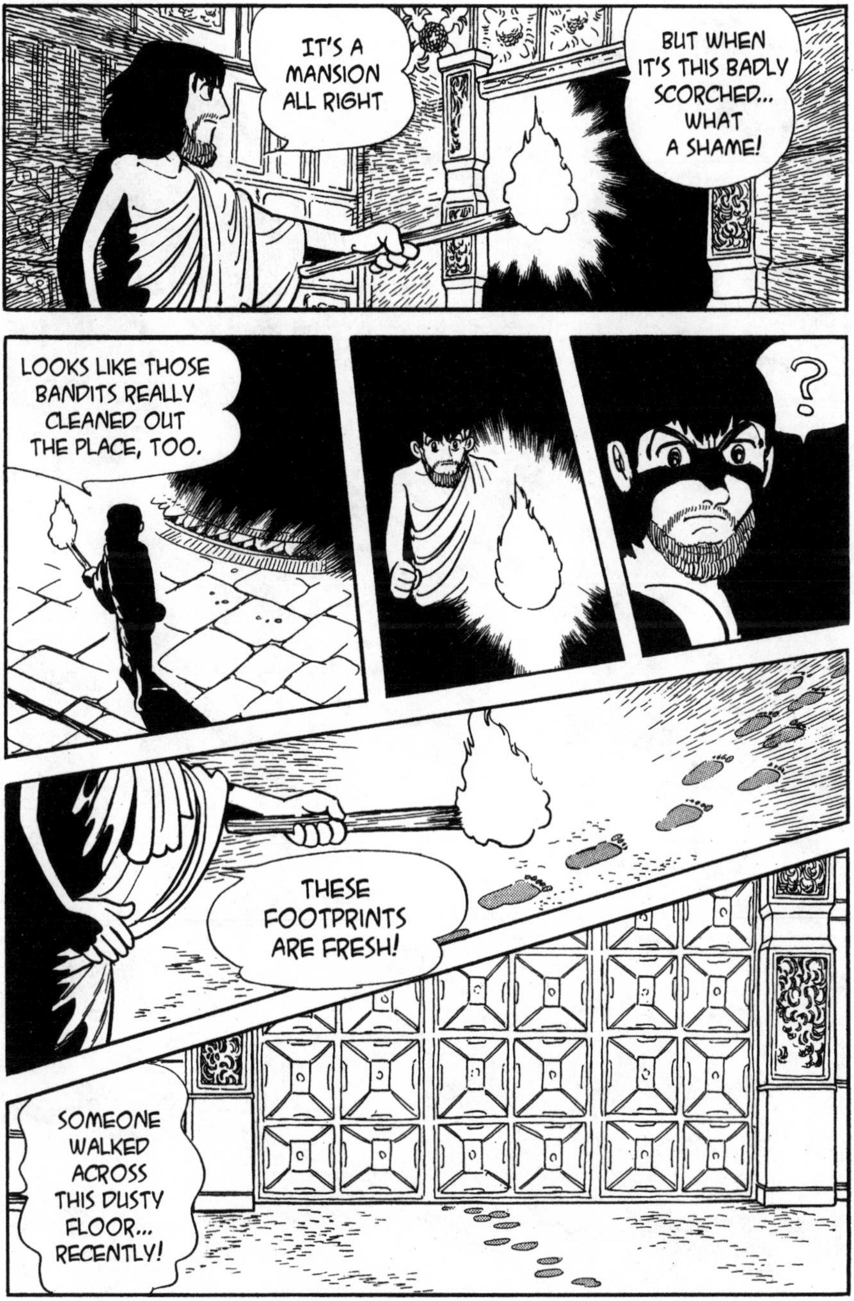

LOOKS LIKE THOSE BANDITS REALLY CLEANED OUT THE PLACE, TOO.

?

THESE FOOTPRINTS ARE FRESH!

SOMEONE WALKED ACROSS THIS DUSTY FLOOR... RECENTLY!

HEY... THIS WALL MOVES...
A SECRET CHAMBER !!
LOOKS LIKE IT ELUDED BOTH THE BANDITS AND THE FIRE
A WINE CELLAR ?
ECH! WHAT IS THIS STUFF?

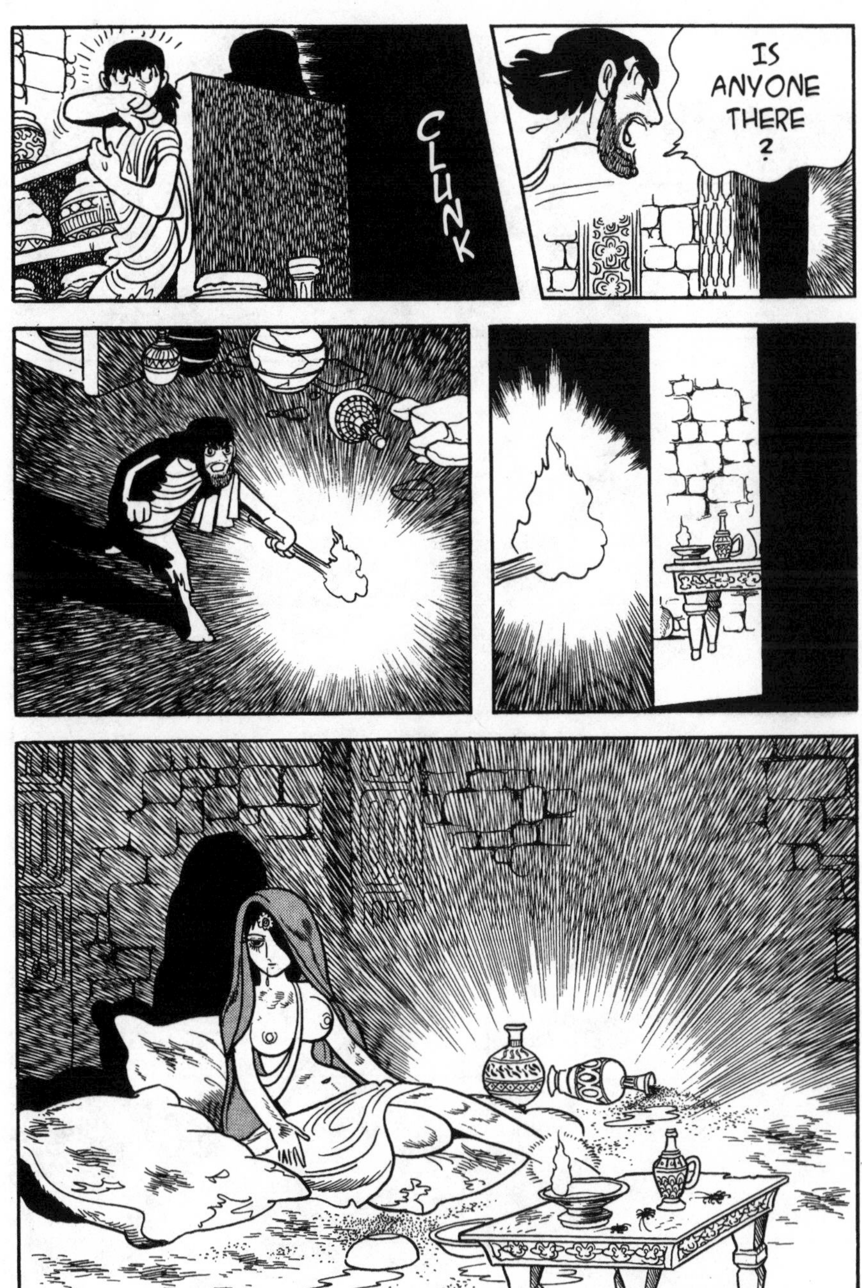
CLUNK
IS ANYONE THERE ?

HOHOHOHOH

HAHAHAHAH

HEEEEEE
HEEEEE
HEEEE
ULP...

UH UHH
UGH
AHH
WHO ARE YOU? YOU AREN'T VISAKHA, ARE YOU?!

AHA?! HA-HA-HAH! HO HOH! TEE HEE!!
...

CHAPTER FOUR

MADWOMAN VISAKHA

GOOD MORNING
ANANDA, WHERE DID YOU SLEEP LAST NIGHT?

LET'S GET OUT OF THIS PLACE! NO USE TARRYING HERE.
WHY THE BIG HURRY? HAS THE RAIN STOPPED?

THE WHOLE PLACE REEKS OF DEATH.

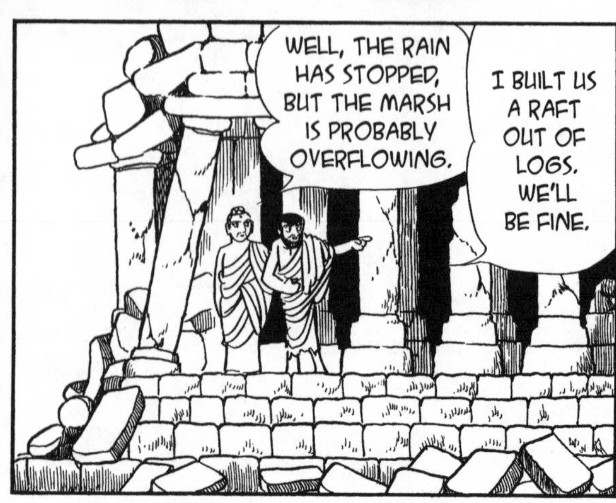
WELL, THE RAIN HAS STOPPED, BUT THE MARSH IS PROBABLY OVERFLOWING.
I BUILT US A RAFT OUT OF LOGS. WE'LL BE FINE.

ISN'T SHE FROM THE TOWN? SO PEOPLE STILL LIVE HERE!

NEVER MIND HER... PLEASE, LET'S HURRY.

HEH HEH HEH HEH
WAIT! THAT'S VISAKHA, ISN'T IT?!
NOT A CHANCE!
ARE YOU VISAKHA ?!
SHE'S JUST SOME CRAZY WOMAN. I FOUND HER IN AN ABANDONED HOUSE LAST NIGHT.
SHE'S CRAZY ?
IT'S A WASTE OF TIME!
SHE JUST BABBLES. DOESN'T EVEN KNOW WHO SHE IS. A TOTAL NUTCASE.

HEEE HEE HEEE!
YOU SEE? IT'S NOT VISAKHA.
HMM, I COULDN'T TELL... AND SHE JUST STARED AT ME BLANKLY.

BUDDHA, WAIT! WHERE ARE YOU GOING?
I'M GOING TO VISAKHA'S MANSION. JUST TO BE SURE.

THIS USED TO BE HER LIVING ROOM

CREAK

THESE ARE STILL HERE!
?
YOU FOUND HER IN HERE?
YES
VISAKHA TOLD ME THAT WHEN SHE DRANK
THESE POTIONS...
THESE MAKE YOU DREAM.

SHE FELT YOUNG AGAIN AND SOARED THROUGH THE SKIES LIKE A BIRD.
SHE BOUGHT EVERY LAST BOTTLE FROM A MERCHANT WHO CAME FROM THE WEST.
WHY DID SHE?

SHE'D SEEN TOO MANY PEOPLE DIE. NEITHER THE TOWN'S BRAHMIN SHRINE, NOR ALL THE PRAYERS, COULD SAVE ANY OF THEM.

SHE LEARNED THAT LIFE IS BUT A PASSING THING. LOSING HERSELF IN DREAMS AND ILLUSIONS, SHE TRIED TO ESCAPE FROM THE FEAR OF DEATH.

DRINKING THESE DAY AFTER DAY WOULD RUIN BOTH YOUR BODY AND YOUR MIND.

BUT WE DON'T KNOW THAT SHE'S REALLY VISAKHA!
SHE COULD JUST BE SOME BEGGAR WOMAN WHO WANDERED IN HERE AND FOUND ALL THESE DRUGS!

EITHER WAY, I'M GOING TO HELP HER.

I WAS AFRAID... YOU WERE GONNA SAY THAT...

ANANDA, I SET OUT ON THIS JOURNEY TO SAVE PEOPLE FROM SUFFERING!

FIRST, WE NEED TO TAKE THESE DRUGS AWAY FROM HER.
WE'LL THROW THEM OVER THE TOWN WALLS.

DON'T LET HER NOTICE. SHE COULD TURN DANGEROUS.

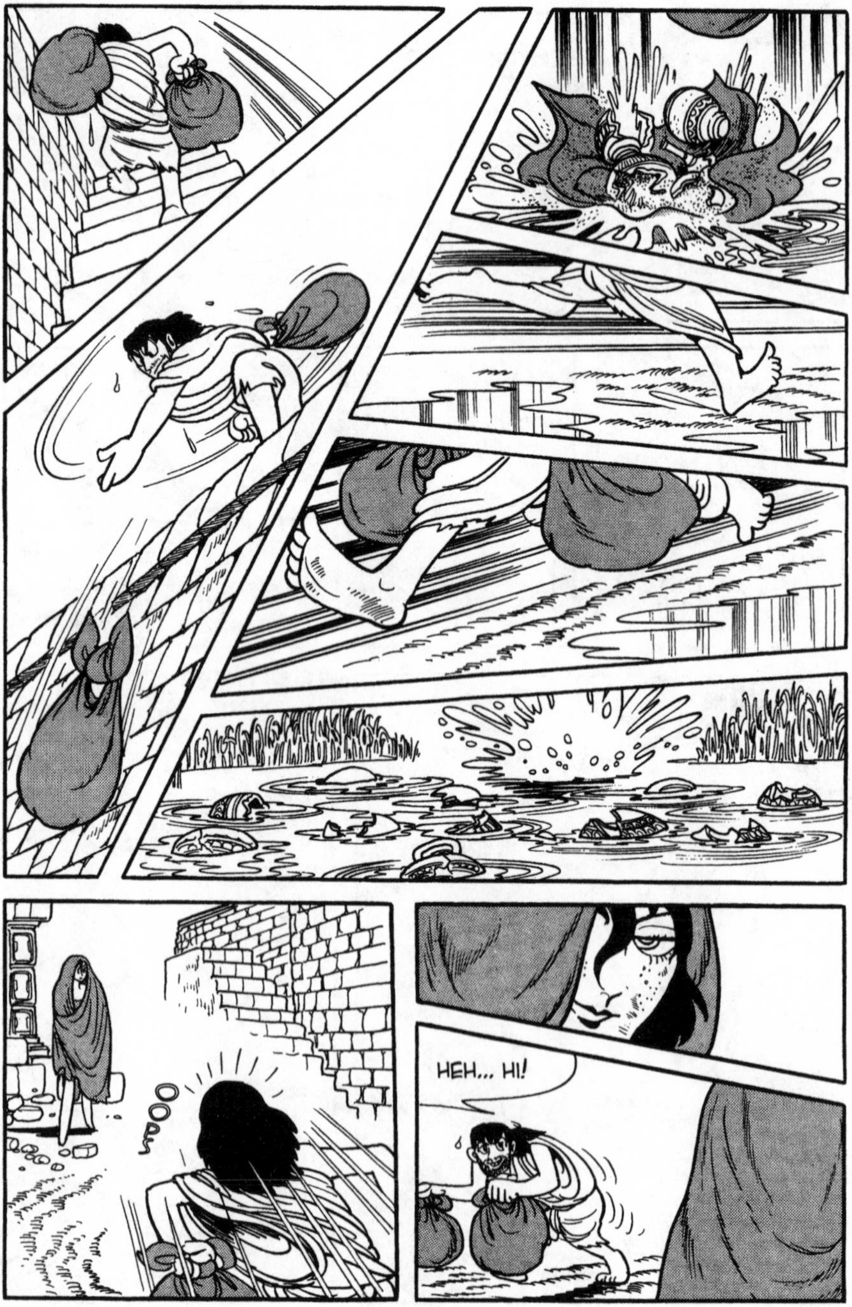

OOPS
HEH... HI!

PLOP
KRAC

UH-OH !!

...
DOES SHE REALIZE ...?

BUDDHA, WATCH OUT! THE WOMAN'S CAUGHT ON!

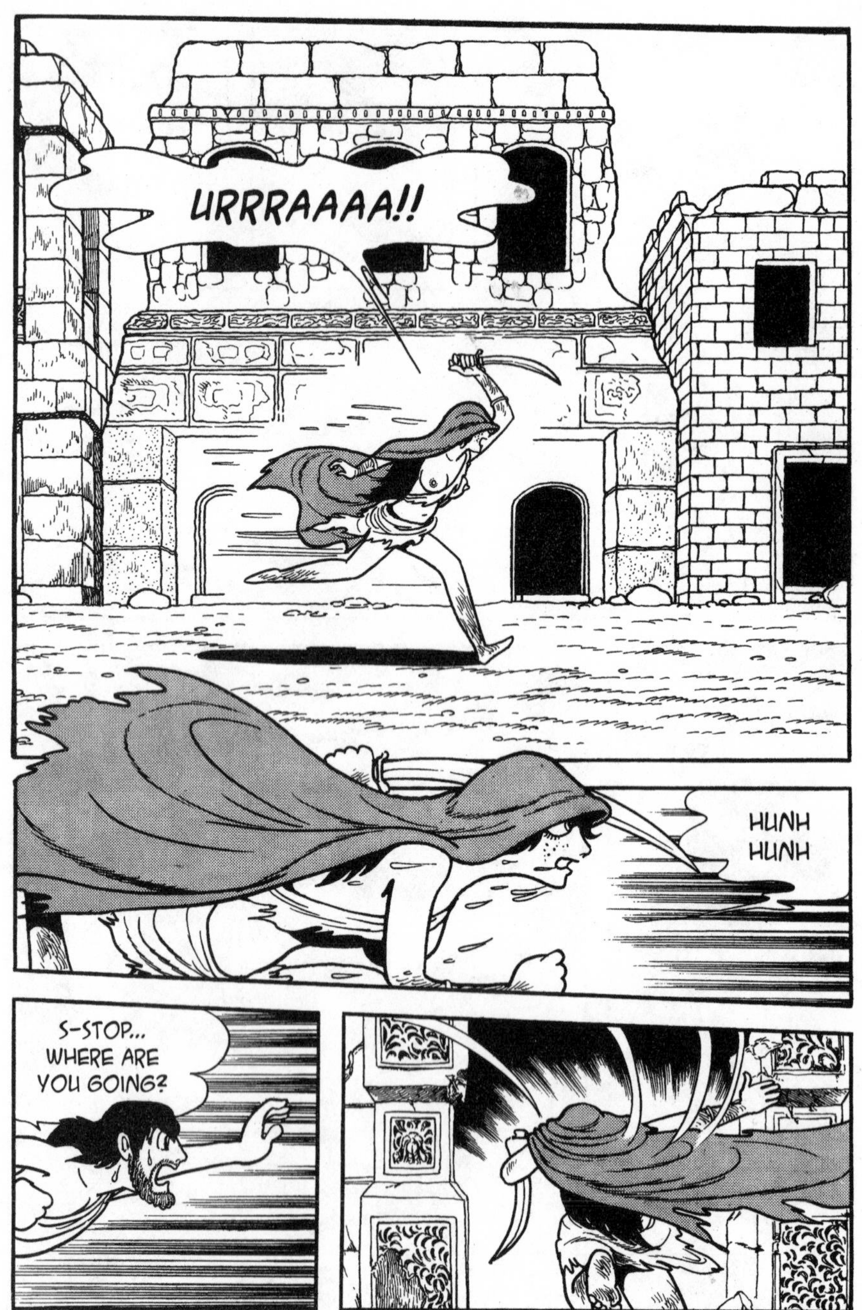
URRRAAAA!!
HUNH HUNH
S-STOP... WHERE ARE YOU GOING?

OHH
!!

GA...
HA?
HA?
UNG,
UNG...
UHHH!

SLAM
BONK

OH... OOOHH !!
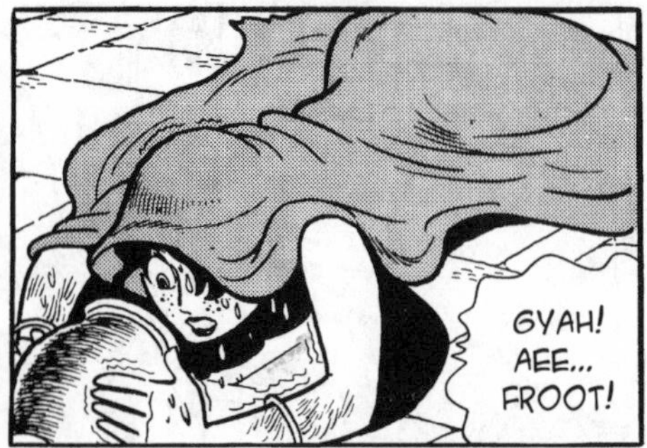
GYAH! AEE... FROOT!

BILBAN-BUH... DAGUM!

BRANF!!

GI...
GINU...
FU...

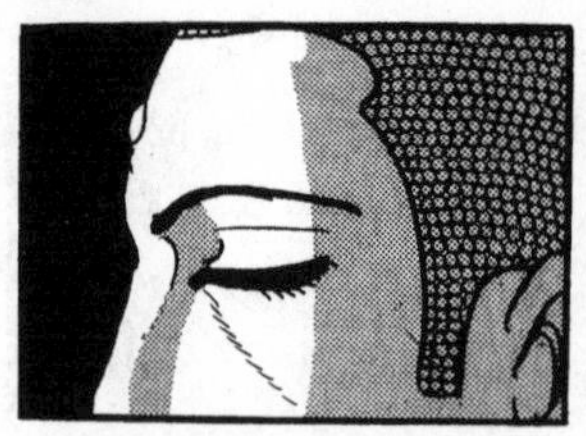

AAHH!!

WH...O
OH, OH...
UHH...

WAAA
WAAA
WAAA
WAAA
WEEP
SOB
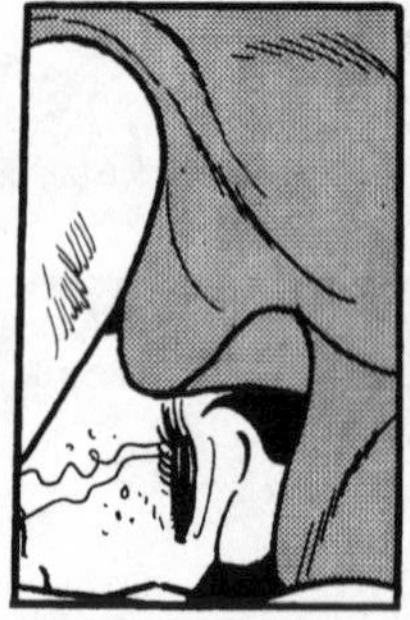

BUDDHA, ARE YOU HURT?

I'M FINE ...
I'LL CHASE HER OUT!
LEAVE HER ALONE.

I CAN SAVE HER. SHE'S NOT ENTIRELY GONE.
WHY ?

A TINY FISTFUL OF SANITY KEPT HER FROM KILLING ME.

SHE'S JUST ILL. HER MIND IS.
THERE'S NO WAY SHE'LL BE CURED...
WITH AN ILLNESS OF THE MIND, YOU MUST FIND THE CAUSE, AND THEN REMOVE IT. THAT TENDS TO BE THE CURE.

FINE, BUT HOW LONG DO WE WANNA STAY HERE?

SHE'LL COME WITH US.

BUT
BUT
WHA WHA WHAT ?!
I DON'T TRAVEL WITH CRAZIES !

HA?
SO YOU'RE SAYING THAT YOU'RE NOT CRAZY?

'COURSE NOT!! I'M PERFECTLY SANE !!

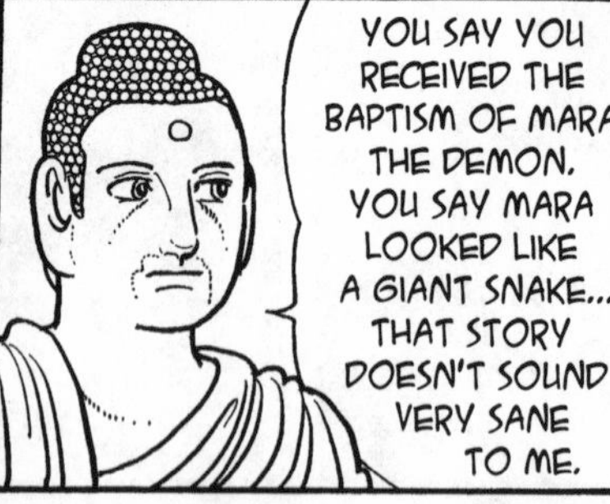
YOU SAY YOU RECEIVED THE BAPTISM OF MARA THE DEMON. YOU SAY MARA LOOKED LIKE A GIANT SNAKE... THAT STORY DOESN'T SOUND VERY SANE TO ME.

YEAH, BUT... UHM...

DON'T BE TOO HARSH ABOUT THE MADNESSES OF OTHERS.
RIGHT...
THINK ABOUT IT. WE ALL HAVE OUR BITS OF MADNESS.

OH... YOU...

I DON'T KNOW WHO YOU ARE, BUT YOU MUST LEAVE AT ONCE.
THIS TOWN IS FULL OF DEATH.
I'M ABLE TO SPEAK TO YOU NOW, BUT BEFORE LONG THE GHOSTS OF THE DEAD WILL POSSESS ME AGAIN.

THEN I WON'T BE MYSELF. PLEASE, YOU MUST LEAVE AS SOON AS POSSIBLE!

ALL RIGHT, WE'LL GO. BUT YOU'RE COMING WITH US.

NO, STOP!
I AM FATED TO DIE! YOU MUST NOT TOUCH ME!!

YES, YOU WILL DIE. IF YOU STAY HERE.

THAT'S WHY YOU MUST COME WITH US.
THEN YOU SHALL LIVE!
NO!!

YOU MUST COME WITH ME, VISAKHA!
...

WHO ARE YOU? WHY DO YOU CALL ME VISAKHA?

BECAUSE I BELIEVE THAT IS YOUR NAME.
VISAKHA? I KNOW I'VE HEARD THAT NAME BEFORE. BUT IT'S NOT MINE... MY NAME IS... I FORGOT MY NAME.

COME ON. CHIN UP! WE HAVE A RAFT READY!
NO!!
I... I... I CAN'T LEAVE!

VISAKHA, YOU MUST!!

NO! NO!! I'M NOT GOING! LET GO OF ME! PLEASE!! LET GO OF ME!!

LET ME OFF! I WANT TO GO HOME!!

MY TOWN... *SOB SOB*

THIS SWAMP IS LARGER THAN I RECALL...

EVERY TIME I THOUGHT WE'D COME TO SHORE, IT TURNED OUT TO BE JUST AN ISLET.

...

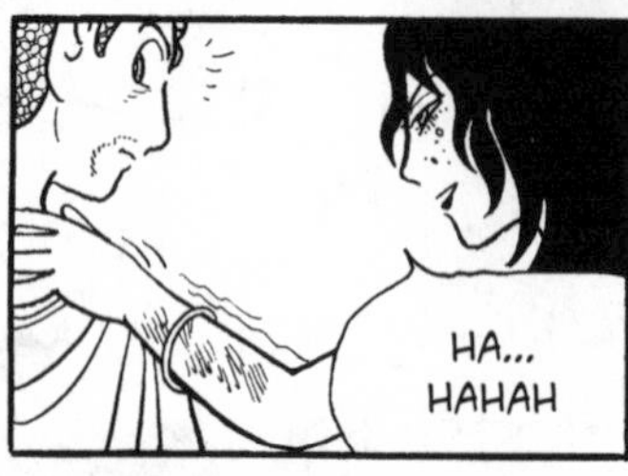

HA... HAHAH

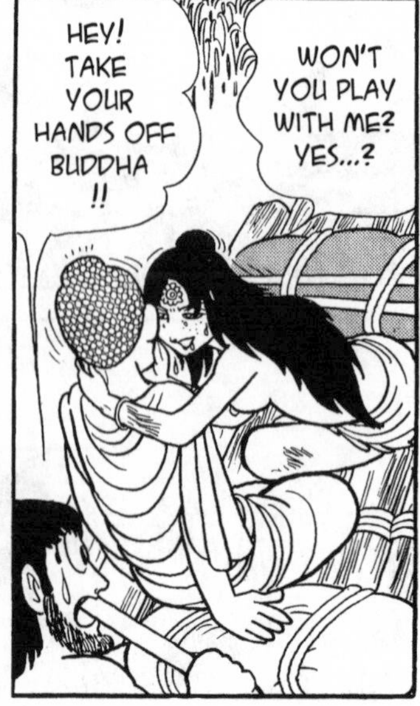

WON'T YOU PLAY WITH ME? YES...?
HEY! TAKE YOUR HANDS OFF BUDDHA !!

KISS ME... WON'T YOU? HEE HEE!
QUIT IT, YOU CRAZY PERVERT! LEAVE HIM ALONE, OR I'LL...
OH YEAH? THIS RAFT DOESN'T OFFER MUCH PRIVACY...
DO NOT HURT HER! LET HER DO AS SHE LIKES.
HUFF HUFF
DON'T WORRY. THIS WOMAN ISN'T CAPABLE.
HEHEH, MAKE LOVE TO ME, BIG BOY... YEAH?
BUT I CAN'T BEAR TO WATCH THIS!
THEN LOOK THE OTHER WAY

BY THE GODS
DON'T WORRY I SAID.
AHH, HAH... AH, AHA?
Y-YOU SURE SHE'S NOT REALLY UP TO IT?
YES...
UHH... HUNH... UHH, UHH
GIMME... GIMME POTION

STOP! STOP IT! WE'LL TIP OVER!

AH! UNH UNHH AAAAH!

HEE HEE HEE HEE HEE!

HEHEH

WHAT DID I...

WHOA

SPLASH!

GAAAH!

SPLOSH
SPLASH!
THUMP

HOW DID YOU KNOW THERE WAS NO NEED TO WORRY?
A LONG TIME AGO, VISAKHA TOLD ME WHAT THE DRUGS DID FOR HER. "WITH THESE," SHE SAID, "I CAN FLY LIKE A BIRD, FLY AWAY TO ANY FARAWAY PLACE I FANCY."
THAT IS TO SAY, THE MIND WANDERS A WORLD OF ILLUSIONS.
BUT OF COURSE, THE BODY STAYS. IN FACT IT IS DULLED.
IT ENTERS A STATE WHERE IT FEELS, BUT CANNOT DO.
EVEN IF SHE FEELS THE URGE TO TAKE ME, SHE SIMPLY CAN'T GO THROUGH WITH IT.
WHAT AWFUL STUFF !!
ARE WE BRINGING HER ALONG FOR THE WHOLE JOURNEY?
I'D LIKE TO...
WE'LL LOOK AFTER HER UNTIL SHE RECOVERS.

BUDDHA GAUTAMA, WELCOME TO KOMADHUSSA, OUR HUMBLE VILLAGE.
THERE ISN'T A SOUL HERE WHO HASN'T HEARD YOUR NAME, SIR.
WE'VE GATHERED IN THE TOWN HALL. PLEASE DELIVER A SERMON FOR US!

TO RELEASE YOURSELVES FROM PAIN, YOU SHOULD FOLLOW THE EIGHTFOLD PATH.

YOU MUST SEE RIGHTLY, THINK RIGHTLY, SPEAK RIGHTLY, WORK RIGHTLY, LIVE RIGHTLY, STRIVE RIGHTLY, PRAY RIGHTLY, AND STAY RIGHT.

HEY, BE QUIET!

HEY, YOU CAN'T GO OVER THERE! SIT DOWN!
WHAT'S WITH HER?
THAT LADY CAME WITH BUDDHA...

AH HAH HAH HAH!
TEE HEE HEE HEE!
HEY!!
WH- WHAT IS THE MEANING OF THIS?
HOLD ME! HUG ME! KISSY KISSY KISSY!
VISAKHA !!
WHAT THE HELL? DO YOU ALWAYS INSERT LOVE SCENES IN YOUR SERMONS?
HEE HEE HEE! I WANT YOU! I WANT YOU...
VISAKHA, NOT HERE! CUT IT OUT! STOP!
THE RIGHT PATH YOU'RE PREACHIN' IS THIS?

WE'VE HAD ENOUGH! PLEASE LEAVE!

KOOCHIE KOOCHIE
WHEE

IF THIS KEEPS HAPPENING WE'LL BE CHASED OUT OF ANY VILLAGE.
VISAKHA IS ILL... FORGIVE HER.

BUT AT THIS RATE YOU WON'T EVER FINISH ANOTHER SERMON!
LET'S CHASE HER AWAY!

WHAT ARE YOU SAYING ?!
DIDN'T YOU TRY TO CHASE AWAY LATA AT FIRST? THE GIRL WHO WOULD ONE DAY MAKE SUCH A FINE NUN?

... VISAKHA CAN BE SAVED
AND I'LL SAVE HER NO MATTER WHAT !

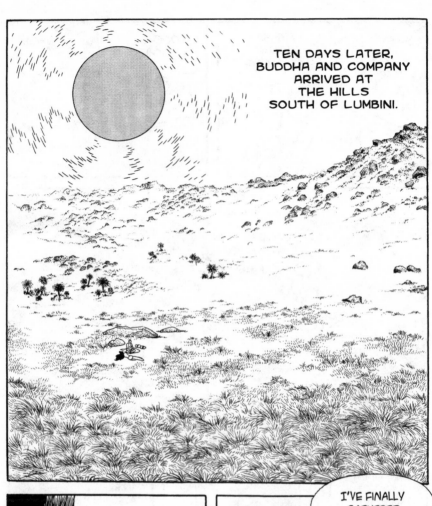

TEN DAYS LATER, BUDDHA AND COMPANY ARRIVED AT THE HILLS SOUTH OF LUMBINI.

DRIP
DRIP

I'VE FINALLY GATHERED JUST THIS MUCH!

JUST ENOUGH FOR ONE PERSON...
THE ONLY WATER I COULD FIND IS WHAT'S DRIPPING FROM THOSE BOULDERS.
TOOK ME AN HOUR TO GET THIS MUCH.

PLEASE GIVE IT TO VISAKHA.

BUT I GOT IT FOR YOU, BUDDHA!

SHE'S HALF-DEAD FROM THIRST. I CAN WAIT.

IT'S NO USE... THIS ISN'T GONNA REVIVE HER.
SHE WAS ALREADY PRETTY WEAK WHEN WE SET OUT.

LOOK. SPILLED EVERY DROP...

PLEASE, WAKE UP...
VISAKHA! DON'T DIE ON ME!

AH

IT'S OVER

LOOK, VULTURES ARE CIRCLING. THEY'VE SMELLED DEATH.

FLIES SWARMING, TOO.

VISAKHA

PLEASE, BUDDHA... SHE'S DEAD.
IT'S TRUE THAT SHE'S NOT BREATHING.
SHE MIGHT LOOK DEAD ON THE OUTSIDE
BUT I'M SURE THAT LIFE AND DEATH ARE CLASHING INSIDE HER, BATTLING FURIOUSLY.
I DON'T THINK SO...

ONLY VISAKHA HERSELF KNOWS FOR SURE.

LET'S GO. AND WE HAVE TO JUST LEAVE HER HERE.
THE VULTURES WILL SEND HER SOUL TO THE SKIES.

I'M GOING BACK TO GET VISAKHA!
WHAT ?!

BUT SHE'S MILES BEHIND US NOW!
NONE TOO FAR.
I CAN'T GET HER OUT OF MY MIND. SHE WASN'T DEAD.
BUDDHA! IT'S NO JOKE WALKING ALL THE WAY BACK THERE.
WAIT HERE THEN
SHE'S ALIVE

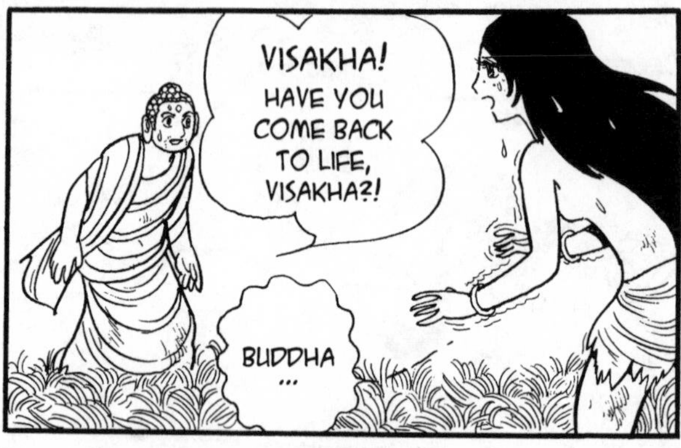
VISAKHA! HAVE YOU COME BACK TO LIFE, VISAKHA?!
BUDDHA ...

WELL DONE! I'M PROUD OF YOU.
MY NAME IS VISAKHA. I'M A RICH MAN'S DAUGHTER, FROM PANDAWA. OH...WHAT WAS I DOING FOR SUCH A LONG TIME? SUCH A LONG, LONG TIME..!

YOU'RE OKAY NOW. CONGRAT-ULATIONS.

LET'S GO. YOU'LL START A NEW LIFE IN KOSALA!

CHAPTER FIVE

Encounter with Prince Crystal

I CAN'T BELIEVE IT! SHE'S LIKE A DIFFERENT PERSON FROM THAT NUTCASE.
NOW LET IT REST, ANANDA. IT'S ALL OVER AND DONE WITH.
AH! WE'RE ALREADY IN ANUPIYA.
AFTER I LEFT MY COUNTRY, THIS IS WHERE I DISMOUNTED, SHAVED OFF MY HAIR, AND BECAME A MONK...
I WAS YOUNG THEN.
WOW

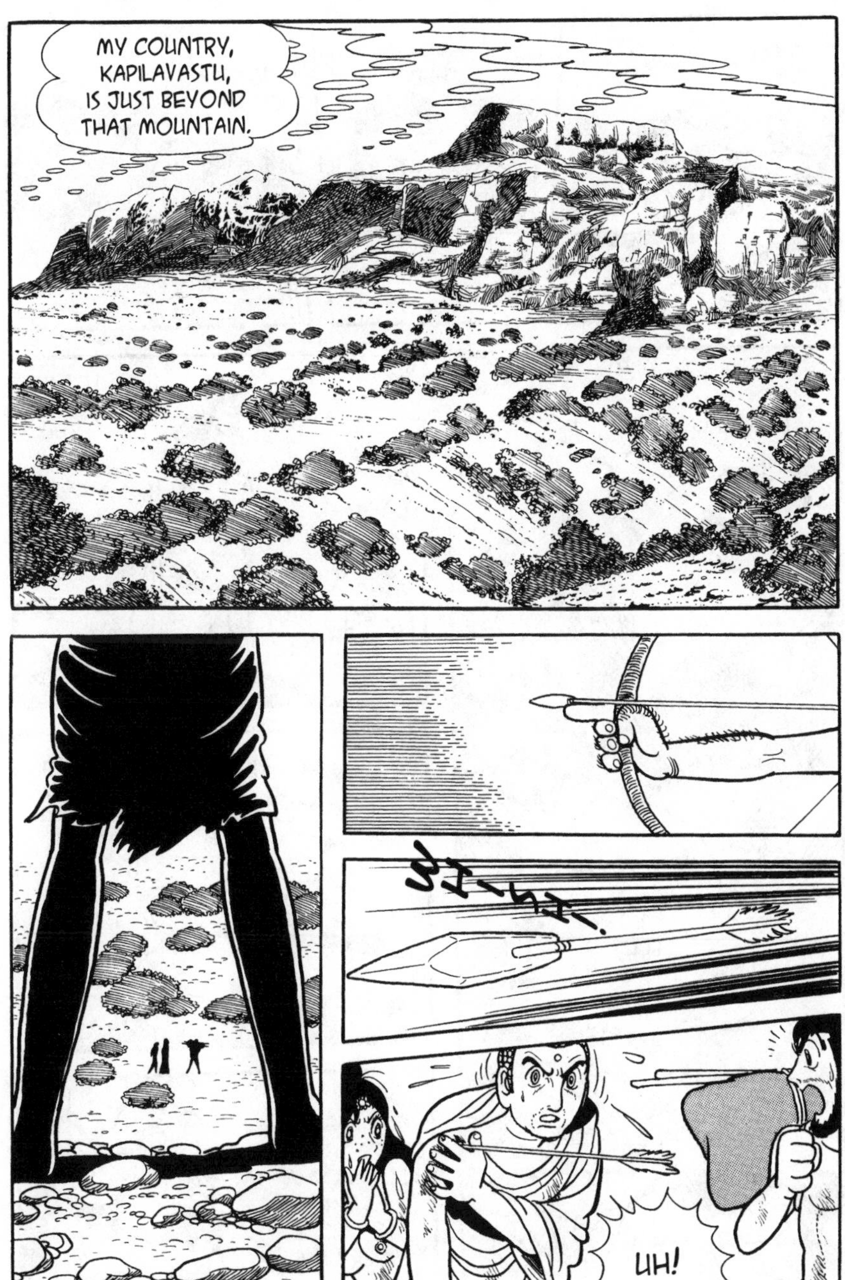
MY COUNTRY, KAPILAVASTU, IS JUST BEYOND THAT MOUNTAIN.
UH!

WHAT THE...!

HANG IN THERE!
UNH!

WHO ?!

YOUR OLD PAL AHIMSA, ALSO KNOWN AS ANGULIMALA.
AHIMSA! YOU'VE BEEN PROWLING AFTER BUDDHA THIS WHOLE TIME?

YEAH, I HAVE. BUT I'M GETTING TIRED OF THIS GAME.
LET ME KILL HIM AND GET IT OVER WITH.

LAY A FINGER ON BUDDHA, AND I'LL MAKE YOU REGRET IT FOR THE REST OF YOUR LIFE!

SHUT UP AND GET THE HELL OUTTA THE WAY. IT'S BUDDHA I WANT, NOT YOUR SORRY ASS.

ONCE HE'S DEAD AND GONE
YOU'LL SNAP OUT OF YOUR STUPOR AND JOIN ME AGAIN.
DON'T! DON'T COME ANY CLOSER, OR...
I'LL KILL YOU!
WHAT A VICIOUS LITTLE LAPDOG YOU GOT HERE, BUDDHA.
STOP THIS !!
IN THE END, MAYBE YOU AND I WERE MEANT TO FIGHT TO THE DEATH. FINE, NO TIME LIKE NOW.
ANANDA, I HAVE DONE MY UTMOST TO AVOID FIGHTING WITH THIS MAN.
DO YOU WANT TO RUIN ALL MY EFFORTS ?
BUDDHA, FORGIVE ME THIS ONE DEED !

HEY PUPPY,
YOUR MASTER'S PISSED.
ROLL OVER AND
PLAY DEAD LIKE
A GOOD BOY.

SHUT UP!
I'LL FIGHT
IF WE MUST!
YOU WILL
NOT LISTEN,
ANANDA
?!

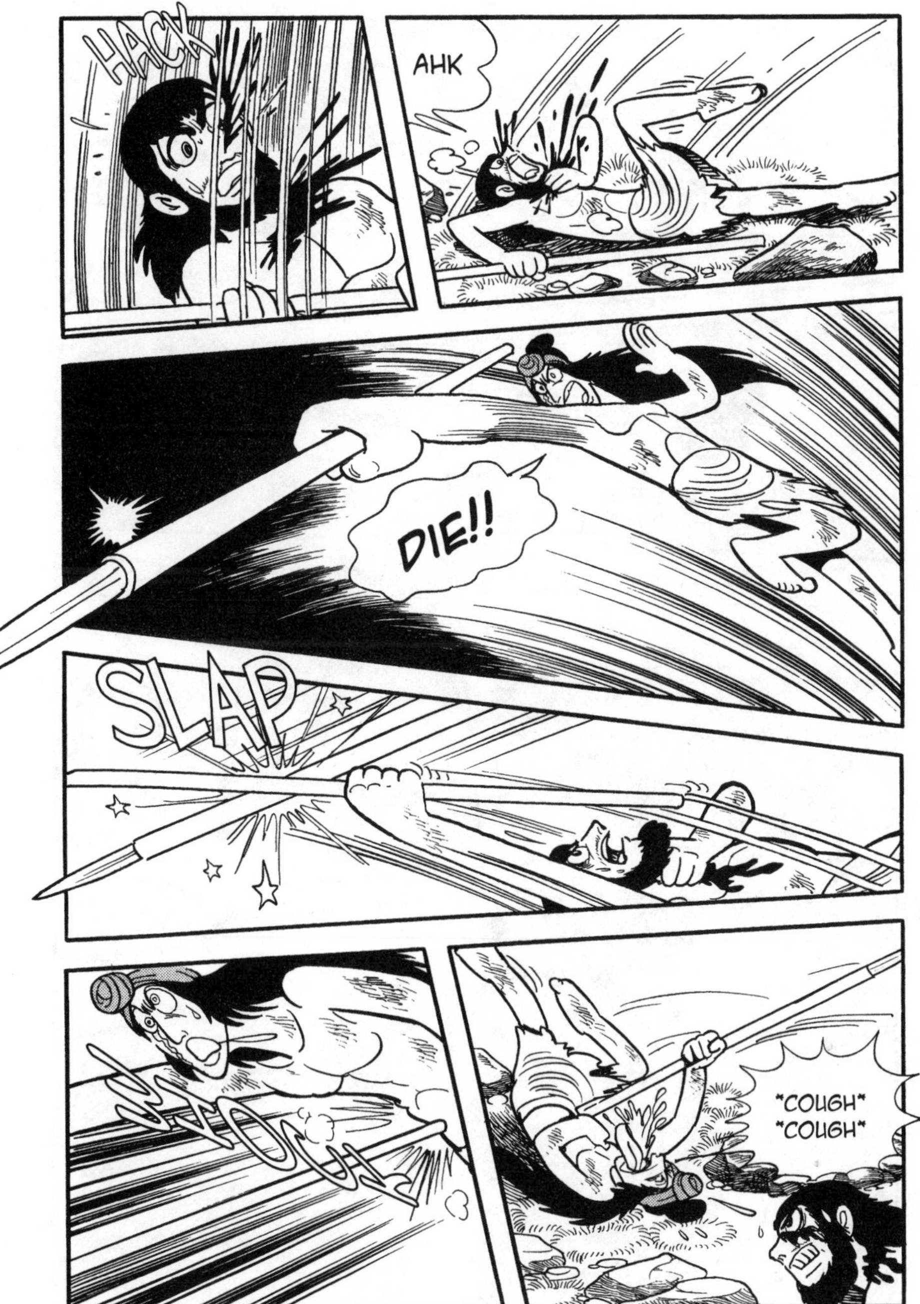
HACK
AHK
DIE!!
SLAP
COUGH
COUGH

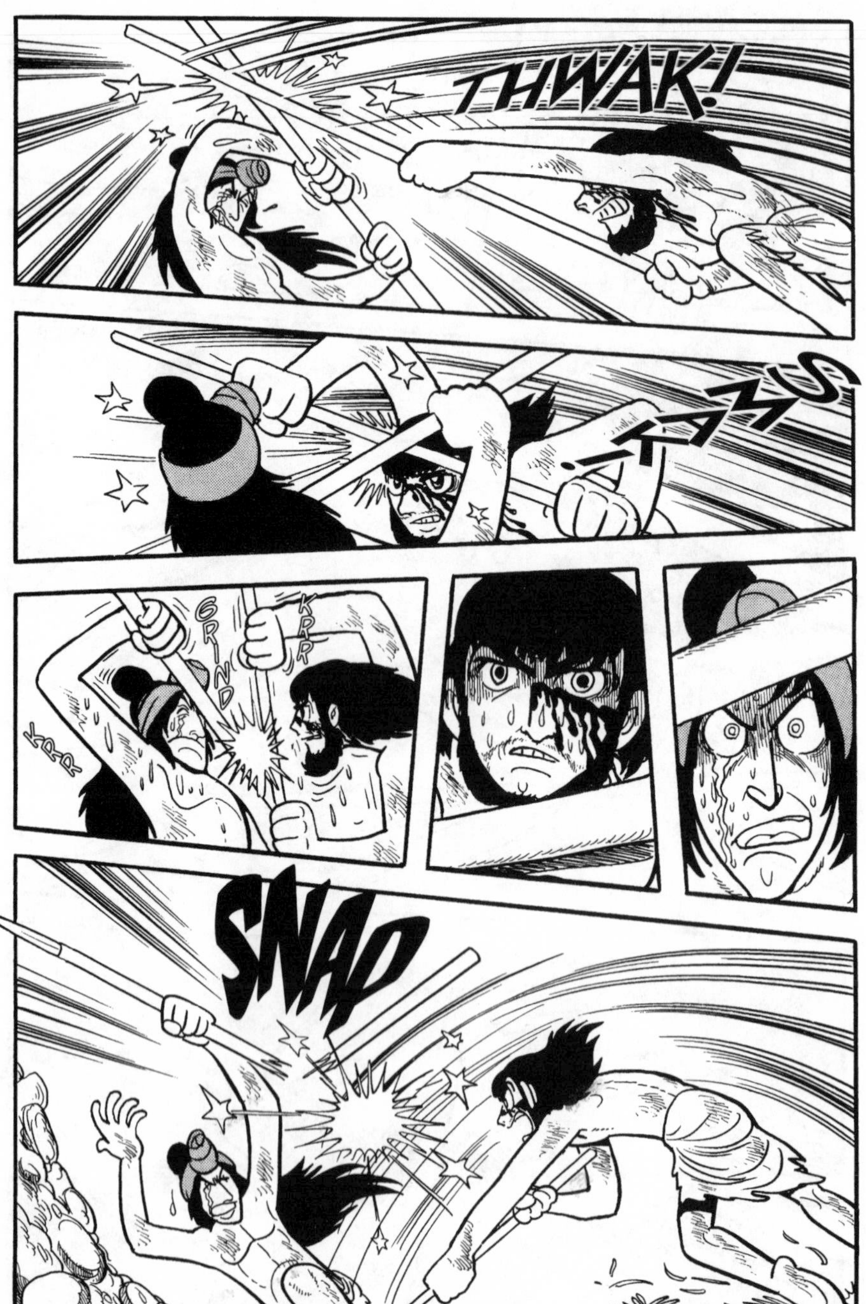
THWAK!
SMAK!
GRIND
KRR
KRR
SNAP

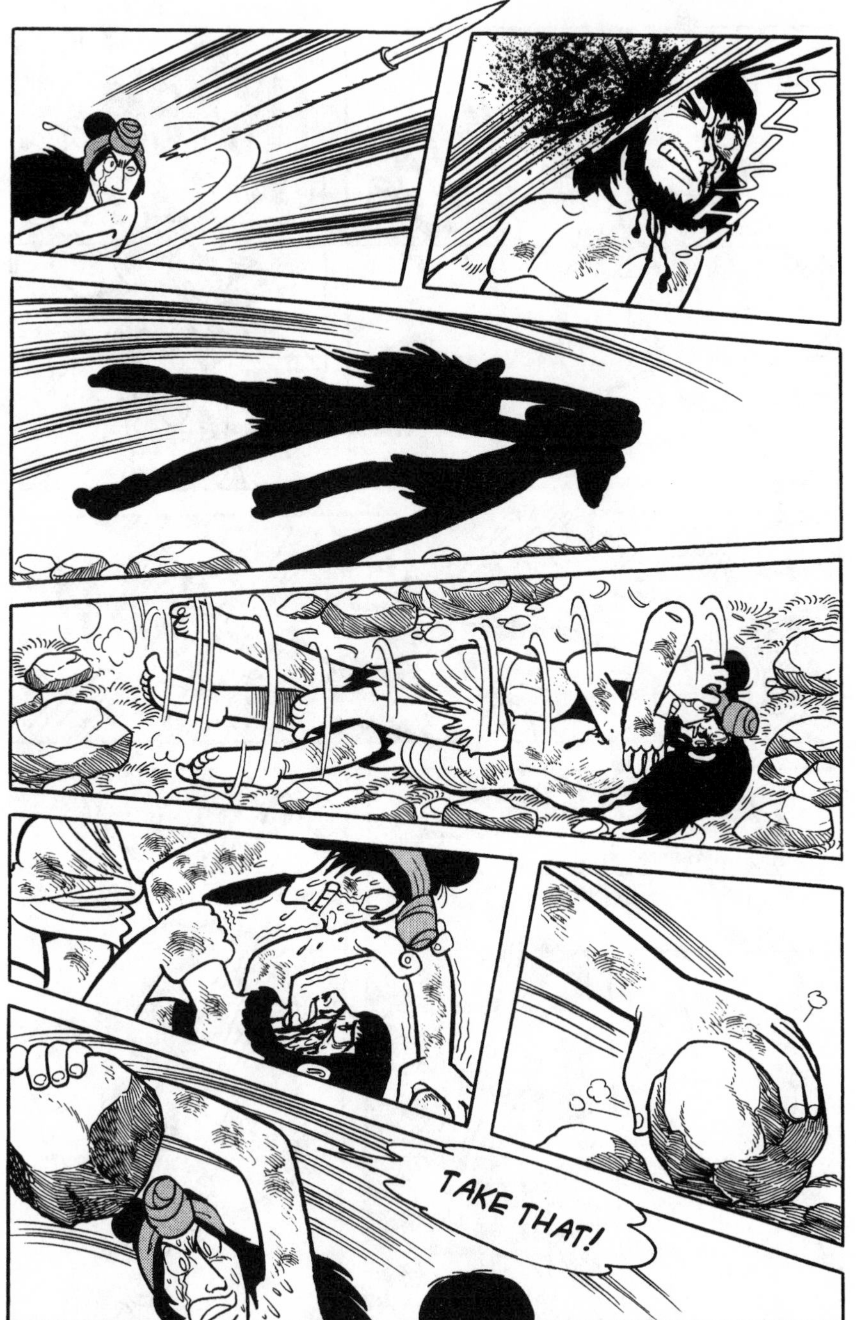
TAKE THAT!

UGH ?!
WHOP

KRAK

POW
BLAM

WHOK
SOK

SLIPP
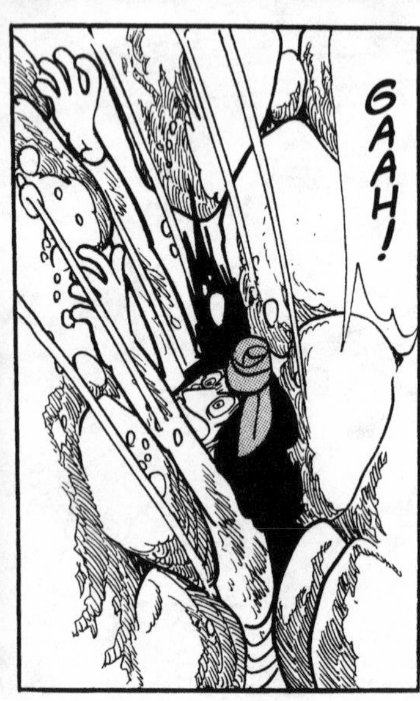
GAAH!

AH! AAAH!
ARGH!
AA...
SHIT... DIE, BASTARD !!
UNH! UH...

UNGH...
URR...

RUN!!

HE FELL DOWN THIS HOLE...

A CRACK IN THE EARTH ?
IT LOOKS PRETTY DEEP...

YO!! CAN YOU HEAR ME ?!

HEEEELP
...G-GET ME OUTTA HERE...

LOOKS LIKE HE'S STILL ALIVE, DAMN HIS LUCK.
LET'S JUST LEAVE HIM THERE!

DON'T LOOK AT ME LIKE THAT!
...
HE WAS TRYING TO KILL YOU, IN CASE YOU'VE FORGOTTEN.

AND SO WE SHOULD WISH HIM DEAD?
BUT...

LET ME TRY
I'M THIN ENOUGH TO SLIP IN

HMM, IT LOOKS LIKE SOME ROCKS FELL IN AFTER HIM AND BLOCKED HIS WAY OUT

CAN YOU MOVE ?
GET THIS OUTTA THE WAY !

HE CAN BARELY STICK OUT ONE ARM.

CAN WE DIG HIM OUT?
NOT UNLESS WE FIND SOME HELP.

I-I CAN'T BREATHE! THERE'S NO AIR DOWN HERE !!

THERE SHOULD BE MANY TROOPS AT THE BORDER FORT.
I'LL BE BACK BEFORE YOU KNOW IT!

GO.

WHAT ARE YOU DOING? WHY'RE YOU ALL SO QUIET? WHAT'S THE IDEA?

WE'VE SENT FOR HELP. THE ARMY WILL BE HERE.

WHAT?! YOU IDIOTS!! I'M A WANTED MAN, ALL RIGHT? THOSE SOLDIERS WILL CUT OFF MY HEAD!

I'LL ASK THEM TO SPARE YOU. I HAPPEN TO KNOW THE OFFICERS AROUND HERE.

AHIMSA, LET ME ASK YOU SOMETHING. SAY YOU HAVE KILLED ME. THEN WHAT?
DUNNO. HAVEN'T THOUGHT THAT FAR AHEAD. I JUST WANT TO KILL YOU!

I SWORE I'D KILL THE WORLD'S GREATEST MONK!

YOU TOLD ME THAT. WHAT FURTHER PLANS DO YOU HAVE?

HA! I DON'T HAVE ANY FANCY PLANS! KILLING YOU'S MY GOAL!

WHAT A BORING LIFE.
OH, SO A MONK'S TELLING ME I'VE GOT A BORING LIFE?

STOP THE TOUGH-GUY ACT. YOU'RE JUST A POOR SOUL WHO GAVE UP ON LIFE.
LIKE I SAID BEFORE, WHEN WE LAST MET. DIE ONCE, AND BE REBORN AS A NEW MAN.

IF YOU WISH, I CAN HELP YOU.

SHUT UP!! I'D RATHER DIE HERE THAN ASK FOR YOUR DAMNED HELP!

THEN WHY DID YOU CRY OUT FOR HELP ?

...

I...BEG YOUR FAVOR... PLEASE...COME HELP US!

WHAT'S THIS NOW? WHERE YA FROM, BEGGAR MONK?
WENT OUT BEGGIN' BUT GOT YOUR BUTT BEATEN INSTEAD?
NO, SIR...A MAN HAS FALLEN DOWN A HOLE...WE NEED YOUR HELP!
YOU THINK WE'LL SEND OUT TROOPS FOR THAT?
WHO IS IT THAT YOU'RE TRYING TO RESCUE?
UHM, YES... A MURDEROUS BANDIT CALLED ANGULIMALA... I MEAN, AHIMSA...
HE'S AN OLD FRIEND OF MINE!
SO, WHAT, YOU'RE SAYING THIS BANDIT'S YOUR PAL?
HE'S SHIFTY. WE'LL TAKE HIM IN FOR QUESTIONING!
WAIT! I'M JUST A MONK IN TRAINING! I JUST WANT TO HELP THIS MAN!
SHUT UP! WE'LL GET YOU TO SPILL YOUR GUTS INSIDE!

SOLDIER! WHAT'S THAT RACKET?!

SIR! AN ODD BEGGAR MONK JUST CAME TO OUR FORT
HE SAYS HE'S FRIENDS WITH A BANDIT AND IS BEING HELD FOR QUESTIONING.

HE ALSO SAYS HE'S THE DISCIPLE OF SOME MASTER MONK NAMED BUDDHA WHO'S NEARBY TOO.
WHAT? BUDDHA?!
I KNOW HIM.

BUDDHA, EH? ...HA HA! GO GET HIM AND BRING HIM TO ME.
TELL HIM PRINCE CRYSTAL EAGERLY AWAITS HIS VISIT!

IT'S GETTING HARD TO BREATHE IN HERE!
GET ME OUTTA HERE QUICK!
PATIENCE. THEY'LL COME DIG YOU OUT SOON.
BUT... THEY'RE TAKING FOREVER.
MAYBE SOMETHING HAPPENED, BUDDHA...
YOU'RE RIGHT. ANANDA OUGHT TO BE BACK BY NOW.
I CAN'T BREATHE! I'M GONNA DIE IN HERE! *COUGH* *COUGH*
AHIMSA, CALM DOWN. EVEN IF THE SOLDIERS ARE TOO LATE, YOU CAN FIND PEACE, IF YOU SEEK IT.
PLEASE, PLEASE GET ME OUT OF HERE!
DOES DYING HURT A LOT ?
AM I GONNA DIE?
THAT DEPENDS ON YOUR OWN STATE OF MIND.

YOU SAY YOU'VE KILLED HUNDREDS OF PEOPLE. DID YOU EVER FIND IT IN YOUR HEART TO SPARE ANYONE AT ALL?
Y-YES... JUST ONE. I LET A LITTLE BABY LIVE!
IT WAS TOO ADORABLE. SO I DIDN'T KILL IT...
THEN, BY THAT ALONE, YOU HAVE DONE GREAT GOOD IN THIS WORLD. BECAUSE THAT BABY WILL GROW UP TO BECOME A MAN AND HAVE CHILDREN OF HIS OWN.

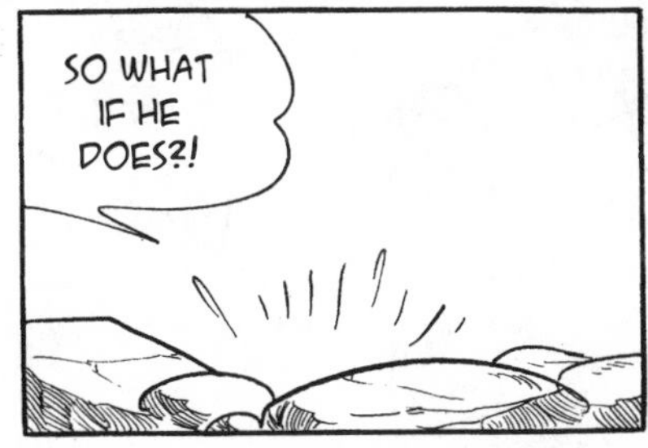
SO WHAT IF HE DOES?!

CENTURIES LATER, HE WILL HAVE A MILLION DESCENDANTS, WHO WILL SAY...

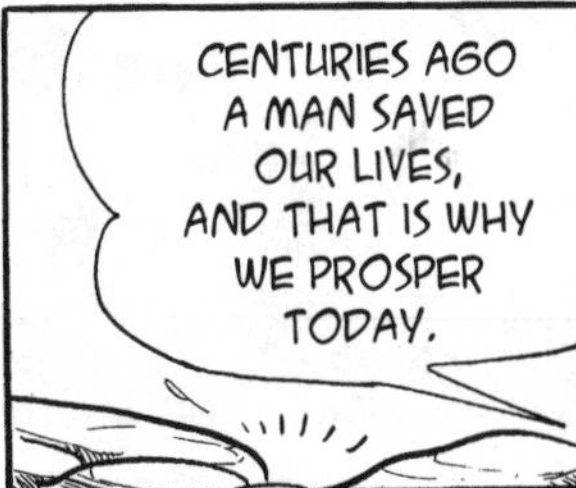
CENTURIES AGO A MAN SAVED OUR LIVES, AND THAT IS WHY WE PROSPER TODAY.

YOU WILL BE REVERED, REMEMBERED BY THAT CLAN ETERNALLY.

M-ME... REVERED... YOU'VE GOTTA BE KIDDING! I'M A RUTHLESS KILLER! I'VE KILLED HUNDREDS OF PEOPLE!

KILLING A HUNDRED IS NOT GOOD. BUT LISTEN, AHIMSA, SPARING ONE FOR LIFE LEADS TO A SACRED MILLION

HUFF... UHH...
BUDDHA... I WON'T LAST MUCH LONGER...

YOU'RE ABOUT TO ENTER A MYSTERIOUS WORLD
WHERE ALL THE SPIRITS OF THE UNIVERSE GATHER.

STAND TALL THERE AND SAY WITH PRIDE, "I AM AHIMSA, THE ONE WHO SAVED A BABY!"

BUDDHA... YOU'VE REALLY MADE ME FEEL BETTER...
I...WANT TO BE YOUR DISCIPLE.

I ACCEPT YOU. BE REBORN AND COME TO ME.

B-BE... REBORN AND...

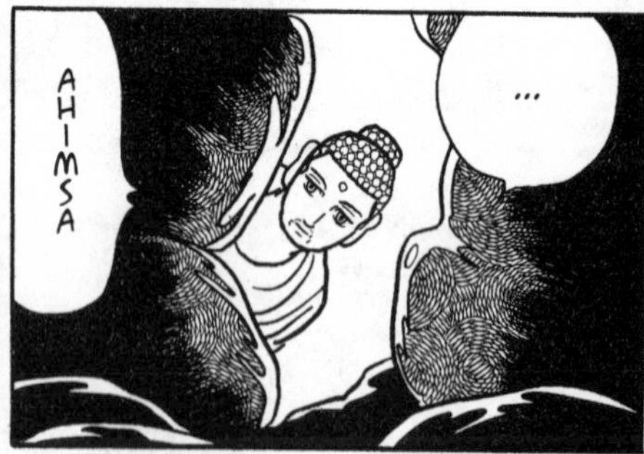
...
AHIMSA

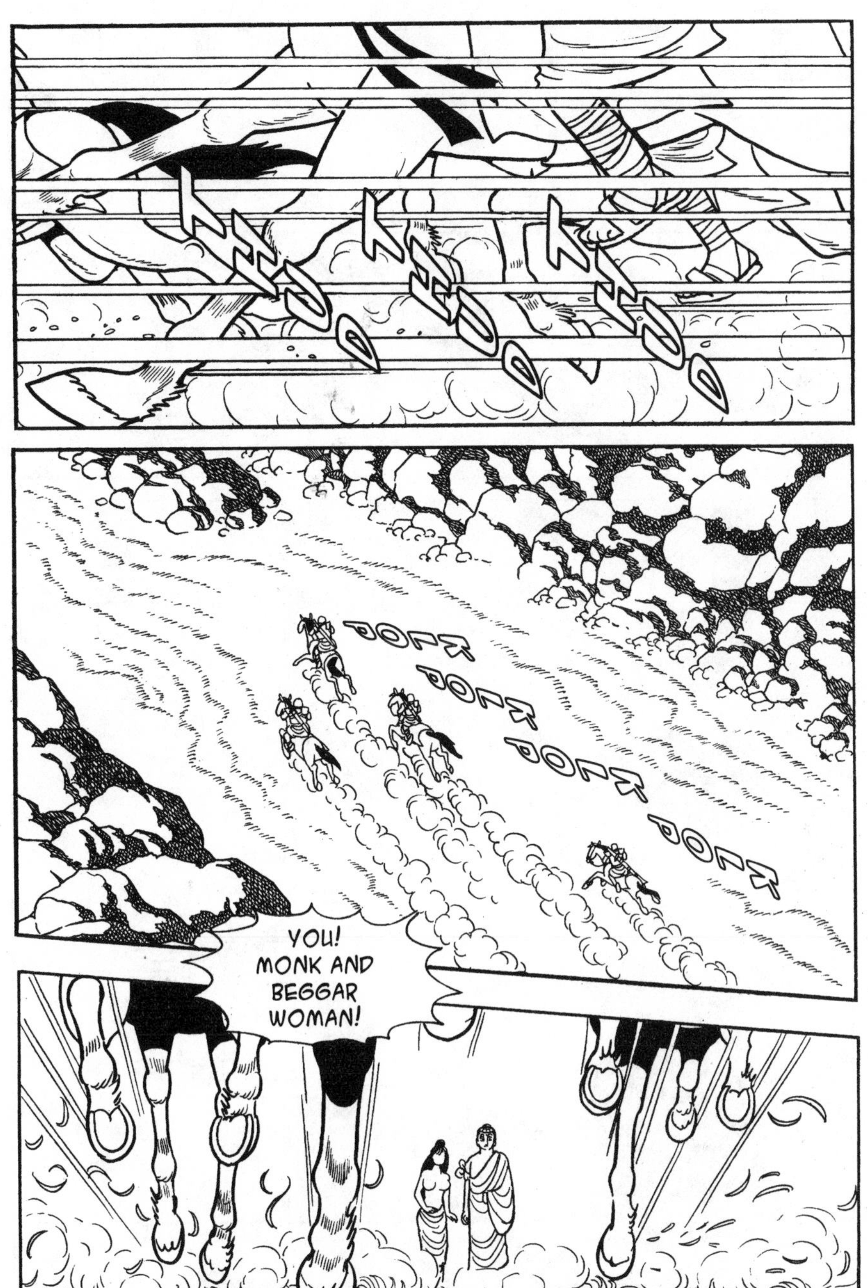
YOU! MONK AND BEGGAR WOMAN!

WELL NOW, BUDDHA. I'D SAY YOU'VE GAINED AN AURA OF IMPORTANCE. YOU LOOK ALL WISE—CUNNING, EVEN. REMEMBER ME?

WE LAST MET IN A FOREST IN SARNATH
DURING OUR WAR WITH MAGA-DHA.

AH. THE YOUNG PRINCE ON THE ELEPHANT ...

I TRIED TO KILL THE IMPUDENT MONK LYING IN MY PATH
BUT THESE DEER JUMPED OUT AND TOOK THE HITS FOR HIM. QUITE A BEAST TAMER!
...

SINCE THEN I'VE HEARD MANY RUMORS ABOUT YOU. YOU'RE SOME HOT-SHOT RELIGIOUS LEADER
WITH OVER 1,000 DISCI-PLES ?

I BET YOU THINK YOU'RE SOME KIND OF KING

SMART ASS !!

NOW YOU WANT TO SPREAD YOUR EVIL FAITH INTO KOSALA?

I DON'T REALLY CARE HOW MANY DISCIPLES YOU GAIN IN MY KINGDOM
BUT THIS JOURNEY WON'T BE A JOYFUL ONE FOR YOU.

FOLLOW ME!

YOU GOTTA SEE THIS.
COME ON!

OVER THERE

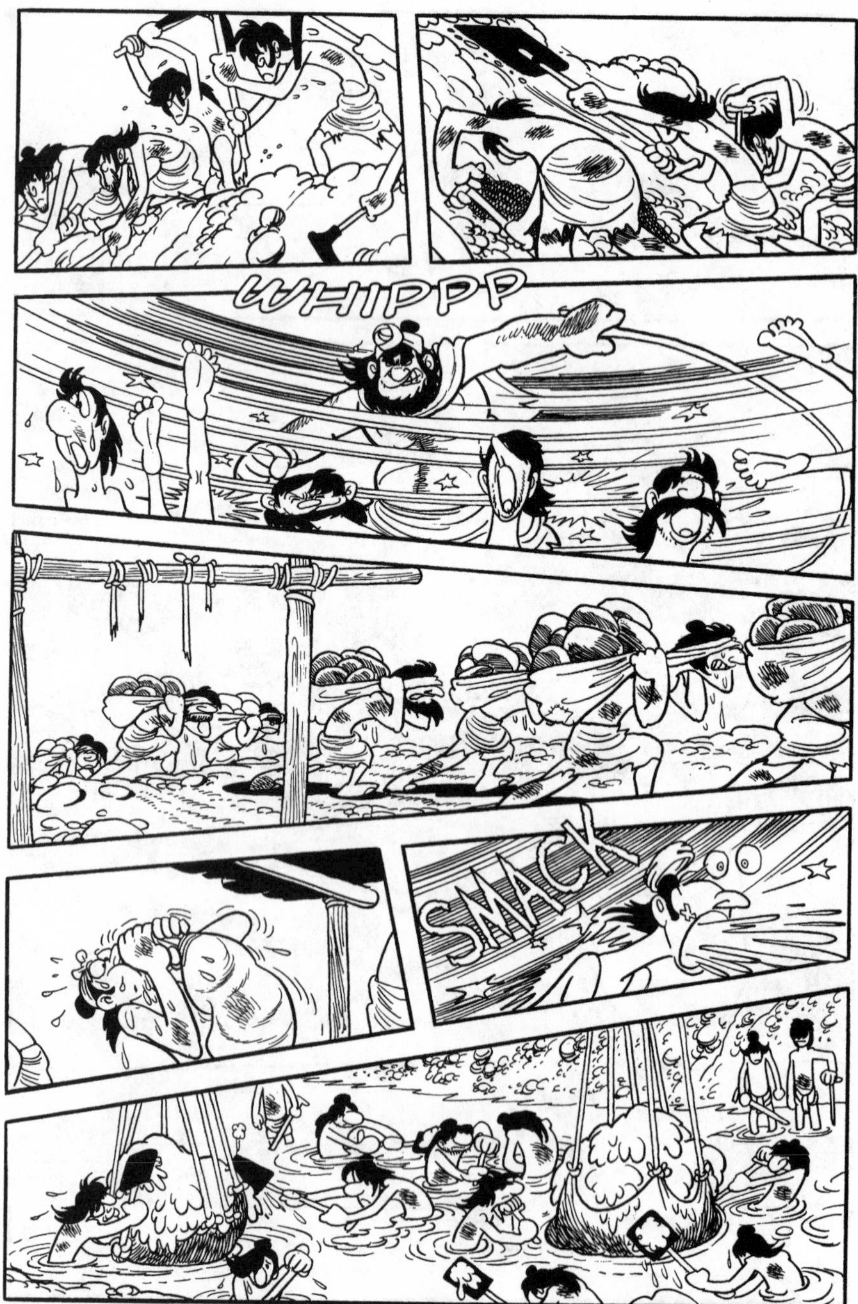
WHIPPPP
SMACK

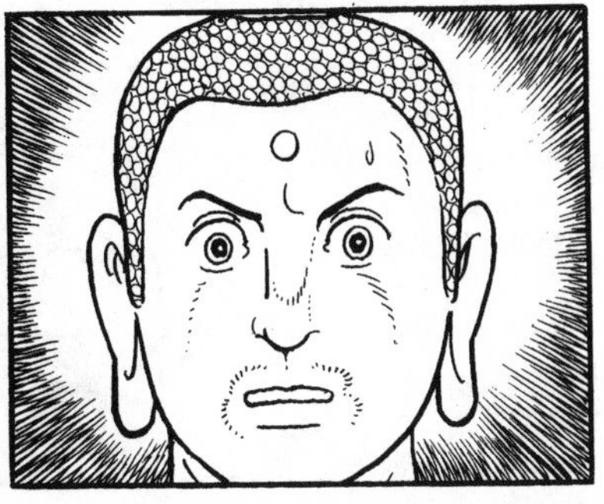

HOW DO YOU LIKE THAT?

ALL THOSE WORKERS ARE SHAKYA. YOUR CLAN.
HAULING MUD SO THE LUMBINI DOESN'T FLOOD OVER.

WE TREAT THEM LIKE ANIMALS AND MAKE SURE THEY SUFFER UNTIL THE VERY END.
THEY DIE PRETTY QUICKLY, WHICH IS GREAT. SAVES US THE TROUBLE OF KILLING THEM.

WE BURY THEM TEN AT A TIME. SEE THOSE MOUNDS?
THERE USED TO BE, WHAT, THREE THOUSAND PEOPLE IN KAPILAVASTU, RIGHT? WELL, NOW IT'S DOWN TO EIGHT HUNDRED.

WHEN THE LAST ONE DIES THE SHAKYA TRIBE WILL BE NO MORE.

HOW DOES THAT MAKE YOU FEEL?

I CONQUERED. THEY LOST AND THE VICTOR DOES WHAT HE PLEASES WITH THEM. IT'S THE WAY OF THE WORLD. DO YOU OBJECT?

ANOTHER THING I WANT TO SHOW YOU...

TAKE A PEEK INSIDE

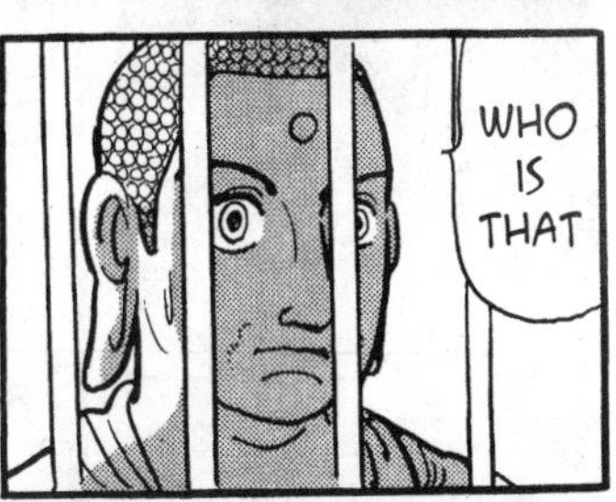
WHO IS THAT

DON'T RECOGNIZE HIM? I GUESS IT'S HARD TO TELL HE WAS ONCE THE KING OF KAPILAVASTU.

FATHER ?

FATHER!!

WHO...
IS THIS WHO CALLS ME "FATHER" ...?

I DON'T KNOW YOU...
ONLY PRINCE SIDDHARTHA AND HIS WIFE YASHODARA CALL ME FATHER.

WHAT'S THE MATTER? WON'T YOU TELL HIM?
NOT THAT YOUR TELLING HIM WOULD SET HIM FREE, YOUR FATHER.

ARE YOU UPSET? ARE YOU IN PAIN?
YOU HATE ME? YOU WANT TO KILL ME?
IF YOU WANT, I'LL CROSS SWORDS WITH YOU!
OR MAYBE YOUR WIFE YASHODARA? THEY'RE ALIVE, YOU KNOW, MORE OR LESS.
AH, WANNA SEE YOUR MAMA PAJAPATI?
OR SHED THOSE ROBES AND PICK UP A WEAPON
GO AHEAD AND TRY YOUR SORCERY
WANT TO SAVE THEM WITH YOUR POWERS?
EVERY MEMBER OF YOUR CLAN IS EITHER IMPRISONED OR ENSLAVED.
SAY SOMETHING, YOU FAT-FACED HUMPTY DUMPTY FAKE SAINT!!
WIMP!!

ROTTEN MONK! HEAD OF CORNS! SCALLION-FACED GEEZER, SAGGING-EARLOBE MAN! YOU FLABBY MONKISH DROPOUT!
THICK-SKINNED BUGGER. ACT HUMAN FOR ONCE.
YOU STILL WON'T GET ANGRY?
YOU ARE A PITIFUL MAN, PRINCE CRYSTAL.
I AM YOUR ENEMY! I WANTED REVENGE, AND I'VE BEEN MAKING YOUR WHOLE TRIBE PAY!
WHY SHOULD I BE PITIED?! YOU...
PITIFUL?!
I FEEL ONLY PITY FOR YOU, NO ANGER.

I WAS BORN OF A LOWLY SLAVE FROM HERE
SO THEY DISDAINED ME. I WAS PRINCE, AND YET I WAS SLANDERED. NOW I'M HAVING MY REVENGE AND I CAN'T HAVE ENOUGH OF IT!

LET ME ASK YOU, THEN. DO YOU ENJOY THIS REVENGE?

WHAT?

HAVE YOU EVER SAID TO YOURSELF, EVEN ONCE: "THIS IS WONDERFUL!"
...

OR RATHER, DO YOU SUFFER FOR IT? AT NIGHT?

...

YOU ARE SUFFERING. I CAN SEE IT IN YOUR FACE.

CUT THE CRAP!

YOUR PAIN WILL ONLY GROW

THROUGHOUT THE REST OF YOUR LIFE. THAT'S WHY I SAY I PITY YOU.

SHUT UP!!

TAKE HIM AWAY
DON'T KILL HIM
LOCK HIM UP WITH HIS LACKEY

KILLING HIM SPELLS TROUBLE; THIS MAN HAS THE KING OF MAGADHA'S BACKING. BETTER TO KEEP HIM ALIVE AND TEACH HIM SOME LESSONS.

AH, BUDDHA!

WHAT DID THEY DO TO YOU?
DON'T WORRY. I'M FINE.
YOU'RE NOT HURT...?

PLEASE REST, BUDDHA... BEATS ME WHY YOU'RE BEING TREATED THIS WAY IN YOUR OWN COUNTRY...
KAPILAVASTU IS NOW OCCUPIED BY KOSALA.

PRINCE CRYSTAL OF KOSALA IS AN ACQUAINTANCE OF MINE, ACTUALLY.

THEN WHY IS HE DOING THIS TO YOU?
ACQUAINTANCES AREN'T ALWAYS FRIENDS.

WHAT'S THE MATTER ?

WHAT IS IT?

I CAN SEE WHEN YOU'RE UPSET. PLEASE, YOU CAN TELL ME!

I SAW MY FATHER.
YOU SAW KING SUDDHODANA? MUST'VE BEEN HAPPY TO SEE YOU!

HE DIDN'T RECOG-NIZE ME...
HE'S GROWN OLD AND DECREPIT. HE LOOKED LIKE A MUMMY.

THEY'VE KEPT HIM IN THE DUNGEON.
HOW... AWFUL !

PERHAPS MY MOTHER AND MY WIFE ARE IMPRISONED, TOO.

LEAVE IT TO ME! I'M AN OLD HAND AT JAIL BREAKS !
I'LL SNEAK IN AND RESCUE THEM !

NO !!
THAT'S NOT WHY I BROUGHT YOU WITH ME!
RIGHT

WE HAVE SPECIAL PERMISSION FROM PRINCE CRYSTAL TO SPEAK WITH BUDDHA.

YOU HAVE SOME VISITORS !!

PLEASE PARDON THE INTRUSION AT THIS LATE HOUR.

MY NAME IS BHADDIYA. I'M THE REPRESENTATIVE OF THE SHAKYA, THE SLAVE KING, SO TO SPEAK.
WE MET ONCE IN THE HOUSE OF LORDS WHEN YOU WERE STILL OUR PRINCE.

BUT UHM ...
WHAT'S WITH ALL THOSE WOUNDS?
AH, WELL, AS KING OF THE SLAVES, I'M HELD RESPONSIBLE FOR THINGS. MY WOUNDS NEVER EVEN HAVE THE TIME TO HEAL.

FORTUNATELY, I'M TOUGH AND CAN TAKE ALL THE BEAT-ING
I GUESS THAT'S WHY I'M THE REPRE-SEN-TATIVE.

PLEASE SIT DOWN, SIR...
I'LL HEAR WHAT YOU HAVE TO SAY.

THE ENTIRE SHAKYA CLAN IS SIMPLY OVERJOYED THAT...
YOU'VE RETURNED AT LAST TO THESE LANDS.
BUT, BEING SLAVES, WE CAN'T GREET YOU PROPERLY.

WE BUILT AN ASSEMBLY FORUM A WHILE BACK.
LUCKILY, IT HASN'T BEEN USED YET.
WE COULD ALL GATHER THERE AND YOU COULD GIVE A TALK TO THE SURVIVING SHAKYA.

A TALK...

YES, SIR, A TALK THAT WILL LIFT OUR SPIRITS AND REVIVE HOPE.
WOULD PRINCE CRYSTAL ALLOW YOU ALL TO ASSEMBLE IN ONE PLACE FOR THIS?

I'LL GET HIM TO AGREE TO IT.
PLEASE, BUDDHA! PLEASE SAY YES!

THIS IS ANURUDHA AND KIMBILA. THEY WILL BE THE ORGANIZERS.
THEY WILL LEAD YOU TO THE FORUM TOMORROW.

VISITING HOURS ARE OVER. NOW GO.

WHAT A SURPRISE... HE WAS SO FEEBLE AND SICKLY WHEN HE WAS PRINCE SIDDHARTHA. HE LOOKS GRAND...

EVERYONE WILL SHOUT FOR JOY WHEN THEY SEE THE MAN HE HAS BECOME.

BHADDIYA, SIR! WE CAN HAVE BUDDHA ISSUE A CALL!
WE CAN RALLY AND DESTROY THE OCCUPATION FORCE!
SIR, THERE WON'T BE ANOTHER CHANCE LIKE THIS!
DON'T BE STUPID. THE KOSALANS ARE ARMED! WHAT WILL WE FIGHT THEM WITH?
BUT THEY ARE ONLY 300 IN ALL, RIGHT?
WE NUMBER EIGHT HUNDRED! WE'LL SUFFER CASUALTIES, YES, MAYBE A HUNDRED OR SO...
BUT WE'LL GET THEIR WEAPONS!
NO
PLEASE, SIR BHADDIYA!
LET US GIVE IT A CHANCE!
DON'T SHOUT!! ARE YOU TRYING TO GET YOURSELF KILLED?!
BE PATIENT! THE TIME IS NOT RIPE.

THINK ABOUT IT! IF THERE'S ANY KIND OF RIOT, THEY'LL PUNISH BUDDHA FOR IT!

...WHATEVER BHADDIYA KING SAYS, WE'LL STICK TO OUR PLAN. DURING THE ASSEMBLY, WE WILL RISE UP AS ONE... AND TAKE BACK WHAT'S OURS...

PRINCE CRYSTAL! HOW COULD YOU AGREE TO LET THAT MONK SPEAK TO THE WHOLE CLAN?!
IF HE NEEDS TO PREACH, LET HIM PREACH. HA HAH...

HAVE YOU FORGOTTEN THAT HE'S ONE OF THEM? WHO KNOWS WHAT HE'LL SAY!
HE MUST NOT!

HOW DO YOU KNOW HE WON'T AGITATE AND INCITE THEM? WE DON'T WANT A REVOLT!

TUMP

A RIOT'S EXACTLY WHAT I WANT
NOW THAT WOULD BE NICE
WHY?!

YOU THINK I HAVEN'T SEEN THROUGH THEIR PLAN TO USE BUDDHA TO STIR UP A REVOLT?
THEY THINK BUDDHA IS THEIR SAVIOR
BUT THEY'RE PLAYING RIGHT INTO MY HANDS. I'LL HAVE CAUSE TO EXECUTE EVERY LAST SHAKYA, INCLUDING BUDDHA!
ORDER ALL THE TROOPS TO BRING THEIR BOWS AND ARROWS TOMORROW TO STAND GUARD AT THE SLAVES' ASSEMBLY.
YES SIR
MOTHER!
MOTHER, SIDDHARTHA HAS COME BACK!
WHAT?! WHERE IS HE?

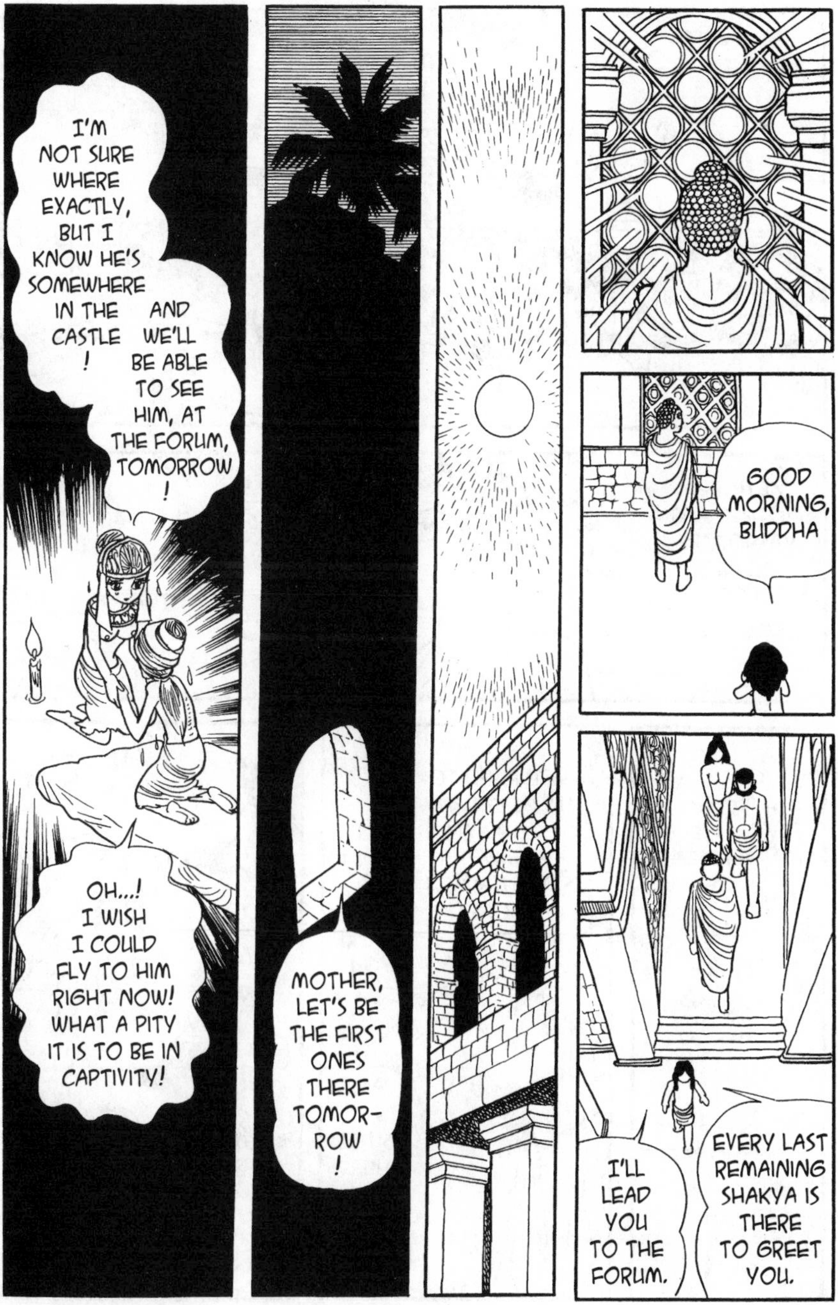

I'M NOT SURE WHERE EXACTLY, BUT I KNOW HE'S SOMEWHERE IN THE CASTLE!
AND WE'LL BE ABLE TO SEE HIM, AT THE FORUM, TOMORROW!
OH...! I WISH I COULD FLY TO HIM RIGHT NOW! WHAT A PITY IT IS TO BE IN CAPTIVITY!
MOTHER, LET'S BE THE FIRST ONES THERE TOMORROW!
GOOD MORNING, BUDDHA
EVERY LAST REMAINING SHAKYA IS THERE TO GREET YOU.
I'LL LEAD YOU TO THE FORUM.

MUR
MUR
MUR
MUR
MUR
MUR
MUR
MUR

I HOPE MOTHER AND YASHODARA ARE HERE, TOO.
I'D LOVE TO SEE THEM AGAIN...
BUT IF THEY'RE AS RUNDOWN AS MY FATHER...
THAT'S RIGHT! MY SON RAHULA! HOW IS HE? IS HE ALIVE?

SILENCE!
OUR PRINCE SIDDHARTHA, AFTER AN ABSENCE OF MANY YEARS

...IS NOW RETURNED TO HIS HOMELAND OF KAPILAVASTU AS BUDDHA, THE CHOSEN ONE!
HE IS ABOUT TO COME BEFORE YOU
AND YOU SHALL HEAR HIS VOICE!

HM... WHAT NOW?

FITCH
FITCH
MUR
MUR
ROAR
BUDDHA
ROAR
ROAR
HURRAY
ROAR
BUDDHA
ROAR
BUDDHA
BUDDHA
BUDDHA
BUDDHA
BUDDHA
BUDDHA
HURRAY
BUDDHA
YES, MOTHER ...!
YOUR FATHER, WHO LEFT US TO BECOME A GREAT MONK.
RAHULA, LOOK WELL. YOUR FATHER!
THAT'S HIM?
...HE'S CHANGED SO MUCH!
SIDDHARTHA
BUDDHA
BUDDHA

HURRAY
YESSS
ROAR
ROAR
ROAR
ROAR
BUDDHAA
BUDDHA
BUDDHA
BUDDHA!
BUDDHA!
BUDDHA!
ROAR
YAY
ROAR
ROAR
ROAR
BANZAI
BUDDHA
BUDDHA
BUDDHA
THEY'RE MAKING ONE HELL OF A RACKET
THIS IS DANGEROUS
STAY ALERT ...

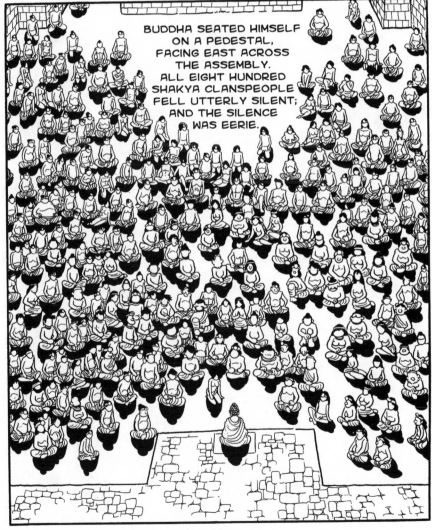

BUDDHA SEATED HIMSELF ON A PEDESTAL, FACING EAST ACROSS THE ASSEMBLY. ALL EIGHT HUNDRED SHAKYA CLANSPEOPLE FELL UTTERLY SILENT; AND THE SILENCE WAS EERIE.

CHAPTER SIX

A Battle of Wills

HUSSHHH

IS THIS WORN-OUT, FILTHY CROWD GATHERED BEFORE ME REALLY THE PEOPLE OF KAPILAVASTU...?
ARE THESE REALLY THE PROUD, BRAVE PEOPLE OF MY HOMELAND ?

THEY'VE CHANGED SO MUCH
IN A MERE TWENTY YEARS HOW COULD THEY HAVE CHANGED SO?

ALL IS IN VAIN...

WHAT TALK COULD EVER OFFER SOLACE AND HOPE
TO SUCH A PITIFUL, TIRED PEOPLE?

HOW CAN I CHEER THEM...

WHEN THEY'RE HEMMED IN BY GUARDS WHO GLARE DOWN AT THEM ?

SOMEWHERE IN THIS CROWD ARE MY MOTHER, MY WIFE AND MY SON RAHULA.
AH YES, RAHULA, MY SON! ...AS HIS FATHER, WHAT DO I NEED TO SAY?

AND THERE IS THAT MAN PRINCE CRYSTAL, SITTING OVER THERE

WHAT CAN I SAY TO EASE A HEART SO KNOTTED IN HATRED?

...BRAHMAN, GIVE ME STRENGTH!

CHITTER
CHATTER
CHITTER
CHATTER

WHAT'S THE DEAL? WHY'S BUDDHA JUST STARING AT THE SKY?
IS IT S'POSED TO RAIN?
FOOL. FORECAST SAID WE'D HAVE A SUNNY DAY.

THAT CLOUD...

?
?

MY FELLOW COUNTRYMEN, LOOK AT THAT CLOUD IN THE SKY !

LOOK LONG ENOUGH, AND YOU'LL SEE HOW ITS SHAPE CHANGES, GRADUALLY.

WOW, THAT CLOUD LOOKS LIKE MY MOMMY'S FACE
NOW IT LOOKS LIKE A PIG
HEY, NOW IT LOOKS MORE LIKE A SEAL
HMM, THIS IS LIKE WATCHING ANIMATION
A CLOUD NEVER STAYS THE SAME SHAPE FOR VERY LONG. MOREOVER, IT SOMETIMES BRINGS RAIN, EVEN THUNDER.
LIKE A CLOUD, A MAN'S FORTUNES ARE EVER-SHIFTING.
SO TOO WITH HUMAN FATE...
NOW HE LIVES LIKE A KING, BUT TOMORROW HE'S JUST A BEGGAR.

A PERSON'S LIFE
CHANGES,
LIKE A CLOUD.
NO LIFE IS
UNIFORMLY HAPPY
OR UNHAPPY
OVER ITS COURSE.

LIKEWISE WITH OUR FATES: THEY HAVE CAUSES...
THERE IS NO FATE THAT DOES NOT HAVE A CAUSE.
TWENTY YEARS AGO, I, TOO
HAD MY COURSE ALTERED, WHEN A WISE MAN SHOWED ME SICKNESS, DEATH, HUMAN MISERY. I WAS SHAKEN, AND THAT WAS THE CAUSE OF MY FORSAKING THE CASTLE.
IT SET ME ON A PATH OF TRIALS...

IF A TREE, SPROUTING WHERE THERE IS AMPLE SUN AND WATER, IS NONETHELESS CHOKED UNDER THE EARTH BY STONES OR IS ROTTING AT THE ROOTS
IT WILL NOT GROW STRONG. SINCE THE CAUSE IS NOT VISIBLE, BEFORE ANYONE WILL EVER NOTICE, IT WILL SHRIVEL AND DIE.

THE PEOPLE OF KAPILAVASTU ONCE ENJOYED RICHES AND LEISURE, AND ONLY INTERRUPTED THE POURING OF WINE AND THE DANCING TO ENGAGE IN FACTIONAL STRIFE...

SHAKYAN SOCIETY WAS ROTTEN TO THE CORE. I KNEW THAT GROWING UP IN SUCH A PLACE I WOULD MAKE NO DECENT KING. I'D JUST BECOME A WRECK, AND DIE.
SO I FORSOOK MY FAMILY, EVEN MY SON RAHULA, AND LEFT...

DID HE JUST SAY MY NAME ...?

I'M RAHULA!
YOU REMEMBER MY NAME !

WHERE ARE YOU GOING? STOP, RAHULA!

FATHER! IT'S ME! I'M YOUR SON!
OH...! YOU'RE RAHULA ?!
SUCH A FINE YOUTH
FATHER... I'VE WAITED FOR THIS DAY... FOR TWENTY YEARS!
MOTHER AND GRAND-MOTHER ARE HERE TOO!
AH
RAHULA, SIT HERE
LISTEN TO ME BY MY SIDE

FATHER
COME DOWN TO SEE MOTHER, RIGHT NOW!
BE QUIET MY SON
I AM TALKING NOW TO THE WHOLE CLAN...
NO, IN TRUTH I'M TALKING TO ALL THE KOSALANS HERE AS WELL!
I... I KNOW ...
NO MATTER HOW TRIFLING IT MAY SEEM, WHERE THERE IS A CAUSE, A RESULT WILL ISSUE! SUCH IS THE LAW OF NATURE.
SHAKYAN PEOPLE! TODAY, YOU SPEND YOUR DAYS IN MISERY. YOU MUST RECALL THE GRAVE CAUSES THAT BROUGHT ABOUT THIS DIRE RESULT!
AND YOU, KOSALANS! TODAY YOU PERSECUTE THESE PEOPLE AS YOU PLEASE... THINK WHAT TERRIBLE RESULTS WILL ISSUE FROM THIS!
YOU SHOULD BE AFRAID !
WH-WH-WH-WHAT?!

THAT REMARK WAS AN OUTRAGE!!
WE MUST SHUT HIM UP!

CALM DOWN! IT'S JUST MONKISH CLAPTRAP!
OUI

SHAKYAN PEOPLE!! I WANT YOU TO START DOING SOMETHING FOR YOUR FUTURE!
PRECISELY IN THESE HARSH TIMES, YOU MUST THINK AND DO RIGHTLY!
DO NOT DESPAIR. IF YOU DO NOT SWERVE, EVEN AS YOU SUFFER,
IT WILL BRING FORTH GOOD RESULTS IN THE FUTURE!

I'M TOO OLD TO LOOK FORWARD TO A FUTURE. MY TIME IS ALMOST UP.

OLD MAN,
DO NOT WORRY. THE END OF ONE LIFE IS THE BEGINNING OF THE NEXT.

REALLY? I'M GOING TO BE REBORN? SHOULD I REALLY BELIEVE IN SUCH A THING?

WHEE, THANK HEAVEN! THEN I'LL DO ALL THE RIGHT I CAN!

BUDDHA, DOING AS YOU SAY WON'T GIVE US PEACE OF MIND! FIRST WE HAVE TO BREAK FREE FROM THE CHAINS OF SLAVERY!
I'VE HEARD ENOUGH!

AND HOW WILL YOU DO THAT?

WITH AN UPRISING

WE'LL FIGHT FOR OUR FREEDOM!

IF YOU FIGHT, MANY MORE OF YOU WILL DIE
HOW IS THAT DIFFERENT FROM KOSALAN CRUELTY?
DIDN'T I JUST TELL YOU ABOUT CAUSES AND EFFECTS?
HAH

THEN HOW ABOUT PRINCE CRYSTAL?! HOW'S HE JUST SITTING THERE WITH A COCKY SMIRK ON HIS FACE?

ALL RIGHT, I'LL TELL YOU!

THERE SITS A MAN WHO SUFFERS MORE TERRIBLY THAN ANY OF YOU PEOPLE
TORMENTED THAT HE HAS KILLED HUNDREDS, INCLUDING HIS OWN MOTHER!
HE WILL ALWAYS REGRET IT. THAT, MORE THAN ANY TORTURE, WOUND, OR ILLNESS, IS INSUFFERABLE!
SHUT UP!!
FZZSHHH

FSHHHH
SHHH
ZSHHH
ZSHHH

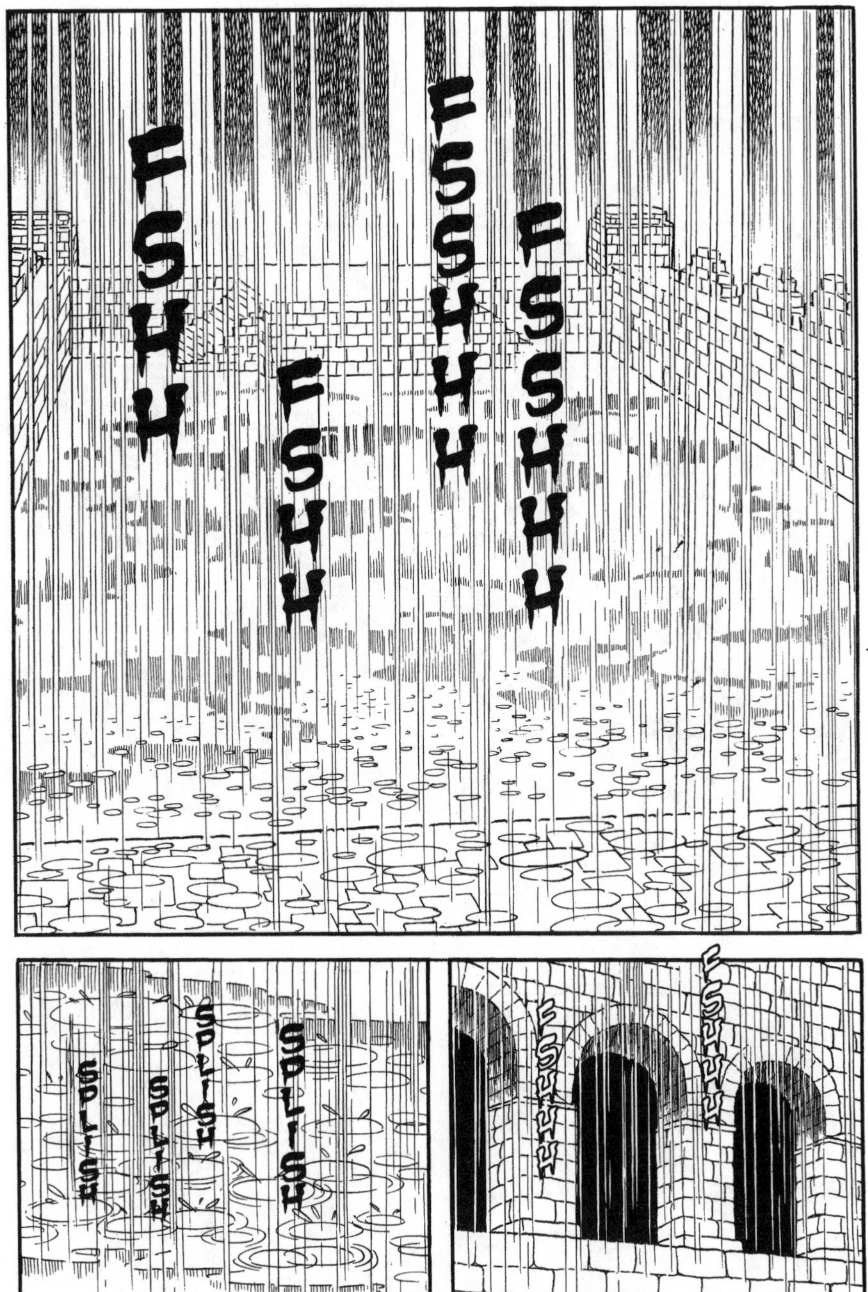
FSHH
FSHH
FSSHHH
FSSHHH
SPLISH
SPLISH
SPLISH
SPLISH
FSHHHH
FSHHH

PRINCE, I'M THINKING TO PUT THAT INSOLENT MONK TO DEATH RIGHT THIS MOMENT...
I TOLD YOU TO LEAVE HIM BE.
MONKS ARE NO MENACE. JUST KEEP AN EYE ON THE RABBLE-ROUSER.

PRINCE, YOU'LL CATCH COLD!
SHUT UP. I'M GOING TO TAKE A NAP.

BLAM

IT'S TRUE, YEARS AGO, I HAD MY CLASSMATES KILLED AS I WATCHED. BUT THEY HAD INSULTED ME, AND THEY HAD TO DIE! WHY WOULD I WANT TO REGRET IT?

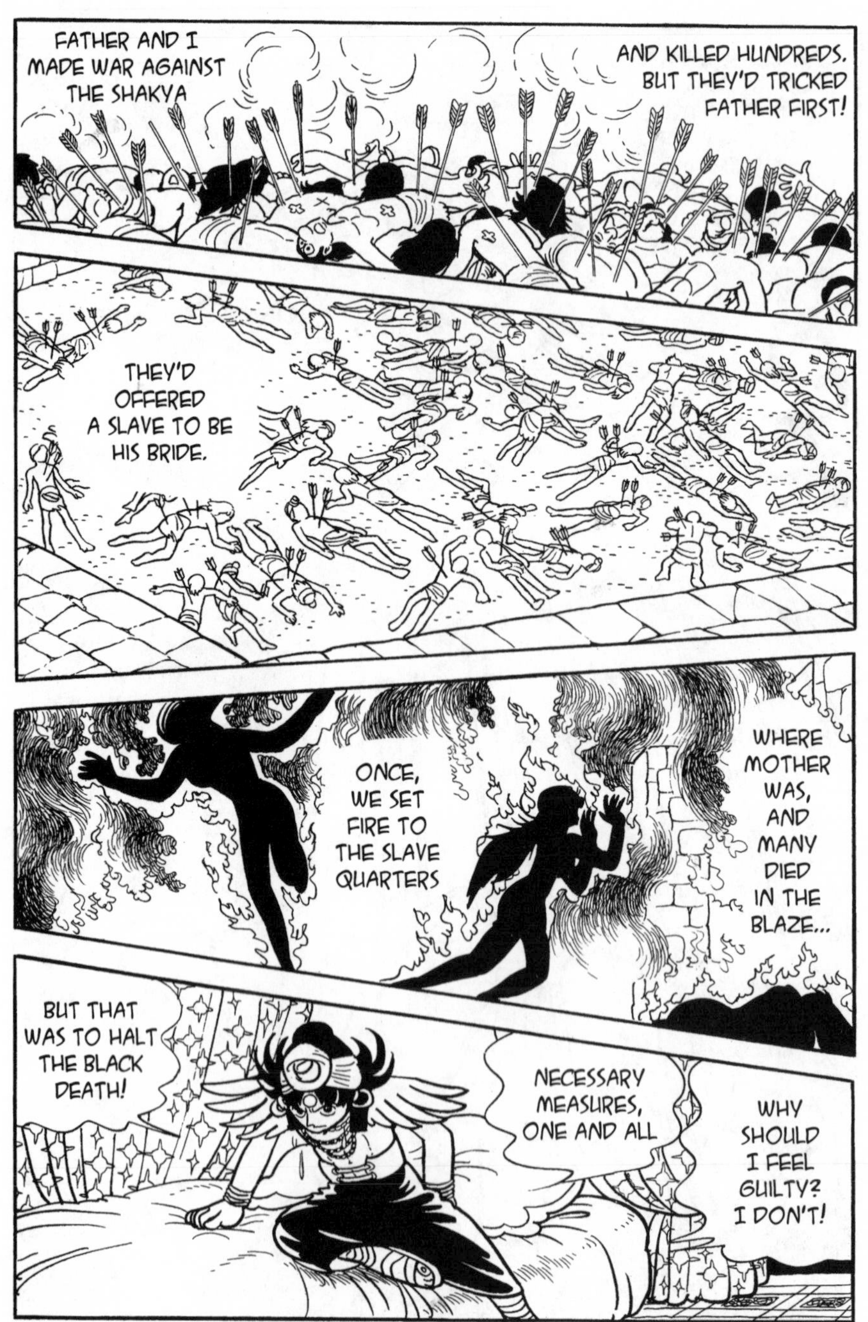
FATHER AND I MADE WAR AGAINST THE SHAKYA
AND KILLED HUNDREDS. BUT THEY'D TRICKED FATHER FIRST!
THEY'D OFFERED A SLAVE TO BE HIS BRIDE.
ONCE, WE SET FIRE TO THE SLAVE QUARTERS
WHERE MOTHER WAS, AND MANY DIED IN THE BLAZE...
BUT THAT WAS TO HALT THE BLACK DEATH!
NECESSARY MEASURES, ONE AND ALL
WHY SHOULD I FEEL GUILTY? I DON'T!

DEAR !!
YASHODARA
YOU DON'T LOOK LIKE MY HUS-BAND...
MOTHER IS HERE TOO
MY MOTHER?
OH, SIDDHAR-THA... I WAITED AND WAITED... FOR SO LONG!
I WANTED YOU TO... COME BACK SOONER... THAN THIS...
HOW DID YOU GET HERE? THEY LET YOU ROAM FREELY?
NO. BUT WE CAN BRIBE THE GUARDS...
DEAR...
WE HAVE NOTHING LEFT, NOT EVEN HOPE

SIDDHARTHA, PLEASE TAKE YOUR SON ALONG WITH YOU ON YOUR JOURNEY
BUT RAHULA, AT LEAST, OUGHT TO BECOME A FINE MAN UNDER YOUR GUIDANCE

FATHER !!
PLEASE ACCEPT ME AS YOUR DISCIPLE !

I WANT TO GO WHERE YOU GO
AND TRAIN, STUDYING LIFE AND THE WAY TO LIVE
TAKE ME WITH YOU!

MY SON
IF YOU REALLY WANT TO UNDERGO TRIALS, WHY NOT STAY HERE IN YOUR COUNTRY?

BUT DEAR, IF HE STAYS HERE, HE WILL ALMOST CERTAINLY DIE!!
THE KOSALANS KNOW THAT RAHULA IS ROYALTY. SO THEY TREAT HIM HORRIBLY, GIVING HIM TOUGH CHORES.

THAT'S YOUR TRIAL! DON'T YOU SEE? PERSEVERE!!
...

YOUNG MAN !!
I'M ANANDA, A DISCIPLE OF BUDDHA. I USED TO BE A THIEF AND A MURDERER.

A THIEF...

AMONG HIS DISCIPLES YOU'LL FIND MANY MONKS WHO ALMOST KILLED THEMSELVES TRAINING OR WHO SURVIVED TERRIBLE HARDSHIPS. COMPARED WITH WHAT THEY'VE SUFFERED, YOU HAVE IT EASY HERE.

DO AS BUDDHA SAYS AND STAY HERE AND ACCEPT YOUR TRIAL.
PERSEVERE, ENDURE IT TO THE END! YOU MUST TRY.
THE STIGMA OF THIEF DOESN'T DIE SO EASY
BUT I'VE ENDURED IT AND I'LL GO ON ENDURING IT...

FATHER, I SEE...
I MEAN... BUDDHA !!
I'LL STAY HERE AND... CONTINUE WITH MY TRIALS...

BUDDHA, THE PRINCE HAS SENT FOR YOU.

WILL YOU BE ALL RIGHT? HE WOULDN'T...
KILL ME? NO. IF HE WANTED ME DEAD, I'D BE DEAD BY NOW.

PRINCE WOULDN'T KILL YOU, BUDDHA. YOU'RE A CELEBRITY.

YOUR TALK THIS MORNING WAS SO MOVING, IT OPENED MY EYES.

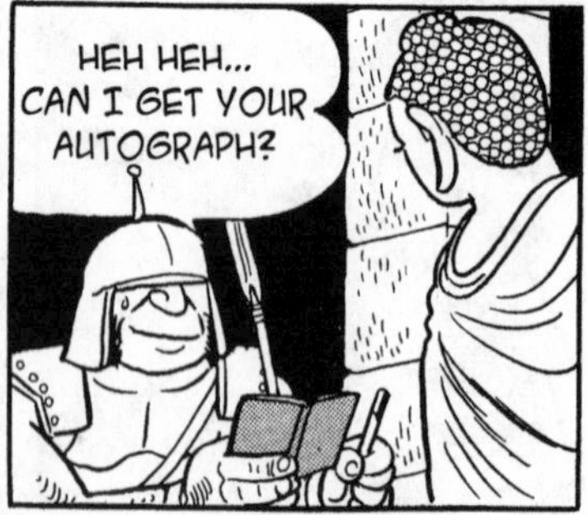
HEH HEH... CAN I GET YOUR AUTOGRAPH?

NO? IN THAT CASE, CAN YOU ADD ME TO YOUR COHORT OF DISCIPLES?
SEVERAL COMRADES OF MINE ALSO WANT TO JOIN
WE'RE KOSALAN SOLDIERS, I KNOW, BUT WILL YOU ACCEPT US?

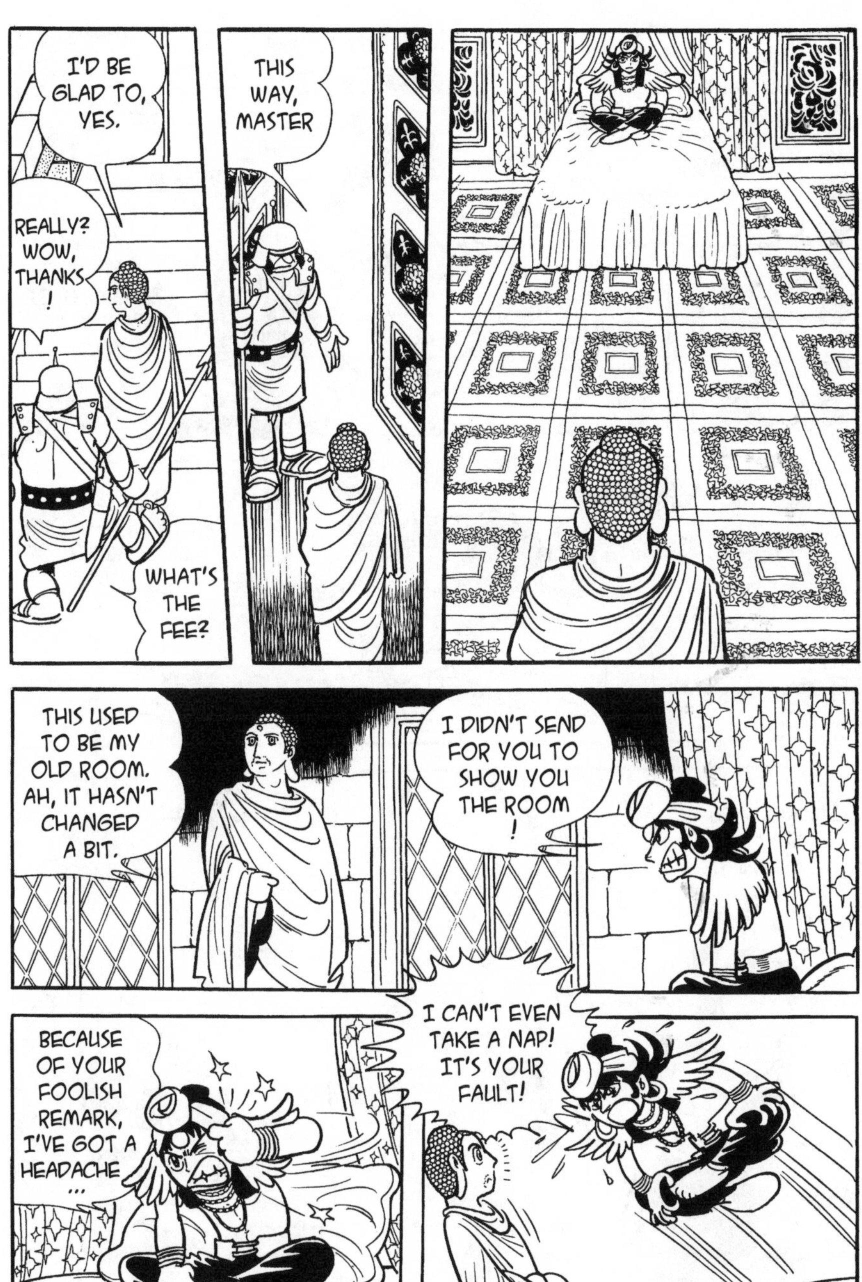
I'D BE GLAD TO, YES.
REALLY? WOW, THANKS!
WHAT'S THE FEE?
THIS WAY, MASTER
THIS USED TO BE MY OLD ROOM. AH, IT HASN'T CHANGED A BIT.
I DIDN'T SEND FOR YOU TO SHOW YOU THE ROOM!
BECAUSE OF YOUR FOOLISH REMARK, I'VE GOT A HEADACHE ...
I CAN'T EVEN TAKE A NAP! IT'S YOUR FAULT!

I'LL SUFFER FOR THE REST OF MY LIFE?
WHAT WERE YOU THINKING? HOW DARE YOU SAY I'M MISERABLE AND IN PAIN?
YOU BIG FAT LIAR! IN FRONT OF EVERYONE, TOO!!

I'LL STUFF THAT LOUD MOUTH OF YOURS!
SHUT UP, YOU !!
BUT I DIDN'T LIE, DID I?

I'LL KILL YOU WITH MY OWN HANDS!
YOU TRIED IT ONCE, IN DEER PARK, PRINCE CRYSTAL.
YEAH, BUT THOSE DAMN DEER GOT IN MY WAY!
THERE ARE NO DEER THIS TIME

CRAKKAKK

KLANG

UHH... OHHH!

PRINCE, WHAT IS WRONG?
TEACH ME!! T-TEACH ME HOW TO...
FREE MYSELF FROM THIS PAIN!

FSSHH
FSSHH
FSSHH
FSSHH

WHAT IS GOING ON?! WHAT IS PRINCE CRYSTAL UP TO?
HE'S BEEN TALKING WITH BUDDHA FOR FIVE HOURS STRAIGHT.
WITH NO BATHROOM BREAKS?

YOU'VE GOTTA BE KIDDING! BUDDHA'S DANGEROUS!
THERE'S NO TELLING WHAT'LL HAPPEN IF HE'S LEFT ALONE WITH THE PRINCE!

FSSHH
FSSHH
FSSHH
FSSHH

CRACK!

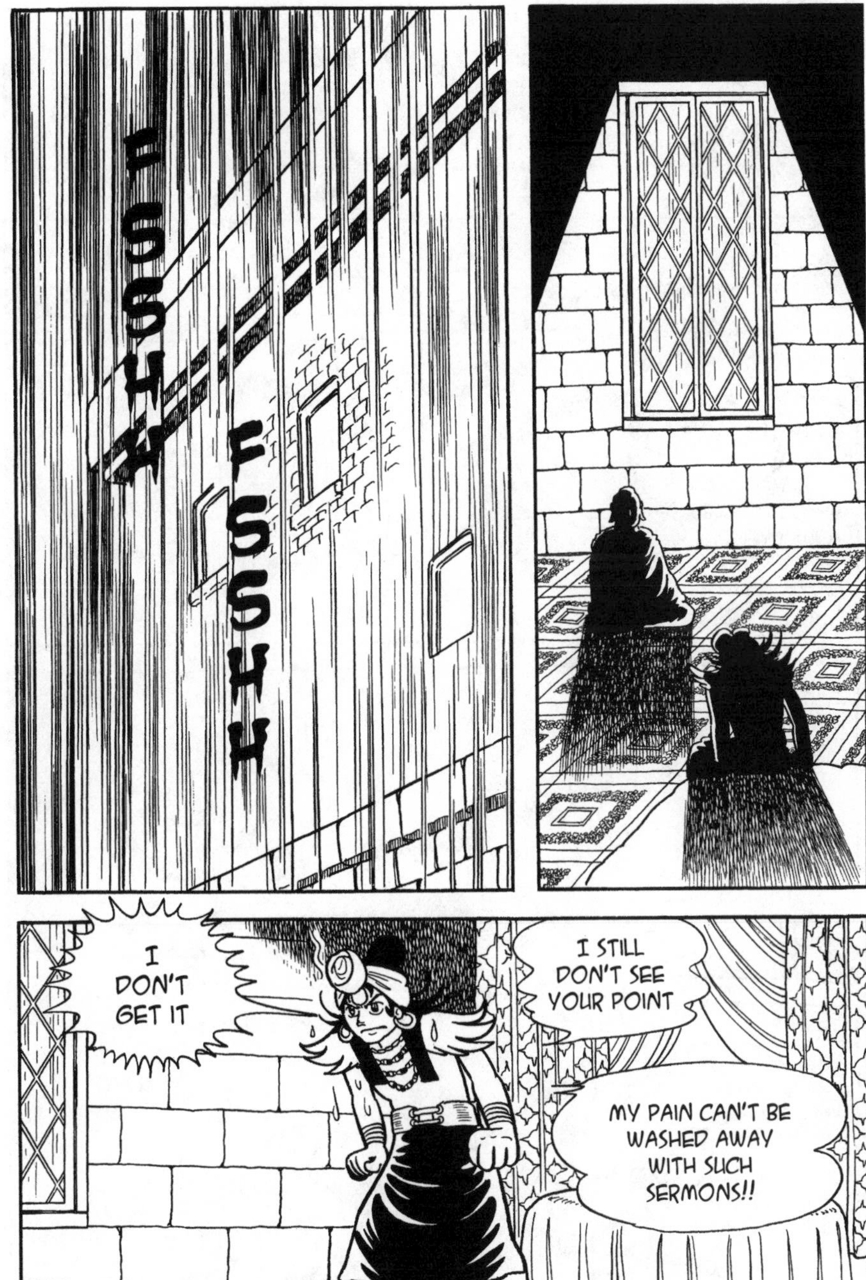
FSSHH
FSSHH
I DON'T GET IT
I STILL DON'T SEE YOUR POINT
MY PAIN CAN'T BE WASHED AWAY WITH SUCH SERMONS!!

I WAS BORN FROM THE WOMB OF A LOWLY SLAVE WOMAN AND THAT IS THE DAY MY SUFFERING BEGAN!!
I DON'T CARE HOW WISE YOU ARE OR WHAT MIRACLES YOU PERFORM, YOU STILL CAN'T CHANGE MY BIRTH!!
EVEN IF YOU WERE SENT BY THE GODS!
HAH! NOW WHAT? HOW WILL YOU GET RID OF MY PAIN?
I'M GETTING BORED OF YOU,
NOW GET OUT OF HERE
YOU USELESS SHIT MONK! OUT!!
I'LL LET YOU LIVE. I EXPECT YOU AND YOUR DAMN DISCIPLES TO BE GONE BY NOON.

YOU DIDN'T LET ME FINISH...
IF YOU WANT TO BE SAVED, COME TO THE FORKED TREE ON THE BANK OF THE LUMBINI. I'LL BE WAITING FOR YOU.
HUMPH

PRINCE CRYSTAL! DID THAT NO-GOOD MONK SAY MORE RUDE THINGS TO YOU?

DID HE SEEM LIKE HE WANTED TO KILL YOU ?
YOU THINK HE EVER COULD?

I WILL HAVE HIM BEHEADED
YOU WILL NOT!!

BUDDHA! WHAT HAPPENED ?
I TALKED WITH THE PRINCE.

RIVER'S RISEN AGAIN FROM THE RAINS LAST NIGHT
LONG RAINY SEASON THIS YEAR

WE'LL NEVER SEE THE LAST OF THESE ROCKS

NEW ONES JUST KEEP ROLLING OUR WAY

SO, WHAT DID YOU THINK OF BUDDHA'S TALK?
THAT SERMON HOOEY IS TOTALLY USELESS

IT WON'T MAKE OUR LIVES ANY EASIER, NOT A BIT

I DON'T KNOW ABOUT THAT

HE REALLY STRUCK A CHORD WITH ME. ALL THAT GOOD STUFF ABOUT HOW TO LIVE...
WHATEVER, MAN! HEARING ABOUT IT NOW WON'T CHANGE OUR WRETCHED LIVES.

QUIT YER YAPPIN! GET TO WORK!

YOU! WHAT ARE YOU DOING OVER THERE?

HE'S DEAD
WHAT?

WE'LL BURY HIM...
NO TIME FOR THAT! THROW HIM TO THE DOGS!

THREE HAVE DIED THIS MORNING
DON'T BOTHER REPORTING EVERY SINGLE DEATH!

WE KNOW THEY'RE DROP-PING LIKE FLIES
THEIR HARD LABOR BRINGS THEIR LAST DAY EVER CLOSER. SAVES US A LOT OF EFFORT.

ISN'T THAT SO, PRINCE?

SLAP!

OUCH! MY LORD, I DIDN'T MEAN TO OFFEND!
I DECIDE WHAT HAPPENS TO THE SHAKYA CLAN
DON'T BE PRESUMP-TUOUS!

I WAS ONLY SAYING WHAT YOU ALWAYS SAY...

NICE TO BE PRINCE, HUH?

WHERE DID ALL THESE DEAD GO?

CHAPTER SEVEN

EMANCIPATION

BUDDHA !!
I TOLD YOU TO LEAVE! WHY ARE YOU HERE?

MORE IMPORTANTLY, WHY ARE YOU HERE ?

I-IT BOTHERED ME THAT YOU'D BE SITTING HERE! I HAD TO COME SEE!

WELL THEN, BE SEATED.
YOU CAN HEAR THE END OF MY TALK.

DAMMIT, I DIDN'T COME TO HEAR YOU PREACH!

...

YOU'RE RAHULA! WHAT ARE YOU DOING HERE?
GET BACK TO WORK!

THAT YOUNG MAN IS NOT JUST BUDDHA'S SON, BUT A NEW DISCIPLE. HE CAME TO HEAR BUDDHA SPEAK.
AND YOU THINK I'D ALLOW IT?!

I'LL MAKE SURE THEY GIVE HIM EXTRA HARD WORK!

ALL DISCIPLES HAVE THE RIGHT TO LISTEN TO BUDDHA, BE THEY SLAVE OR BEGGAR.
YOU MUST LET HIM BE...

... HUNH

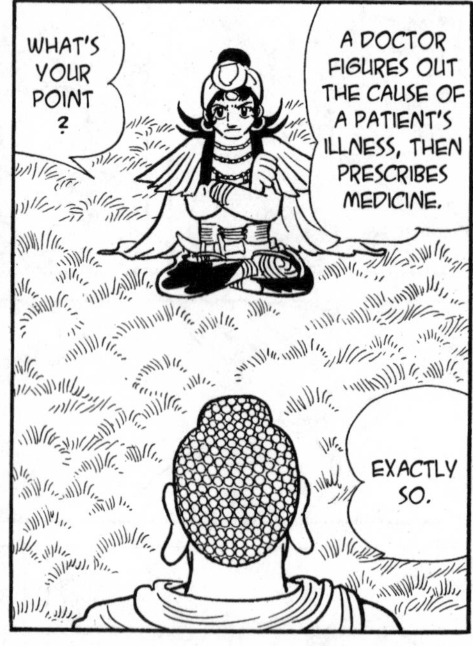
A DOCTOR FIGURES OUT THE CAUSE OF A PATIENT'S ILLNESS, THEN PRESCRIBES MEDICINE.
WHAT'S YOUR POINT ?
EXACTLY SO.

PRINCE CRYSTAL, HOW IS IT THAT A DOCTOR IS ABLE TO HEAL PEOPLE?

IF THE PATIENT MERELY WRITHES ABOUT CRYING IN PAIN, THE DOCTOR CANNOT LEARN THE CAUSE. THE DOCTOR MUST TALK WITH THE PATIENT, AND THEN EXAMINE HIM, TO DISCOVER THE CAUSE.

I KNOW ALL THAT! WHAT'S THAT GOT TO DO WITH ANYTHING?!

IN OTHER WORDS, I'M A DOCTOR.

EEP

I'M A DOC-TOR
WHO HEALS THE SICKNESS IN PEOPLE'S SOULS, SO TO SPEAK.

YOU ARE MY PATIENT.
YESTERDAY, I LISTENED TO YOUR COMPLAINTS.

YOU BELIEVE THAT YOUR SUFFERING IS SOME KIND OF FATE THAT YOU SHOULDERED UPON BIRTH. YOU'RE MISTAKEN.
YOU DO NOT SUFFER BECAUSE YOUR MOTHER WAS A SLAVE WOMAN...

YOU SUFFER BECAUSE YOU SHUNNED YOUR MOTHER AND LET HER DIE MISERABLY, AND YOU REGRET IT.
HOLD A PROPER MEMORIAL SERVICE IN HER HONOR
AND YOUR PAIN WILL VANISH.
AH, AND THERE IS YET ANOTHER CAUSE...
YOU REGRET THAT YOU'VE MASSACRED THE SHAKYAN PEOPLE.
ENDING THIS OTHER PAIN OF YOURS WILL REQUIRE GREAT RESOLVE. FORGIVE THE SHAKYA AND RETURN TO KOSALA WITH YOUR ARMY. THEN THE PAIN WILL END.
WHAT DID YOU SAY?!

RESTORE THINGS TO THE WAY THEY WERE!
THEN YOU WILL NOT HAVE TO KILL. YOUR MIND WILL BE CURED.
THAT'S ONE JEST TOO MANY, BUDDHA!!
YOU WANT ME TO PULL OUT MY TROOPS AND GO BACK TO KOSALA?!
YOU WANT ME TO FORGIVE EVERY LAST ROTTEN SHAKYA?!
TAKE IT AND SHOVE IT!!
DIDN'T I JUST EXPLAIN HOW THIS WORKS? I'M THE DOCTOR. YOU'RE THE PATIENT AND I MERELY OUTLINED THE PROPER TREATMENT FOR YOUR ILLNESS.
IF YOU REFUSE TO IMPLEMENT MY REGIMEN, PRINCE CRYSTAL, YOU'LL SUFFER FOR THE REST OF YOUR LIFE.
JUST SHUT UP. I CAN'T BELIEVE THIS. WHAT A WASTE OF TIME.

THIS IS YOUR LAST WARNING. BE GONE WITHIN THE HOUR! IF YOU'RE STILL HERE, MY TROOPS WILL KILL YOU ALL.
I MEAN IT.

DOUBLE THE LEVEE WORK!
VERY GOOD, SIR

I WILL NOT LOSE! THIS IS NOW A MATTER OF HONOR AND AUTHORITY AND I WILL SHUN NO PAIN!!

ARE WE ALL MET?

GATHER 'ROUND. LET US BEGIN THE PLANNING.

THANKS TO BUDDHA'S UNNECESSARY SERMON, EVERYONE IS CONFUSED. SOME HAVE LOST THE WILL.

IF WE DON'T ACT NOW, WE'LL NEVER PULL OFF A REBELLION!

THE NEXT NEW MOON IS 12 NIGHTS AWAY. WE WILL RISE ON THAT MOONLESS NIGHT.
FIRST, TEN MEN ATTACK THE ARMORY AND SET IT ON FIRE.

THE REST SNEAK INTO THE KOSALANS' BARRACKS WITH STONE AXES WE'LL HAVE ON HAND.

WHAT ARE YOU DOING?!!

YOU CAN'T WIN AGAINST KOSALAN REGULARS! IF YOU START A REBELLION

EVERY LAST MAN, WOMAN AND CHILD WILL BE KILLED. OUR CLAN WILL BE WIPED OUT!

LORD BHADDIYA, IT'S TOO LATE.

THE PLAN IS UNDER-WAY. YOU CAN'T STOP US.

FOOL !!

FOO-OOL!

WHAT WILL IT TAKE TO GET THROUGH YOUR THICK SKULL?
DON'T MAKE A MOVE WHEN BUDDHA'S STILL WITH US. LIE LOW AND KEEP YOUR CALM!
BUDDHA! WHAT USE ARE HIS SERMONS ANYWAY?!
WATCH YOUR MOUTH
DON'T FORGET THAT BUDDHA USED TO BE OUR PRINCE!
STAMP
SEIZED
PSST
NIGHT WATCH COM-ING
BHADDIYA, WHAT ARE YOU ALL DOING HERE AT THIS LATE HOUR?
AH, WELL SIR, SOMEONE DROPPED SOMETHING HERE THIS AFTER-NOON.
WE'RE HERE TO HELP HIM LOOK FOR IT.

HAH? WHAT DID HE LOSE ?
UHM, A MONTH'S WORTH OF MEAL TICKETS, SIR...
WE CAN'T EVEN EAT WITHOUT THOSE, Y'KNOW?

WELL, I'LL HAVE TO REPORT THIS INCIDENT TO THE BRASS ...
WAIT WAIT WAIT WAIT

PLEASE DON'T REPORT THIS... IF THIS IS ENOUGH?

'NIGHT
I KNOW
HURRY UP AND GET BACK TO BED.

UNDER-STOOD ?

PUT ASIDE YOUR REBELLION FOR NOW. IT'D BE NO BETTER THAN SUICIDE.

WOOOOO...

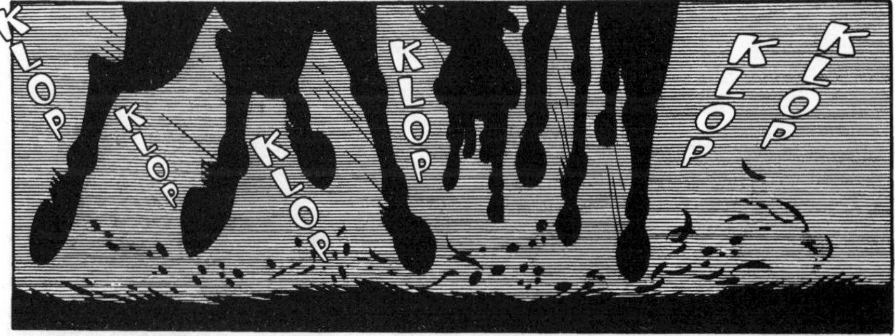
KLOP
KLOP
KLOP
KLOP
KLOP
KLOP

GALLOP
GALLOP
GALLOP
GALLOP
GALLOP
GALLOP

GALLOP
OVER THERE
GALLOP
GALLOP

PLEASE COME BACK WITH US TO KAPILAVASTU

WE'VE BEEN EXILED FROM KAPILAVASTU. IF WE GO BACK WE'LL BE KILLED.

YOUR BANISHMENT HAS BEEN REVOKED!
WHY?

WE DO NOT KNOW. OUR TASK WAS SIMPLY TO COME TELL YOU.
IF YOU'D LIKE TO RETURN RIGHT AWAY, PLEASE FEEL FREE TO USE MY HORSE.

IF YOU DON'T LIKE HORSES, I'LL HAIL A CAB FOR YOU.
WHATCHA TALKIN' ABOUT?

ALL RIGHT, I'LL RETURN IN THE MORNING. TO BE HONEST, I DIDN'T RELISH LEAVING MY COUNTRY IN SUCH A WAY.

DID HE REALLY SAY HE'D COME BACK?
THE ORDERLY DID TELL US SO.

DO YOU THINK HE'LL COME BACK?

I DON'T SEE WHY HE WOULD. HE HAS NOTHING LEFT HERE, HIS COUNTRY IS GONE. WHAT GOOD WOULD COME OF IT?
SHUT UP !!

BUT PRINCE, WHY DO YOU BOTHER WITH A MAN LIKE BUDDHA?

HIS WAY OF THINKING IS DANGEROUS, SIR. YOU MUST SEE THAT HE IS NOT JUST USELESS BUT TRULY HARMFUL TO YOU.

BUDDHA AND COMPANY ARE APPROACH-ING THE CASTLE!

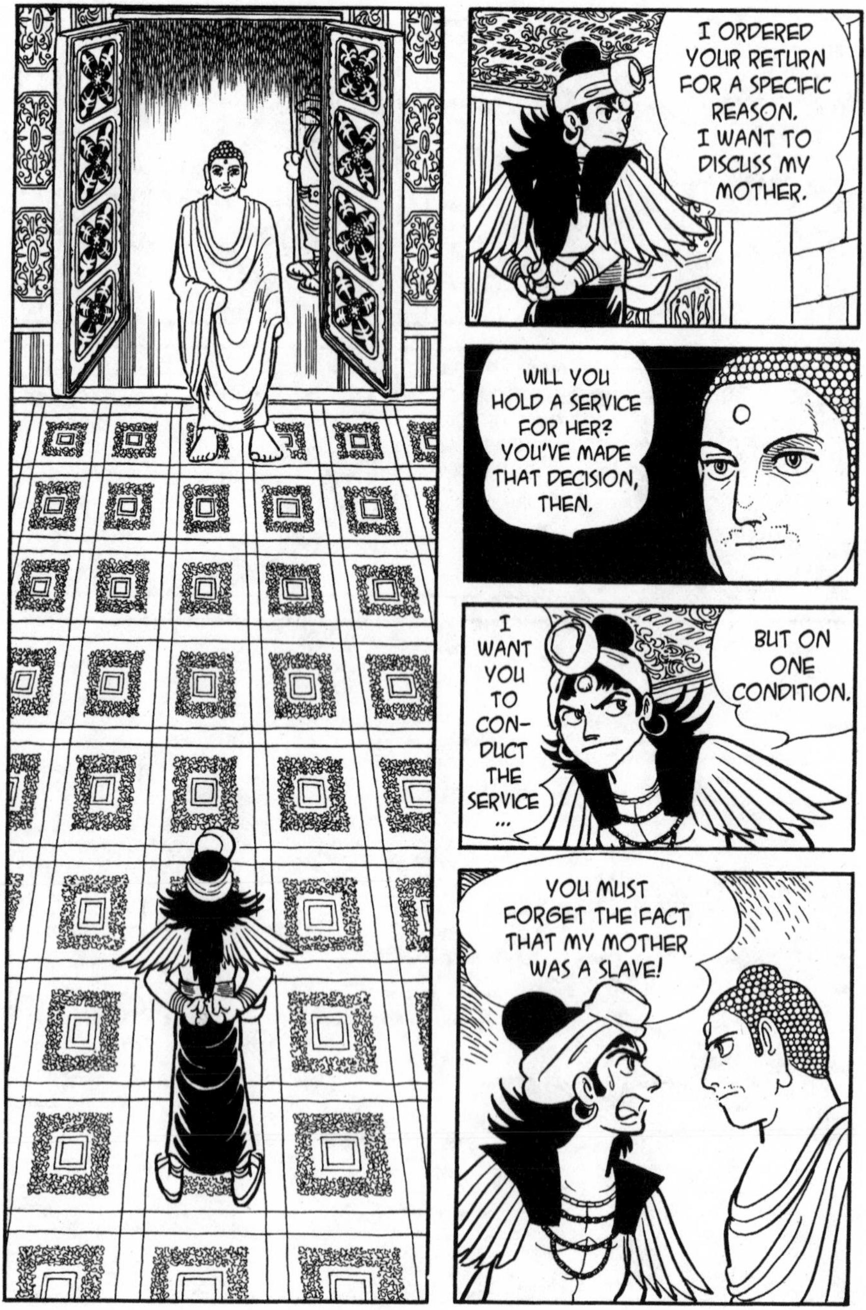

I ORDERED YOUR RETURN FOR A SPECIFIC REASON. I WANT TO DISCUSS MY MOTHER.

WILL YOU HOLD A SERVICE FOR HER? YOU'VE MADE THAT DECISION, THEN.

I WANT YOU TO CON-DUCT THE SERVICE ...
BUT ON ONE CONDITION.

YOU MUST FORGET THE FACT THAT MY MOTHER WAS A SLAVE!

WHY MUST I?

SINCE I'M DOING THIS AT ALL, I WON'T BE STINGY ABOUT IT. WE'LL HAVE A REAL FESTIVAL WITH NOBLES AND CELEBRITIES IN ATTENDANCE.
WE CAN'T POSSIBLY ANNOUNCE THAT SHE WAS A SLAVE.

I HAVE MY PRIDE, YOU KNOW.

HE WILL BE KILLED ON THE SPOT!
I'M GOING TO RECASTE MY MOTHER. SHE WILL NO LONGER BE A SLAVE, FOR I WILL GRANT HER THE TITLE OF NOBILITY. IF ANYONE DARES TO SLANDER HER HENCEFORTH...

PRINCE, YOU SEEM OBSESSED WITH APPEARANCES, LOSING FACE AND SUCH TRIFLES.

WHAT ?!

CHANGING YOUR MOTHER'S CASTE WON'T CHANGE A THING FOR YOU.

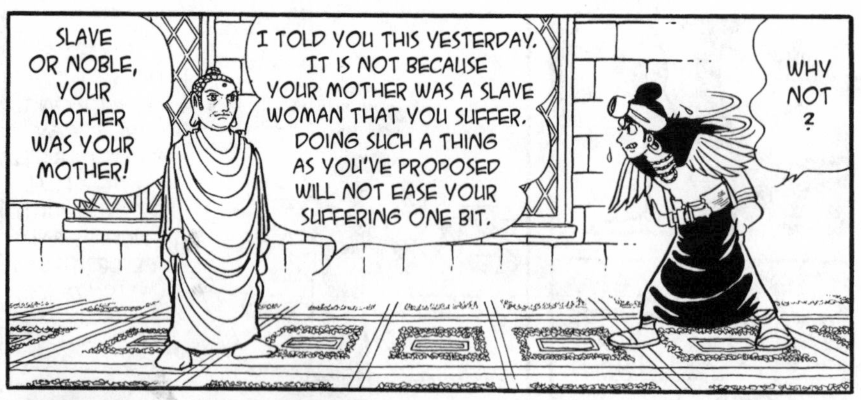
WHY NOT?
SLAVE OR NOBLE, YOUR MOTHER WAS YOUR MOTHER!
I TOLD YOU THIS YESTERDAY. IT IS NOT BECAUSE YOUR MOTHER WAS A SLAVE WOMAN THAT YOU SUFFER. DOING SUCH A THING AS YOU'VE PROPOSED WILL NOT EASE YOUR SUFFERING ONE BIT.

LET ME TRY AN ANALOGY. WHICH WOULD YOU ENVY MORE, PRINCE: AN UGLY SOOT-COLORED ELEPHANT BORN IN A WEALTHY LORD'S GARDEN, OR ONE WHITE AS SNOW BORN IN A GARBAGE DUMP?

MM...

THE WHITE ONE, RIGHT?

...

A WHITE ELEPHANT DOESN'T GET BORN IN A GARBAGE DUMP!
BUT SUCH A WHITE ELEPHANT GAVE BIRTH TO YOU!!

WHETHER IT IS BORN
ON TRASH OR ON FLOWERS,
AN ELEPHANT IS AN ELEPHANT.
THE SAME IS TRUE FOR HUMANS.
YOU SAY YOUR MOTHER WAS A SLAVE,
BUT WHATEVER HER BIRTH OR CASTE,
SHE WAS YOUR MOTHER.
WHERE IS THE SHAME IN THAT?

GET UP!!

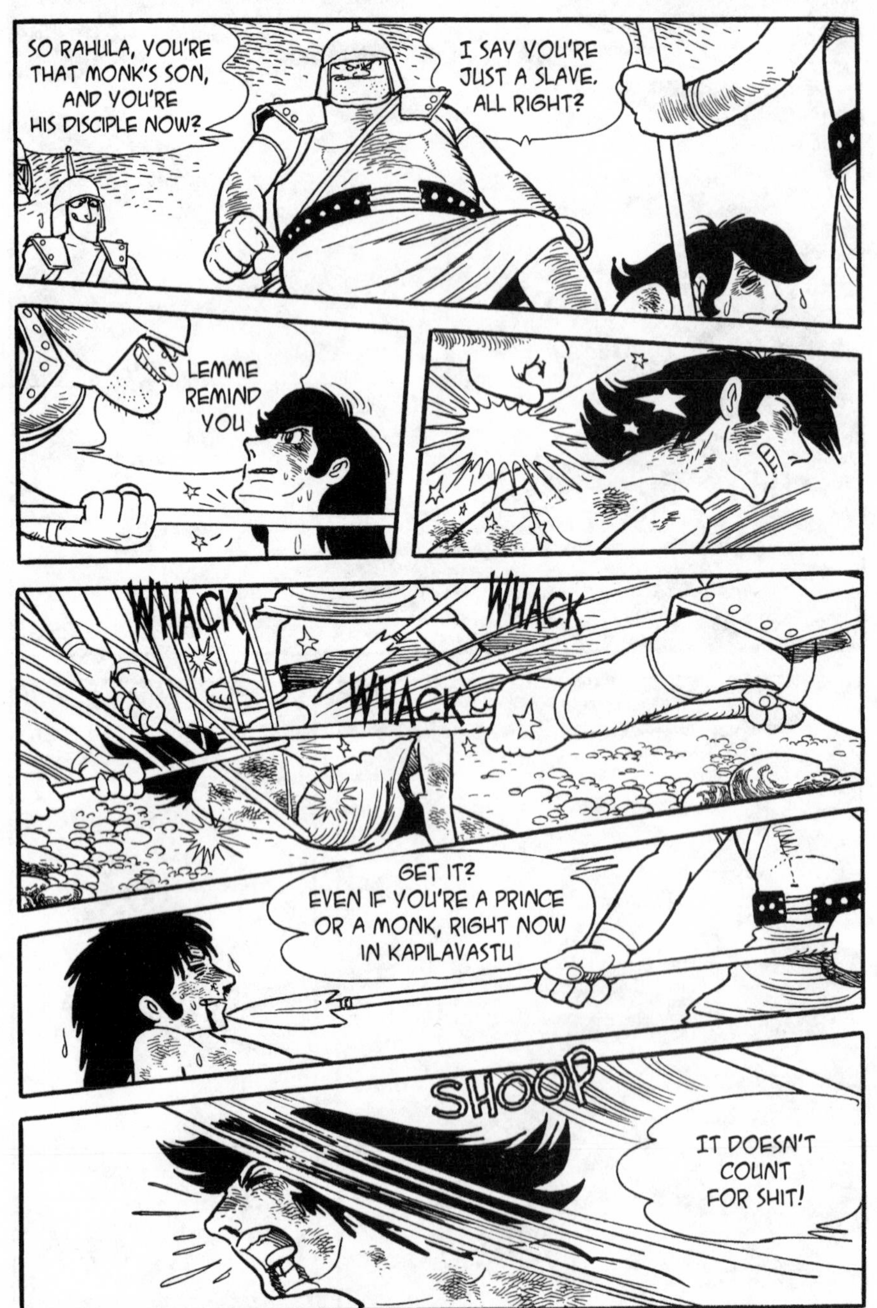
SO RAHULA, YOU'RE THAT MONK'S SON, AND YOU'RE HIS DISCIPLE NOW?
I SAY YOU'RE JUST A SLAVE. ALL RIGHT?
LEMME REMIND YOU
WHACK
WHACK
WHACK
GET IT? EVEN IF YOU'RE A PRINCE OR A MONK, RIGHT NOW IN KAPILAVASTU
SHOOP
IT DOESN'T COUNT FOR SHIT!

UGH !!
SWAP
GOT IT? GOOD. NOW WORK TWICE AS HARD.
ECH
UNG...

RAHULA... WHAT HAVE THEY DONE TO YOU?
M-MOTHER?

GLUG
UG
GLUG
UG

MY POOR BOY! IF THE WORLD WERE ITSELF, YOU'D BE RULING THIS COUNTRY...

MOTHER! MUST YOU GO ON SPOUTING SUCH FANTASIES? WHEN I BECAME A SLAVE, I UNDERSTOOD SOMETHING.
A MAN NEEDS NO CASTE! THAT'S WHY I ACCEPT THIS LABOR.

GO HOME, MOTHER. THEY'LL PUNISH ME IF THEY FIND YOU HERE.

...

SIDDHARTHA... YOUR SON IS BOLDLY FACING HIS SUFFERING...
PLEASE PRAY FOR HIM!

PRINCE CRYSTAL WAS HOLED UP WITH BUDDHA...

THE TWO ARGUED
FOR MANY DAYS
AND NIGHTS—
A FIERCE CLASH OF WILLS
THAT SEEMED TO
SET OFF SPARKS...

ON THE TWELFTH NIGHT, AN EXHAUSTED, BLEARY-EYED PRINCE CRYSTAL SUDDENLY ROSE TO HIS FEET.

THE PARLEY WAS OVER.

MINISTER !!

W-WHAT DID YOU SAY?
Y-Y-YOU CAN'T POSSIBLY MEAN IT...

SEND WORD AT ONCE TO BHADDIYA
SPREAD THE NEWS TO ALL CORNERS OF THE CITY, TO TROOP AND SLAVE.

P-P-PRINCE! I BEG YOU TO THINK THIS OVER!

I'VE MADE UP MY MIND
NOW GO. SEND WORD TO BHAD-DIYA!

BUDDHA ...

I DID IT, BUDDHA!

AT LAST, OUR MOONLESS LIGHT. IS EVERYONE PREPARED?

ATHNAJA, YOU HAVE ENOUGH MEN TO RAZE THE ARMORY?

11 MEN, SIR

I'M COUNTING ON YOU, BONDAKHA, TO KILL THE PRINCE!
HEH

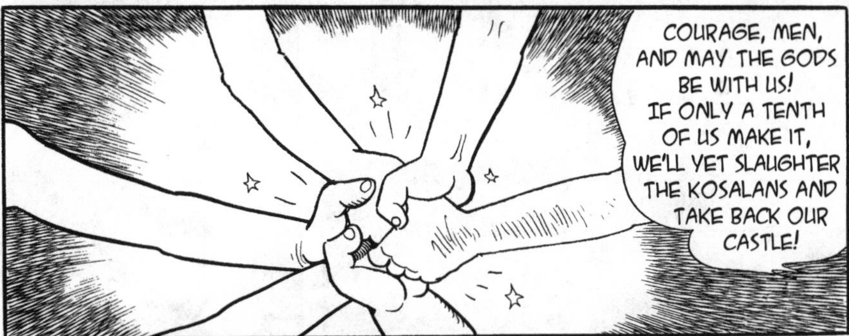
COURAGE, MEN, AND MAY THE GODS BE WITH US! IF ONLY A TENTH OF US MAKE IT, WE'LL YET SLAUGHTER THE KOSALANS AND TAKE BACK OUR CASTLE!

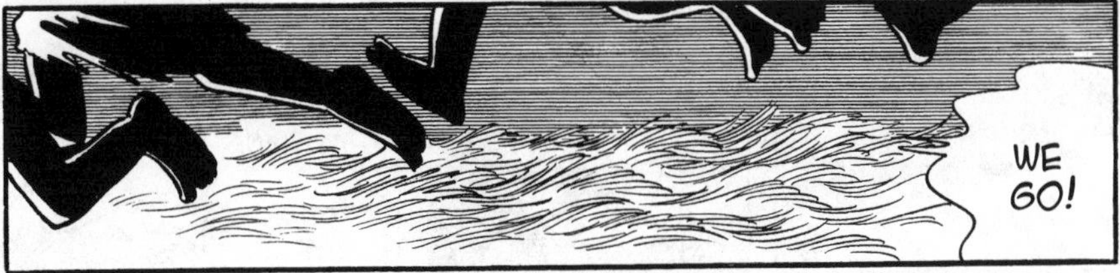
WE GO!

THAT'S THE ARMORY!

DON'T FAIL ME

SCRAPE
SCRAPE

HANG ON A SEC. THEY'RE JUST ABOUT TO ANNOUNCE SOME BREAKING NEWS.
WHERE DID YOU FIND THAT THING, YOU ANACHRO-NIST...

PRINCE CRYSTAL ISSUED THE FOLLOWING STATEMENT AT 9:10 P.M.!
"WITHIN THREE DAYS, THE ARMY OF KOSALA..."
"...WILL WITHDRAW FROM KAPILAVASTU AND HEAD BACK TO THE KINGDOM OF KOSALA!"
WE WILL BE FREED FROM SLAVERY!! WE SHAKYA HAVE SURVIVED!

IT CAN'T BE TRUE!!
PRINCE CRYSTAL IS PLAYING SOME TRICK ON US!
RAHULA!
WE'RE FREE?!
WE'RE SAVED?!
WE'VE BEEN LIBERATED?!

LIBRE ♡

FREE!
FREEDOM

NO WAY

WE'RE FREE !!
HURRAY!

HUR-RAY !
HURRAY!
HOORAY
HOORAY FREEDOM !
HOORAY
BRAVO! TRES BIEN!
HOORAY

WOOHOO
YEAH
YAH
HOORAY
YES
YEAH
YES
YAH
HOORAY
YAH

HOORAY
BRAVO
ROAR
CHEERS
ROAR
HOORAY
BANZAI

WELL DONE, PRINCE CRYSTAL. YOU'VE MANAGED TO ACCOMPLISH, IN THE COURSE OF YOUR LIFE, A TRULY INVALUABLE DEED.

BUDDHA ...

THESE PAST FEW DAYS, I'VE LEARNED FROM YOU THE HIGHEST THINGS.

PLEASE, COME WITH ME TO KOSALA! I'D LIKE TO HEAR MORE OF YOUR TEACHINGS! I'M SURE MY FATHER WOULD, TOO!
THANK YOU. I WOULD BE DELIGHTED TO VISIT KOSALA.

LEAVING ONLY A SMALL DETACHMENT, THE KOSALAN ARMY EVACUATED AS PROMISED.

THAT THIS WOULD CAUSE AN IRREVOCABLE TRAGEDY, NEITHER BUDDHA NOR PRINCE CRYSTAL COULD FORESEE.

HERE ENDS VOLUME SEVEN

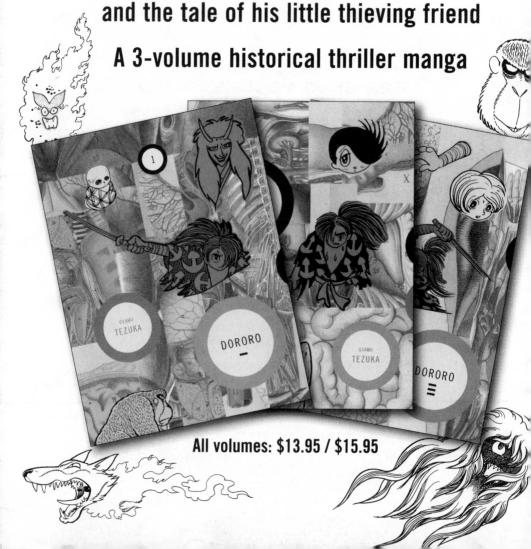

PRAISE FOR OSAMU TEZUKA:

"Thanks to the seminal influence of comics creator Osamu Tezuka, Japanese comics have a long, rich history of iconic characters."
—Eisner Award-winning author Scott McCloud, *Understanding Comics*

"There's manga and then there's manga. More explicitly, there's manga and then there's Osamu Tezuka... Tezuka more or less invented the form as we know it... It's a mark of his artistic singularity that almost 20 years after his death, we are still playing catch up with his achievements." —*Newsweek*

"His works deal with the most profound questions of human existence." —*Publishers Weekly*

"One does not speak of Tezuka's weaknesses. There aren't any."
—*AnimeNewsNetwork.com*

"There would be no manga as we know it without Tezuka."
—*Advanced Media Network*

T O T E

IN SPACE, NO ONE CAN HEAR YOU CR

VERTICAL INC, publisher of BUDDHA and ODE TO KIRIHITO presents TO TERRA... The hit sci-fi emo-manga by

KEIKO TAKEMIYA

R R A . . .

Volume 1

Volume 2

Volume 3

AND...
BUDDHA 8: THE FINAL VOLUME

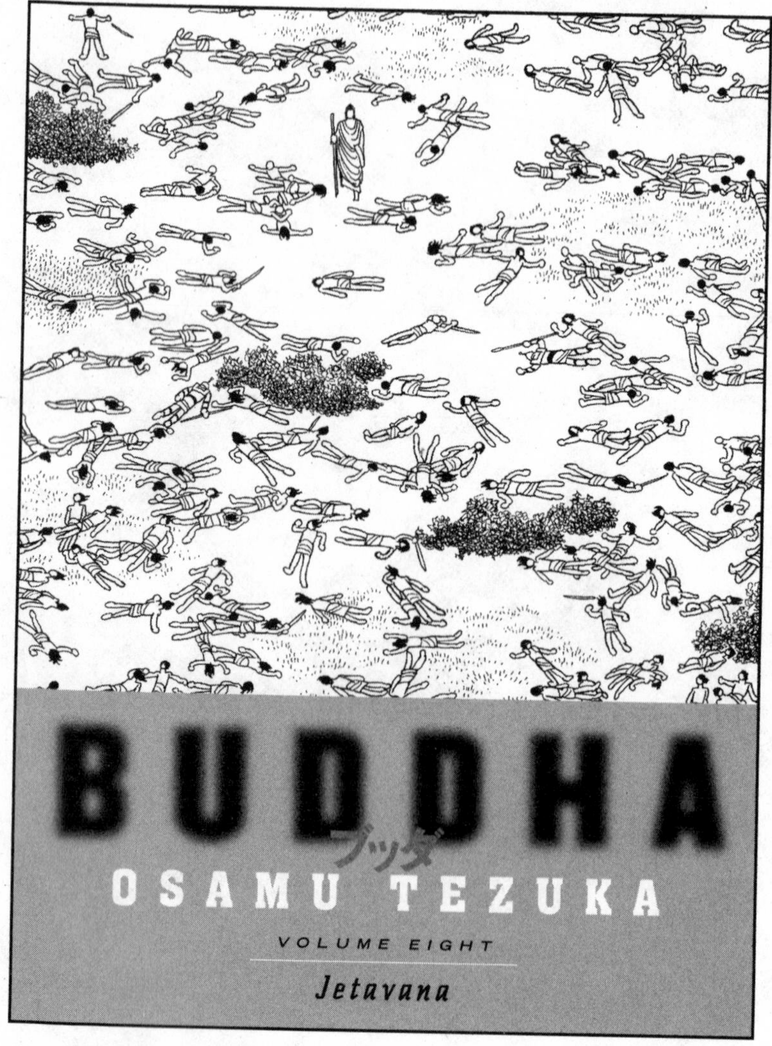